East Asian Direct Investment in Britain

Studies in Asia Pacific Business
1369-7153

Editors: Robert Fitzgerald, Chris Rowley and Paul Stewart

**Greater China: Political Economy, Inward Investment and
Business Culture**
Edited by Chris Rowley and Mark Lewis

Beyond Japanese Management: The End of Modern Times?
Edited by Paul Stewart

**Management in China: The Experiences of Foreign
Businesses**
Edited by Roger Strange

**Human Resource Management in the Asia Pacific Region:
Convergence Questioned**
Edited by Chris Rowley

Korean Businesses: Internal and External Industrialization
Edited by Chris Rowley and Johngseok Bae

East Asian Direct Investment in Britain
Edited by Philip Garrahan and John Ritchie

East Asian
Direct Investment
in Britain

Editors

Philip Garrahan
University of Northumbria at Newcastle
John Ritchie
Durham University Business School

Routledge
Taylor & Francis Group

LONDON AND NEW YORK

First published in 1999 in Great Britain and in the United States of America by
FRANK CASS P UBLISHERS

Published 2013 by Routledge
4 Park Square, Milton Park, Abingdon, Oxon OX14 4RN
605 Third Avenue, New York, NY 10017

Routledge is an imprint of the Taylor & Francis Group, an informa business

British Library Cataloguing in Publication Data

East Asian direct investment in Britain. – (Studies in Asia
Pacific business ; no. 6)
1. Investments, Japanese – England, Northern 2. Investments,
Foreign, and employment – England, Northern
I. Garrahan, Philip II. Ritchie, John
332.6'73'5'0427

Library of Congress Cataloging-in-Publication Data:

East Asian direct investment in Britain / edited by Philip
Garrahan and John Ritchie.
    p.cm. – (Studies in Asia Pacific business)
Includes bibliographical references and index.
ISBN 0–7146–4981–3. – ISBN 978–0–7146–8044–6 (pbk.)
1. Investments, East Asian–Great Britain. I. Garrahan,
Philip. II. Ritchie, John, 1949– . III. Series.
HG5432.E17 1999
332.67'35041–dc21   99-34090
                                                                            CIP

This group of studies first appeared in a special issue of *Asia Pacific Business
Review* [ISSN 1360-2381], Vol.5, No.2, Winter 1998

ISBN 13: 978-0-7146-4981-8 (hbk)
ISBN 13: 978-0-7146-8044-6 (pbk)
ISSN 1369-7153

Contents

Introduction: Arresting Development – East Asian FDI and Regional Change

PHILIP GARRAHAN AND JOHN RITCHIE

THE UK, THE EUROPEAN UNION, AND FOREIGN DIRECT INVESTMENT

This collection puts East Asian foreign direct investment (FDI) into a United Kingdom context by making more critically apparent the course of its inception and realization in the North of England region. Beginning with an overall account of the position of the UK, alternative regionally related scenarios assess the role of FDI within different localities and sectors. The collection was first conceived amid growing calls for a better understanding of the complexities of FDI, especially as the so-called Asian crisis took hold. The North of England is clearly a leading case in point, since it attracted the highest proportion of all FDI coming into all UK regions between 1994 and 1997. Further, within the wider European Union (EU), the UK has been regarded as highly placed and competitively advantaged where East Asian FDI has been concerned. By thus making its particular course more critically apparent within this leading UK host region, this volume aims to stimulate fresh insights and debates into the still sensitive process by which FDI influences future development prospects.

That process has already been understood very differently even within the last decade alone. At the outset East Asia appeared to be verging upon an economic miracle rarely thought possible before. As progenitor for globalization at large, this economic miracle idea virtually somersaulted into popular consciousness thereafter. Soon formal economic league tables designated likely winners, followers and losers, and concerned states sought to reposition their economic prospects accordingly. For example, the US claimed more growing

Philip Garrahan, School of Social, Political and Economic Sciences, University of Northumbria at Newcastle; John Ritchie, Durham University Business School.

allegiance with the Pacific than with the Atlantic, and on the edges of the Pacific Rim both Australia and New Zealand did the same. Any EU approach appeared almost distant by comparison, and as the world's largest trading block the EU concerned itself more with its own internal matters.

As Louise Amoore's article shows, the UK acted opportunistically by promoting its more peripheral regions in securing East Asian FDI. This approach soon drew criticism from other EU member states, since the UK was regarded as privileging itself as the 'enterprise centre of Europe'. After the EU launched its 'Towards A New Asia Strategy' document in 1994 some of the formalities changed and three years later the preferred theme for all EU member states became 'Sharing Asia's Dynamism' (UNCTAD, 1997). As the 1990s ended, however, that very dynamism was thrown into serious question. Both the East Asian economic miracle, and the national and regional repositioning strategies that went with it, were increasingly doubted. Ironically, where East Asia had previously appeared the progenitor for globalization, now it seemed the prisoner and victim of these self-same forces: an economic *volte-face* almost without parallel. So, if an East Asian economic miracle could indeed falter (while further collapses happened in former Soviet states), then the interests of those such as the UK, which had been deliberately positioned to benefit from it, were at risk. Not surprisingly, top think tank-backed calls for rethinking this entire phenomenon were soon forthcoming, requiring much better EU/East Asian related dialogue (Maull, Segal and Wanandi, 1998; Pape, 1998; Sideri, 1995).

In a number of key matters the EU benchmarked the US and Japan, rather than other East Asian countries. For example its 1998 assessment of European competitiveness drew almost exclusively upon these benchmarks alone (EU, 1998). On the other hand these other East Asian countries also regarded the volume and relative shares of their trade and investment with Japan and the US as the more important (Anderson and Francois, 1998). In addition, East Asian fears about non-contingent, exclusionary 'Fortress Europe' protectionism matched EU apprehensions about Japanese and US ascendancy across East Asia generally. Subsequent studies suggest that, especially compared with the US, EU interests in East Asian countries excluding Japan are more complex and expansive than is sometimes supposed. This is despite continuing criticisms about unsatisfactory investment rates (Longhammer, 1998). For example Segal (1998) maintains that, while the overall value of trade remains limited, EU aid to Pacific Asia far exceeds that of the US, while 30 per cent of all IMF crisis relief, notably that directed towards ASEAN states like Thailand and Indonesia, comes from EU member states and is double the US contribution.

Yet even before any prospective eastward enlargement, the significance of the EU for individual member state relationships with East Asia varied considerably. Although the existing EU member states appear relatively homogeneous compared with their East Asian counterparts, Henry Kissinger's famous dictum that the EU 'does not have a telephone number' where certain affairs are concerned could well apply to overall FDI policy. From that standpoint, the overall approaches towards East Asian relationships are still mainly decentralized with considerable scope for individual manoeuvre. As regards incoming FDI, the UK has touched upon important collective sensitivities in this respect. Any sense of undue competitive striving and regional privileging has led to it being labelled unduly economically nationalist as a result. Other observers consider that its overall approach towards all inward FDI has been more concerned with the quantity than the quality and realization of such flows, while other important questions about any symmetry with outgoing FDI remain (Hood and Young, 1997). All this serves to underline the importance of further specifying the course, conduct and performance of East Asian FDI all the way from inception to realization in leading regions like the North of England, where the full nature of its workings can be made more critically clear.

A REGIONAL EXEMPLAR

Against this backcloth, the articles in this volume examine the relationship between the emerging economies of East Asia and the relatively declining regional economy of the North of England. This comprises the counties of Cleveland, Durham and Northumberland in the eastern part of the region, and Cumbria in the west. In recent years, there has been a significant outflow of capital investment from several countries, notably Japan, into this, the poorest of the English regions. The most pronounced impact of FDI has been in the north eastern part of the region, and the contributions here take account of this. From this regional perspective, FDI has been a fairly constant feature of economic development since the Second World War. The major change that has occurred of late is the shift in the origins of this FDI. Whereas previous FDI had been dominated by American and European companies, in the last decade the region has become the focus of East Asian FDI. The recent crises in the financial markets and economic activity of many East Asian countries have thrown this, and the themes of this volume, into special relief.

We began by asking how the region had met the challenge of its long-term decline, especially with regard to the part played by FDI in boosting successive phases of post-war regional economic development planning. Against the background of profound changes in the regional economy in the last decade and a half, the North has also claimed more inward investment from East Asia than any other region in the country, or indeed any region in the other member states of the European Union. So, in key respects how has the North of England changed in the last decade and a half? What are the main indicators of change, and what has been the interaction with FDI from East Asia? How has this FDI influenced change in the region? Have there been specific aspects – for example, private and public sector collaboration, local government, or employment relations – which have been more directly affected than others? Are there other areas of regional development which have been only indirectly affected? We have intentionally not posed the question as to whether regional changes in the North of England would have developed in the same/different way without this FDI. However, now that this source of FDI is levelling off, what are the implications for the region?

For the purposes of this introduction, our discussion engages with three significant themes: first, the region's historical development and the recurring attempts to redefine its political economy, stimulated anew by the current global crisis; second, the relationship between notions of the global imperatives for change and the experience of regional development; and third, the expectation that East Asian FDI would have a transforming effect on employment relations in the region. These three themes arise from the contributing authors' shared interests, which cumulatively highlight the critical juncture at which the North of England and many similar regions now stands. Having witnessed East Asian FDI into the region arresting the attention of all concerned, now we see the growing trend towards disinvestment bringing into question the prudence of economic development strategies that are too heavily dependent on FDI.

REDEFINING THE REGION

Despite its history as a state-managed region, heavily dependent on primary and manufacturing industries (Robinson, 1990), there have been few overall analyses of the economic development of the region since the end of the Second World War (Northern Region Strategy Team, 1977; Chapman, 1984; Hudson, 1989; Garrahan and Stewart, 1996; Sadler, 1992; Evans, Johnson and Thomas, 1995) A major feature of the region's experience in recent decades has been the push away from traditional to new industrial activities. Against the background of accelerated closure in the state-owned coal, steel and shipbuilding industries, new plants assembling cars, consumer electronics and micro-processors were opened especially by East Asian companies investing in the UK. Stone provides a careful overview in this volume of the relative importance of FDI in the region and in the wider context.

Yet, by the spring of 1998 doubts had begun to arise, not least given the reported collapse of profits at Nissan Motors UK from £600m to £21m. The subsequent announcements of the closure of two semi-conductor plants, one in Sedgefield in Durham owned by the Fujitsu corporation (600 jobs) and the other in North Tyneside owned by the Siemens group (1100 jobs), are in sharp contrast with the progress apparently promised on the back of FDI. Previously Samsung, in announcing the halting of its expansion programme on Teesside, took care to say that this was in response to the economic conditions in Korea. No blame was attached to the performance of the business operation in the region. While FDI companies do not want to expose their corporate strategies to unnecessary criticism, there is little reason to underestimate the effect of these setbacks on the potential for developing supply chains in the region. The collapse of world markets in the late 1990s is the major reason cited for plant closures, and this leaves the region without two of its showpiece plants, a third calling a halt to its investment programme, and a fourth barely profitable and forced to merge with a major competitor. Other speculation surrounds the growing competition for investment by Central and Eastern Europe.

Whatever the combination of explanations, there is a direct effect on regional employment, just as rapidly as the buoyancy of FDI impacted favourably on the North of England during the 1980s. There is now good cause for the strategy of the last decade and a half to be seen in crisis as disinvestment grows.

In the national economic development context, the region is out of step with some important trends: while the collieries, shipyards and heavy engineering plants have disappeared, there are few signs that the North of England is enjoying the British boom in information services. The evidence nationally that more people are employed now in information technology services than worked in the coal mining industry at its peak seems to confirm the UK's arrival as a service economy (*The Observer*, 23 August 98). There is a heavy regional bias to this that does not favour the North of England, despite the rise in the number of new telephone call centres being opened (*Regional Economic Prospects*, 1998). As the region's latest report acknowledges (*Competing in the Twenty-First Century*, 1998), although new jobs have been created in the service sector the region has a below-average proportion of jobs in financial services. The same report notes that the region lost 55,000 jobs in primary industry and 81,000 in manufacturing between 1981 and 1996; and that even the benefits of growth in foreign direct investment were offset by the closure of other externally owned branch plants during the same period. Having once been the location for a major national coalfield and for employment in manufacturing, the region is now heavily de-industrialized. The report of the Labour Party's Regional Policy Commission published in 1996, prior to Labour being elected to government, was the latest in a long line to confirm this. It identified the North as a problem region: its per capita GDP is the lowest of any English region, with future growth expected to be behind the rest of the country.

The North of England is relatively weak in terms of small and medium sized enterprises, and the largest single area for employment continues to be the public sector embracing education, government and health. A consequence of the branch plant trend that has affected the region is the relative absence of major company headquarters or strategic functions. As a result, the level of externally-owned businesses continues to be very high and is well above the national average. This is not to be read as a necessary indicator of the increasing effects of globalization. Indeed, in the national context the signs are that the controlling influence of multinational companies over the British economy has not grown significantly since the 1980s (Lovering, 1997).

GLOBALIZATION AND REGIONAL ECONOMIC CHANGE

The particular concerns of the North of England may seem parochial in the context of global economic upheavals towards the end of the twentieth century. Like other regions in advanced industrial societies it has had its own structural problems arising from a long history of industrial activity based on mineral extraction, processing and export – the so-called 'carboniferous capitalism'. Yet the North of England has been tied in to developments in many different parts of the world since the early phases of industrialization, as the article by Conte-Helm demonstrates. For example, the North of England has had a trading relationship with Japan in ships and armaments that began more than a hundred years ago when the region was at the heart of the country's industrial domination of world markets. However, after decades of decline, interrupted by brief resurgence, the region is now exposed more than most in the UK to the vicissitudes of global economic change.

The ability of capital to transfer easily and quickly between markets is a defining characteristic of the present era of globalization of economic relations. The North's long-term economic decline has been matched in recent years by the growth of the emerging economies of East Asia, many of which have invested in the region. As with the UK generally, the region has been the focus for external investors, making it the major recipient of FDI from Japan, for example. Against this backcloth, it will be no surprise if the reversals in the economic fortunes not just of East Asia, but also of Eastern Europe, Russia and Latin America, have negative consequences for the North of England. The much lauded integration of the world economy, whose benefits were taken for granted during the growth phases associated with globalization, now serves to put a brake on those economies which sought inflows of external capital. 'Think globally, act locally' was once the mantra of integration, rising expectations and over-confidence in the stability of the new era; but 'think globally, think again' might replace it as a more cautious and realistic response (Ruigrok and Van Tulder, 1997).

Within the North of England, as in other older established industrial regions undergoing fundamental re-structuring, key agencies have emerged for economic development. As the UK has a relative lack of regionally devolved powers of government, there has been no single and effective body for the governing of the North of England. Unlike the Scottish and Welsh cases, this region does not share the history of a stateless nation, so there has been less political momentum for devolving economic development powers (although the article by Cumbers suggests a degree of convergence in other respects). Nevertheless, a discernible economic development position was voiced in the region in response to the onset from the mid-1980s of major East Asian inward investment into the North of England. During the decade and a half since then, an establishment position emerged that both presumed the benign qualities of such investment in steering economic growth and denied the utility of public debate. In this sense public sector and private sector approaches to economic development overlapped, and the dominant support for FDI went largely unquestioned in the region (Hudson, 1995). The hegemony of the notion that an economic miracle was being performed on the North of England region is subjected to a critical analysis in the article by Ritchie. In the parallel case of South Wales, which was subject to many of the same powerful forces to change from its former industrial character, an 'Inward Investment Service Class' has prevailed in public policy debates (Phelps, Lovering and Morgan, 1998).

When the election of the first Thatcher government in 1979 signalled the end of the post-war settlement around the mixed economy and the welfare state, the North of England was bound to suffer given its earlier character as a state-managed region. After the claims and counter-claims have been debated about the economic miracle being wrought in the region, the North of England remains approximately where it was in the 1970s compared to other English regions: it has the lowest economic activity rate, the highest unemployment, the lowest average weekly earnings, the lowest disposable household income, the lowest gross domestic product, and the largest concentration of derelict land (Regional Trends, 1996). There is now much concern therefore to retain the FDI that has already arrived. The object of regional policy debate increasingly has switched from attracting new inward investment to further embedding existing investment in the host economy, as Burdis and Peck consider in their article under the heading of 'aftercare services'. Of course, while there has been this shift in response to a steady reduction in the inflow of FDI into the region, the regional implications of plant closures have never been fully assessed.

Since the early 1980s, the region has been promoted elsewhere – for example to Eastern Europe – as an example of how to manage the run down of older established industries with less regulation, more open competition, more local small businesses, a privatized public sector and generally reduced government intervention in social as well as economic life. Just as the end of the Soviet empire brought the need to install new forms of social and economic relations, so in a timely way these seemed to have been tested out in the North of England and made ready for easy transplanting. During this imposed transformation of the region, the onset of investment flows from East Asia was unexpected: there were no predictions that it was to happen, since it was not considered to be the state's role to plan how and at what pace the economy should develop. Instead, the economies of regions such as the North of England were to be modernized by withdrawing state support for industries in decline, promoting small businesses and opening up the economy to market forces. These same market forces that promised so much to the region in the form of East Asian FDI now question the durability of recent developments. While as recently as the mid-1980s the major task for economic development agencies was to seek and respond to unprecedented investment prospects from East Asia, the question now being raised is how such investment can remain the foundation stone of the regional consensus, and how might regional development agencies respond to contraction?

At the local level, these changes have had far-reaching consequences for the political economy of local development. In their analysis of one local authority area, Tomaney and Pike are critical of the role of FDI in local economic development. Their conclusion is that much of this investment is reminiscent of the branch plant economy problems of previous decades. This echoes Hudson's (1995) remark that depending too heavily on FDI is akin to looking 'back to the future'. More than ever, the need to support business development through effective networks confronts the core question of who is in charge of developing the local economy.

This is being answered by the New Labour government's policy of establishing Regional Development Agencies for England with strong local representation.

THE 'NEW' EMPLOYMENT RELATIONS

In addition to contributing to new economic growth in the region, East Asian FDI has been widely held to spearhead fundamental changes in employment relations. There are bound to be problematical aspects of any project to introduce new management techniques, but in many instances this was facilitated along the lines of Japanese techniques on greenfield sites (Garrahan and Stewart, 1992). Largely a matter of assumption to date, rather than of objective evidence, has been the belief that these successes would produce an imitative effect whereby innovation also followed on brownfield sites and indeed in businesses not directly affected by East Asian investment. The article by Roberts and Strangleman arises out of one of the few empirical studies into this aspect of regional development, and concludes that there are drawbacks to be balanced against the advantages within the firm.

Ownership and control can pose sensitive issues for both investors and hosts alike and the North has its own changing agenda in this respect. With the eclipse of nationalization the recent combination of privatization, corporate reorganizations, and the influx of FDI from diverse sources has raised some important questions. As a consequence, matters concerning absentee ownership, investment/disinvestment strategies, local managerial autonomy, and associated effects upon local workforces and trade unions are still at issue, and often figure high upon popular regional development agendas. In terms of country of origin the sources of FDI appear increasingly notably diverse. However, as Stone's article here points out, the relative importance of East Asian sources has latterly increased, while the Siemens and Fujitsu cases demonstrate foreign direct dis-investment still continues. In broader terms, the very diversity of these FDI sources raises the fundamental issue of whether, in terms of country of origin, ownership subsequently imparts distinctive 'vintage effects', which then shape the character and performance of whatever firms result. In asking 'does ownership matter' regarding Japanese multinationals in Europe, Mason and Encarnation (1994) have elsewhere concluded that more such 'vintage effects' were likely to materialize through time. In this case Stone has identified the different sources, forms and trends of FDI into the North, with particular reference to country of origin, in order that more suitable comparisons can be drawn and any distinctively East Asian connected features duly identified.

In other respects FDI has become closely associated with bringing – or otherwise galvanizing – newer forms of management into action. Unlike the case of older established regional industries like coal mining and shipbuilding, this management task is considered to be the building and growing of organizations rather than their rundown and closure – at least until similar rundowns and closures materialize among inwardly invested plants. Ritchie suggests in this volume that the idea of a 'New' North supports the re-presentation of its leading managements and workplaces as undergoing transformations where 'new' shopfloor industrial relations prosper. In particular, key regional 'hub' firms like Nissan have been promoted as leading management 'flagship' investments in this respect. Such firms are thus more than just tangible investors for this region; they are also considered 'intangible' investors for their assumed beneficial 'demonstration effect' upon other managements. Exactly what effect East Asian – especially Japanese – invested firms actually demonstrate compared with others, and how beneficial that might be, is still at issue. While this clearly coincides with any switch of emphasis from continuity to change in the conduct of British workplace industrial relations in general, it is important that any East Asian contribution is put into proper perspective. Indeed, Ackroyd and Procter (1998) have argued that larger British manufacturers pursue independently evolved approaches towards workplace change, whatever these – and other – inward investors do.

It is important in this assessment of regional change not to lose sight of the comparative picture. For this reason, the article by Cumbers presents a comparative analysis of the North East of England and South Wales. The particular focus is again the effect of this investment on employment relations, examining how this is configured by on-going processes of employment restructuring. While there is some variation in impact between regions, it is nevertheless clear that transformations in the work environment are occurring and that FDI from Japan plays its part in this. The analysis concludes that while the rhetoric of change is ambitious about goal harmonization between employers and employees, this is not happening in practice given the nature of broader changes in employment practices. As Stewart (1998) has argued, there is in any case little evidence of a single paradigm operating in practice, and the notion of the 'Japanization' of industrial relations as a way of breaking with the bad habits of the past is highly contestable.

Changes in employment relations have been promoted at the same time as heralding the age of the new worker who, under the mantle of lean production, would 'work smarter, not harder'. This notion of the character of work supposedly changing has prevailed as much in the North East of England as in other regions, and primarily by association with the new directions offered by FDI from East Asia. It has been accompanied by a different approach to marketing the country's workforce, especially when seeking to attract overseas investment into the UK. When she became President of the Board of Trade in 1997, Margaret Beckett, MP, judged that competitiveness depended on modern companies succeeding in new markets with new products. She stressed that competition should be on the basis of '...strengths in design, science and ideas, not on cheap labour'. Yet, cheap labour, together with de-regulation, docile trade unions and labour flexibility are key national strengths promoted by the government in practice. The attractiveness of the UK to investors in call centres, for example, is illustrated in the marketing by the government's publicity office – the Invest in Britain Bureau. Among the benefits cited in answer to the question, why are there more call centres in the UK than anywhere else in Europe, the IBB lists the following: the UK has the most advanced deregulated commercial telecommunications market in Europe; world class networks and services; the lowest telecom costs in Europe; price improvements driven by competition, not government subsidy; the most flexible and practical working practices – no restrictions on working hours or 24-hour working; the least unionized country in Europe; the highest levels of network resilience; the lowest labour costs in main EU markets; and the British 'get-it-done' approach – get projects up and running quickly, hassle free.

THE LIMITS TO FDI-LED REGIONAL ECONOMIC DEVELOPMENT

The first signs of the East Asian economic crisis became evident during the summer of 1997 with the collapse of the Thai currency. The growing evidence of economic difficulties (evidenced especially in the banking sector) in Japan saw the Yen getting weaker, with speculation about the devaluation of the Chinese currency. This led to further speculation that the US would intervene to support the Yen, and this happened with a surprise intervention on foreign markets in June 1998. Despite this, the Yen reached an eight-year low against the dollar during the summer of 1998. The article by Henderson, Hama, Eccleston and Thompson in this volume reviews the crisis through the medium of a debate: this allows the participants to examine competing macroeconomic and international explanations. It concludes with a commentary on some of the likely long-term effects of the crisis for East Asia and for the global economy more generally.

With the analysis of macro-economic and international forces in mind, it is increasingly inadequate to refer simply to the crisis as an East Asian one. References in the media to *Asian 'flu* epitomize the tendency to see crisis as someone else's virus, which others have caught so far, but which perhaps might be contagious. All of the articles collected here have an important sub-text in this respect concerning the growing realization of the limits to East Asian capitalism and its modus operandi. This puts the very idea of an East Asian economic miracle in dispute and few anticipate that such seemingly limitless economic growth will continue. More now focus on its economic, organizational and managerial limits instead, believing this realization to be long overdue. Many others find East Asia's current economic predicament to be a surprise, however. Any popular idea of a rapidly risen new East Asian economic powerhouse, headquartered in Japan, but with growing overseas tie-ups, including European bridgeheads within regions like the North, thus no longer holds sway. Rival images and metaphors of an East Asian economic crisis and retreat increasingly dominate instead. Of course the East Asian economic miracle idea always had its critics. Whether deemed 'ersatz', 'cronyist', 'authoritarian command' or 'Confucian', they have considered East Asian capitalism both different and flawed. Such criticism did not really disturb the widely received wisdom about East Asia's own rising, and latterly newly globalizing 'economic dynamism'. Such wisdom then fuelled the belief that the future fortunes of far distant regions like the North could revive through injections of this dynamism. Not surprisingly, then, any possible East Asian economic crisis casts doubt upon this revivalist thesis and whatever economic future it projects.

Although most of the articles in this volume deal with inward investment, the North's actual economic relationship is also based upon the two-way trade of goods and services. The UK, as one of Europe's largest single investors in, and traders with, East Asia has been seeking to develop this relationship further. Nevertheless, it is not possible to particularize the exact outflow of trade and investment specifically from the North to this area from available statistics. Neither is it yet possible to specify the precise effects on these that an East Asian crisis may have upon likely future trends and possibilities. Quite clearly this is an issue which deserves further research. Otherwise the very idea of an East Asian crisis provides a ready-made instant alibi-cum-explanation whenever business and market performance disappoints. The North currently bears witness to this phenomenon across a wide range of sectors. Not only has this alibi-cum-explanation been widely cited within the recent Siemens and Fujitsu decisions, it has also arisen across other sectors ranging anywhere from bank-note printing to textile machinery and clothing manufacture. Of course it is in the nature of crisis 'contagion' that few ever really specify precisely what effects it actually had. What matters for these purposes is the way this has triggered further beliefs that the North's own economic future has been very much tarnished in consequence.

ACKNOWLEDGEMENTS

We would like to thank Lorna Kennedy at the University of Northumbria for her support in producing this volume.

REFERENCES

Ackroyd, S. and S. Proctor (1998), 'British Manufacturing Organization and Workplace Industrial Relations: Some Attributes of the New Flexible Firm', *British Journal of Industrial Relations*, Vol.36, No.2, pp.163–83.
Anderson, K. and J. Francois (1998), 'Commercial Links between Western Europe and East Asia: Retrospect and Prospects' in P. Drysdale and D. Vines (eds), *Europe, East Asia and APEC: A Shared Global Agenda?* Cambridge: Cambridge University Press, pp.31–52.

Chapman, R.A. (1984), *Public Policy Studies: The North East of England*. Edinburgh: Edinburgh University Press.

Competing in the 21st Century. Newcastle: Government Office North East.

EU (1994), *Towards a New Asia Strategy*. Netherlands.

EU (1998) *The Competitiveness of European Industry*. Netherlands.

Evans, L., P. Johnson and B. Thomas (eds) (1995), *The Northern Region Economy: Progress and Prospects in the North of England*. London: Mansell.

Garrahan, P. and P. Stewart (1992) *The Nissan Enigma: Flexibility at Work in a Local Economy*. London: Mansell.

Garrahan, P. and P. Stewart (eds) (1996) *Urban Change and Renewal*. Aldershot: Avebury.

Hood, N. and S. Young (1997) 'The United Kingdom' in J. Dunning (ed.), *Governments, Globalisation and International Business*. New York: Oxford University Press, pp.244–82.

Hudson, R. (1989), *Wrecking a Region: State Policies, Party Politics and Regional Change in the North East of England*. London: Pion.

Hudson, R. (1995), 'The Role of Foreign Inward Investment' in L. Evans *et al.*, op. cit., pp.79–95.

Longhammer, R. (1998), 'Europe's Trade, Investment and Strategic Policy Interests in Asia and APEC' in P. Drysdale and D. Vines (eds), op. cit., pp.223–54.

Lovering, J. (1997), 'Global Restructuring and Local Impact' in M. Pacione (ed.), *Britain's Cities: Geographies of Division in Urban Britain*. London: Routledge.

Mason, M. and D. Encarnation (1994), *Does Ownership Matter? Japanese Multinationals in Europe*. Oxford: Clarendon Press.

Maul, G., G. Segal and J. Wanandi (eds) (1998) *Europe and the Asia-Pacific*, London: Routledge.

Northern Region Strategy Team (1977), *Strategic Plan for the Northern Region*. London: HMSO.

Pape, W. (ed.) (1998), *East Asia by the Year 2000 and Beyond: Shaping Factors*, A Study for the European Commission. Surrey: Curzon.

Phelps, N.E., J. Lovering, and K. Morgan (1998), 'Tying the Firm to the Region or Tying the Region to the Firm?', *European Urban and Regional Studies*, Vol.5, No.2.

Regional Economic Prospects: The North (1998), Cambridge: Cambridge Econometrics.

Regional Trends (1996) London: Office of National Statistics.

Robinson, F. (1990), *The Great North*, Report for the BBC. Newcastle.

Ruigrok, W. and R. van Tulder, *The Logic of International Restructuring*. London: Routledge.

Sadler, D. (1992), *The Global Region: Production, State Policies, and Uneven Development*. Oxford: Pergamon.

Segal, G. (1998) 'A New ASEM Agenda' in *The Pacific Review*, Vol.11, No.4, pp.561–72.

Sideri, S. (1995) 'The Economic Relations of China and Asia Pacific with Europe' in *Development Policy Review*, Vol.13, pp.219–46.

Stewart, P. (1996), 'Beyond Japan, Beyond Consensus? in P. Stewart (ed.) *Beyond Japanese Management: The End of Modern Times?* London and Portland, OR: Frank Cass, pp.1–20.

Stewart, P. (1998), 'Out of Chaos Comes Order: From Japanisation to Lean Production' in *Employee Relations*, Vol.20, No.3, pp.213–21.

UNCTAD (1997) *Sharing Asia's Dynamism: Asian Direct Investment in the European Union*. Geneva: United Nations Publications.

1

Fast but Fragile: British Restructuring for Foreign Direct Investment in a Global Era

LOUISE AMOORE

When the Fujitsu Corporation announced the closure of its North East semi-conductor plant in September 1998, Prime Minister Tony Blair declared that the British government could not 'do much about the twists and turns of world markets in an increasingly globalized economy'. In the same statement, Blair announced that a further £100 million would be made available for the forthcoming Northeast Development Agency. This political statement provides considerable insights into the contradictions of globalization. On the one hand, there is the image of the forces of globalization 'squeezing' state authority into 'retreat' and reducing the ability of governments to exercise 'command over outcomes' (Strange, 1996: 3). On the other, the state participates in a kind of 'beauty contest' to attract foreign direct investment (FDI) through the agencies of the 'competition state' and, thus, actively involves itself in globalization (Cerny, 1990). Thus, the attraction of FDI is viewed as a legitimate political activity of the competition state, while the 'exit' of FDI is presented as an unfortunate but inevitable reality of globalization beyond the political control of the state.

The interrelationships between the much-debated and contested processes of 'globalization', the restructuring of the state and the politics of FDI, must surely draw some insights from the contradictions outlined above. For the case of Britain over the past 15 years, this exercise is of particular significance. Academic, political and corporate debates in the early 1990s tended to present the Anglo-American panacea of 'fast' restructuring for a 'competitive' state, 'lean' firm and 'flexible' labour market, as the best-practice response to the pressures of globalization (World Bank, 1995; OECD, 1994). However, the East-Asian economic

Louise Amoore, Division of Goverment and Politics, University of Northumbria at Newcastle crises of the late 1990s has precipitated a widespread questioning, both of the export-oriented 'Asian model' of development, and of the possible contagion in Western financial markets and 'FDI-attracting' Western states. In this sense, the 'fast but fragile' nature of Anglo-Saxon style restructuring has been rendered increasingly visible by the political-economic and social crises experienced by East Asian state-societies with consequences for the wider world economy.

The discussion here seeks to demonstrate that the British approach to restructuring, geared towards attracting foreign industrial and financial capital, reflects and embodies both a distinctive set of historical state-societal relations and a distinctive understanding of what globalization implies for these relations (Streeck, 1997; Albert, 1993). In short, the equation that 'globalization' equals 'attract FDI' constitutes an oversimplification that neglects the historical specificity and social and political agency of processes of restructuring. The first part outlines the orthodox reading of neo-liberal globalization, with an emphasis on how the Anglo-American 'FDI-centred' approach to restructuring has become a kind of accepted 'best practice'. The second part seeks to critically reassess our understandings of FDI through a process of 'embedding' strategies of attracting FDI in a specific state-society context. In this way we seek to problematize the British 'ideal type' model of restructuring and to make visible some of the contradictions of neo-liberal globalization, particularly the inherent failure of British restructuring to attract 'dedicated capital' (Watson and Hay, 1998). Finally, the third part explores the 'fast but fragile' nature of British restructuring. This is addressed at the interrelated levels of restructuring within state and society, and within the firm.

NEO-LIBERAL GLOBALIZATION AND THE FDI 'BEAUTY CONTEST'

The concept of globalization has become rather an overused and totalizing label for multiple aspects of social, political and economic change (Jones, 1995; Hirst and Thompson, 1996; Boyer and Drache, 1996). Indeed, some scholars have suggested that the concept should be abandoned to prevent its reification in political, academic and corporate debates.[1] However, there is a central problem associated with 'forgetting globalization'. Though the term may indeed have come into general usage as a rather 'empty' and vague concept, it has become 'filled' with meanings that have significant implications for political-economic and social life. Globalization has become inextricably associated with a discourse of imperative restructuring so that the 'global era' is defined in terms of a need for states, firms and societies to restructure their basic institutions and practices around a 'neo liberal' model of competitiveness. For states,[2] this restructuring has been variously described as shifts to the 'competition state' (Cerny, 1990; Palan and Abbott, 1996), the 'marketization' of the state (Strange, 1996), and the 'hollowing out' of the state (Jessop, 1994). The emphasis here has been on the need for political policy agendas that actively create a competitive, low cost and 'firm friendly' location for 'footloose' industrial and financial capital. For firms, the restructuring prescriptions that have been most dominant in the globalization discourse have called for the 'lean', 'flexible' and 'adaptable' organization (see Womack, Jones and Roos, 1990). Such restructuring imperatives send similar messages to individuals and social groups. In the grip of globalization, we are told, there is little alternative but to transform our working practices, our employment expectations, and our overall sense of security and stability (see Beck, 1992).

In this way, the 'empty' concept of globalization has been filled with a set of neo-liberal policy implications. Ideas as to the competitive state and the competitive firm emerge as symbols of efficiency, flexibility and leanness so that the boundaries between public management and private management appear blurred (see Cerny, 1991). Academic analysis of globalization and restructuring thus tends to focus either on the borrowing of private sector doctrines by the state (see Weiss, 1998) or on the bargaining relationships developed between large firms and agencies of the state (see Stopford and Strange, 1991). In both instances symbols of restructuring success in states and firms are selectively drawn into a model of 'best practice'. Throughout the 1990s, the 'best practice' for attracting FDI has turned on an axis of 'business focused' state subsidies and packages, flexible and low cost labour, deregulated telecommunications infrastructure, and 'room for manoeuvre' for incoming firms: in short, a state-sponsored promise of 'no strings attached'. As Streeck (1997) has emphasized, for example, the 'triumph' of this Anglo-Saxon 'low cost deregulatory' model has positioned neo-liberal restructuring practices as 'outcompeting' the 'high cost–high quality' practices of the German social market.

There are many problems with the assumption that Anglo-Saxon restructuring for FDI, as exemplified by Britain through the 1980s and 90s, offers some kind of 'best practice' response to intensified global competition with the potential for emulation by other state-societies. Two sets of these problems are central to our investigation of the British quest for FDI. First, in the wake of the East Asian crises, the Anglo-Saxon 'best practice' has begun to show its fragility and vulnerability. We are increasingly reminded that the very policies that attract foreign firms through a promise of 'no strings attached' make Britain 'as easy to exit as it is to enter' (Observer, 2 August 1998). Second, there are many countries in the advanced industrialized world who not only provide few signs of policy convergence around the Anglo-Saxon model, but also actively pursue alternative strategies with divergent emphases from those in Britain, often with the 'strings' of regulation remaining very much intact (Albert, 1993; Streeck, 1997; Casper, 1999; Berger and Dore, 1996). In this sense, the British approach to restructuring through the attraction of FDI, particularly as compared to continental European state-societies, has distinctive and 'exceptional' dynamics. The questions raised in British debates as to the 'right' response to globalization have tended to focus on the attractiveness of Britain to foreign industrial and financial capital. If we are to understand the origins of these questions then we must reassess our understandings of FDI so that we may view restructuring as embedded within a distinctive set of historical political and social institutions and practices.

RE-EMBEDDING FDI

The dominant image of globalization presents FDI flows as accelerating and increasing in line with the trans-border movements of multi-national corporations (MNCs) (Dunning, 1995), the internationalization of the division of labour, the standardization of products (Chan, 1995), and the trends towards regional groupings in the world political economy (Ohmae, 1990). Indeed, it is clear that, from the 1970s, reductions in barriers to flows of goods and capital have contributed to a rapid increase in the volume of FDI stock in the world economy.[3] Viewed from this perspective, FDI appears as both the 'product' of intensified global competition and as a 'vehicle' for increased globalization as political economies become ever more closely interlinked via investment flows. FDI can, then, take on the guise of a process that 'decouples' or 'disembeds' production, investment and work from bounded national territories.

The image of FDI as a disembedded global force has not, however, gone unchallenged. Commentators from diverse fields and perspectives have sought to emphasize the 'embedded' nature of FDI in specific sets of social power relations, institutions, ideas and practices. For these scholars, FDI is not 'global' in the sense of an all-encompassing and totalizing force. For example, it has been widely demonstrated that the bulk of FDI flows originate from the advanced industrialized countries and are received by other advanced industrialized countries, with the exception of a select group of East Asian and Latin American states.[4] Insights such as these serve to demonstrate one level at which FDI is 'embedded' in social power relations: in the intensification of linkages within and between a grouping of predominantly western states.

A concern with the embeddedness of FDI in the state-societal relations of a particular group of states provides a route into the politicization of our understandings of FDI. That is to say, we are reminded of the political and social agency that underpins economic flows of investment across the borders of nation states:

> So-called globalization needs to be viewed as a politically rather than technologically induced phenomenon... a number of states are seeking directly to promote and encourage rather than constrain the internationalization of corporate activity in trade, investment and production. From this perspective, the internationalization of capital may not merely restrict policy choices, but expand them as well.
>
> (Weiss, 1998: 209).

In a general sense, then, we are reminded that the perceived 'global' economic FDI activities are bound up in political decision, corporate strategy, a dense array of institutional constraints such as financial and innovation systems and, 'from below', in the everyday experiences of change in the workplace. In this way, the 'myth of the powerless state' is exposed (Weiss, 1998), revealing the extent to which the state actively politically participates in the generation, reproduction and receipt of FDI.

At the level of the firm we can also find considerable evidence to counter the image of the global 'footloose' and disembedded MNC carrying FDI across borders. Sally (1994: 162) calls for the MNC to be 'located and analysed in its outer politico-economic environments' so that aspects of the restructuring of overseas plants reflect the dominant embedded institutions and practices of the home nation. Indeed, as Watson and Hay argue, contrary to the 'footloose' image of MNCs, there is at least the potential for a degree of underlying embeddedness in host nation states:

> Even the giants of the multinational world still need to put down roots in their host localities.... Yet the myth of 'hyper-mobility' may well be a necessary and certainly a strategic myth for firms to maintain if they wish to maximise their hold over governments. Capital tends to talk up the possibility of disinvestment through mobility in order to secure a capital-friendly economic climate with as few regulatory constraints as possible on its activities.
>
> (Watson and Hay, 1998: 417).

Thus, the bargaining hand of firms may be strengthened by the maintenance of a 'footloose' image. In such instances, governments may offer subsidies and incentives to curb the perceived wanderlust of the firm. This practice can be seen in the example of the British government's 'aid' package to the BMW-owned Rover plant at Longbridge. The threat in this instance was perceived to be the ability of the firm to move with relative ease to a lower cost/higher subsidy location in Hungary.

The insights provided here suggest that FDI should be studied not as an automatic globalizing phenomenon, but as a debated, negotiated and contested set of practices within specific state-societal contexts. In the British context, the entrance and exit of FDI has been highly debated and contested in social, political and corporate forums. In the regions characterized by a decline in traditional industrial employment, the quest for FDI has been the central plank of policies of regeneration (Sadler, 1992). The vulnerability of the FDI-centred approach has been strongly emphasized by the after-shocks of the East Asian crises, particularly in the 'old industrial regions' of the North of England and South Wales. East Asian multinationals have announced plant closures, capital freezes and the cancellation of UK expansion plans.

The British experience of outflows of capital in the wake of the East Asian crisis is not a simple contingent phenomenon. Since 1979, outflows of capital from the UK have consistently exceeded inflows in FDI (Economist Intelligence Unit, 1998), and redundancies in British-owned multinationals have far exceeded employment creation in FDI implants (Coates, 1999). As Weiss (1998) argues, a large proportion of FDI flows are constituted of 'paper entrepreneurship' in the form of portfolio purchases involving mergers and acquisitions of existing assets. For Weiss, such investment flows are speculative rather than strictly productive and, thus, represent evidence 'less of a growing global economy than of an embattled productive system' (1998: 174). Thus, we may be led to ask whether the impacts of the East Asian crisis on FDI are isolated and unique phenomena, or if perhaps they provide a glimpse of a deeper fragility in restructuring for FDI.

In the light of such contemporary questions of the potential fragility of restructuring for FDI 'attractiveness', it is important to critically reconsider the historical context of the British approach. If the East Asian crisis has punctured a deep hole in the Anglo-Saxon 'attraction' model, then it would seem important to seek to understand the specific social institutions and practices that have informed that model over time.

THE BRITISH APPROACH TO ATTRACTING FDI

Exceptionalism and the British State

It is notable that over recent years, despite the ascendancy of 'globalization' as an 'explain all' concept, there has been a simultaneous revival of attention paid to the distinctiveness of that peculiar creature - British capitalism. Perhaps most elegantly articulated by Nairn and Andersen in their New Left review 'exceptionalism' thesis,[5] the idea that British capitalism has historically privileged financial capital over industrial capital, has enjoyed renewed prominence in recent years (see Cox et al., 1997; Albert, 1993; Ingham, 1984; Hutton, 1995). The relative isolation of British financial capital from the process of industrialization, its historical international orientation, and the short-term relationship between banks and industry, are all frequently-cited and broadly accepted features of the British industrial order (Hall, 1986; Hutton, 1995; Cox, 1986; Woolcock, 1996). In the context of early industrialization, Britain's industries could be financed privately from non-bank and local bank sources and, in particular, from accumulated profits. Thus, the organized and universal banking systems characteristic of Germany, for example, were not developed, or indeed required, in Britain's first industrial revolution (Cox et al., 1997). The City of London had established itself as the world's centre for commodity trade by the late eighteenth century and, thus, was relatively decoupled from the industrial revolution. Ingham's (1984) analysis demonstrates that, as a commercial centre, the practices of the City of London were designed to protect the short-term requirements of commercial activity. Thus, in the British case, the political-economic and social requirements of industrialization may be viewed as distinct and separate from the interests of the City as a world financial centre: British capitalism has maintained a distinctive dual character – as the first industrial economy and as the world's major commercial entrepot (Ingham, 1984: 6).

Ultimately, then, the 'dual' nature of British capitalism has meant that the two faces of industrial and financial capital have competing and contradictory needs. British financial capital is oriented towards securing high short-term returns on investment for shareholders. Thus, the state tends to protect a strong and stable currency, a balanced budget and relatively high interest rates. For indigenous industries, this locks firms into raising capital on the stock market with its emphasis on short-term returns. As Hutton argues, the City's need for liquidity clashes with industry's need for some medium to long-term planning (1995: 132). Thus, it has been widely argued, British systems of corporate governance are preoccupied with financial soundness to the detriment of longer-term manufacturing ideas and innovation (Woolcock, 1996). Such constraints tend to limit the opportunities for a restructuring strategy based on the export competitiveness of indigenous industries, and favour the strategy of attracting overseas capital investment.[6] Indeed, the 'hands off' state stance is actively promoted to attract foreign firms with the tacit promise of 'fast and free' entrance and exit opportunities.

The British predilection for 'shareholder capitalism' (Seccombe, 1999), 'cost reduction' restructuring (Esping-Andersen, 1996), and neo-liberal industrial relations (Coates, 1999), has been a particularly visible aspect of the debates surrounding the British response to globalization. Indeed, many scholars, apparently seeking to critique the 'retreat of the state' thesis (Strange, 1996), have asserted the explanatory power of comparative political economy in highlighting the importance of state traditions, institutions and practices in defining restructuring responses (see Crouch and Streeck, 1997; Streeck, 1997; Berger and Dore, 1996; Rubery, 1993; Vogel, 1996). The use of cross-national comparisons effectively demonstrates the diverse range of restructuring responses that have emerged in the era of globalization. Vogel's analysis of the restructuring strategies of advanced industrialized states suggests that they will tend to favour one of two strategies. The first is a programme of 'pro-competitive disengagement' where the state actively deregulates its financial and labour markets to attract foreign capital and shifts the state support from indigenous industries to the promotion of FDI zones. The second is a programme of 'strategic reinforcement' where the state seeks to reinforce the competitive advantage of indigenous industries through concerted support and industry-centred restructuring (Vogel, 1996: 263). From this perspective, the restructuring programmes of successive British governments have represented a 'pro-competitive disengagement' so that in the restructuring of industrial relations, for example, the emphasis has been on a devolution of bargaining and negotiation to the level of the individual firm.

From a different perspective, the literature concerned with the overseas location decisions of firms, similarly emphasizes perceptions of a distinctive British environment for incoming direct investment. With regard to the location decisions of US and East Asian firms, it has become widely accepted 'common sense' knowledge that the central motivation for European location is a foothold in the European market (Barrell and Pain, 1997; Dunning, 1993; Pickernell, 1998). However, within the European region itself, the location decisions of foreign firms demonstrate clear perceptions of a distinctive British policy context. Here we find an emphasis on the importance of cost competitiveness, the deregulated structures of the UK labour, financial and telecommunications markets, and the willingness of the state to provide 'aid' to encourage company 'entry' and to prevent company 'exit':

> The key objective was to locate within the EU to gain access to the wider regional market. Particular locations within the EU were then chosen on the basis of their cost competitiveness with other possible EU locations, with the UK gaining the largest share of such investments.
>
> (Barrell and Pain, 1997: 67)

In the context of the consideration of the British approach to FDI, the 'exceptionalism' perspective provides some key insights into the distinctive relationship between the British state and overseas firms. However, it would be problematic to assume that there is historical 'path dependency' in the British model of restructuring. Rather, it is argued here that contemporary restructuring for FDI should be understood in the light of wider historical social relations between the state, financial institutions, business organizations and the interests of labour. While it is clear that such relationships may transform, or indeed be radically restructured over time, it is not the case that the forces of globalization decouple the policy agendas of the competition state from their embedded historical institutions and practices.

The Firm and Restructuring in the British Context

A central problem in the critical investigation of the nature of FDI location in Britain is that we cannot sketch a model of one single and 'ideal type' FDI firm. Indeed, as Barrell and Pain argue (1997), the bulk of new direct investments tends to be in non-manufacturing industries, though academic, political and media attention tends to be directed at the high profile manufacturing FDI firms such as those in the automotive sector (see Stewart and Garrahan, 1997; Pickernell, 1998; Elger, 1991). However, a central theme in studies of British inward FDI across diverse sectors is the observation that such firms tend to represent footloose and fickle sources of investment that tend to evade long-term ties (see Watson and Hay, 1998). Indeed, a dominant theme seems to be that the inward investing firm can effectively blackmail governments with threats of capital flight:

> In circumstances in which the threat of capital flight is perceived to be a real one, inward investors may well be rewarded (with extra economic subsidies and political favours) merely for staying put.
>
> (Watson and Hay, 1998: 417)

In this way linkages between firms and their host localities tend to be 'bought' by states, raising questions as to whether longer-term connections between inward investors and their host regions are sustainable. It is these connections (or lack of them) that have provided a central theme for this volume. A key observation linking the articles is the paucity of 'real' social connections between the overseas firms that locate in British regions and the social groups whose everyday lives are influenced by their location. In essence, the policy agenda of the 'FDI competitive' state actively invites firms to abstain from long-term connections with their host society. The absence of such connections can be viewed in terms of three sets of relationships: between the inward investor firm (IIF) and the state; between the IIF and other firms in the production chain, such as suppliers, contractors and the like; and between the IIF employer and groups of employees, extending to their families and communities.

Inward investor firms and the state: The institutions, social power relations and political policy agendas of a particular nation-state provide a set of parameters which offer opportunities and constraints to the firms that locate there (see Sally, 1994; 1996). From this perspective, we may consider that firms establish operations overseas precisely to broaden or transform the range of possible solutions to the 'what' and 'how' questions of production. Questions such as 'will the state allow access to key markets? 'can the employer freely access a flexible external labour market?' or 'will the specific regulations governing labour allow for periodic lay-offs?' may be critical to location decisions.

The British context provides answers to these questions that emphasize the ability of investor firms to externalize some of their costs onto the state-society. The externalizing of social costs is clearly evident in the prevalence of so-called greenfield sites in the British case. The establishment of such sites with no existing embedded patterns of industrial relations, production or working practices, is a key illustration of the relationship between the British competition state and the IIF. Locations effectively become greenfield through active deregulatory government policies which minimize the restrictions on, for example, planning, the use of labour and corporate taxation. Thus, in terms of the use of land, labour and capital, the IIF is effectively given concessions from some of the 'bonds' that link production to a particular locality.

Inward investor firms and inter-firm relations: It was suggested in the second part of this article that the centrality of equity finance and shareholder value in the British context tends to impose a short-term time-frame on investment decisions. This short-termism has particular implications for the relationships between inward investor firms and their suppliers, contractors and outside agencies such as training or innovation institutions. In effect, the British approach to attracting FDI actively promotes Britain as a location that enables rapid responses to fluctuations in global markets. The rapid responses of Siemens and Fujitsu to fluctuations in global semi-conductor markets provide a case in point here. This emphasis on 'speed' of response tends to promote an atmosphere of uncertainty between firms in a supply chain. As a manager of a component SME reported:

> Just-in-time production relies on a minimization of inventory stock. But the fact is, your large production plant may have low inventories but the slack has to be taken up somewhere. In effect, we as suppliers of components, hold reserve inventory for our client purchasers. It is quite a risk we take in doing this.
> (Production manager, British components supply firm)[7]

Thus, the courting of FDI on the basis of flexibility of response does have considerable implications for the security of local supply SMEs. In general, the much-lauded 'uncertainties' and fluctuations of globalization are actually exacerbated by some of the strategic responses put in place by the state.

Inward investor employers and their employees: As has been suggested, a central plank of the British restructuring strategy for attracting FDI has been the provision of a deregulated and 'flexible' labour market. Indeed, prominent international organizations have raised the profile of Britain as having a flexible, low cost labour market, which should be emulated by other nation-states seeking to be FDI competitive (see OECD, 1991; 1996; 1998; World Bank, 1995). The pursuit of such flexibility policies, not unsurprisingly, has considerable implications for industrial relations as we have conventionally understood such relations (Amoore, 1998).[8] Following Herrigel, restructuring practices that are designed to create flexibility, taken to their ultimate conclusion cause 'the old style firm to disintegrate entirely into an infinitely recombinable set of roles and relations that the participants themselves reflect upon and restructure' (1994: 6). In this way, the basic unit of relations between employer and employee in the British context has become the individual.

The individualized contract that characterizes such 'enterprise labour market' social relations tends to have wider implications for skills, job security and the stability of the wider community in which the firm is located. The reduction in labour costs and the increase in flexibility which the employer seeks to gain from restructuring is not without considerable price. The costs of losing trained and skilled workers in lay-offs are widely recognized by management groups (see McCabe, 1996; Rubery, 1996). The use of contract labour and the proliferation of lay-offs not only has implications for the costs of formal training, but also reduces the lines of communication between employer and employee, and between worker groups, so that information-sharing becomes increasingly difficult to promote. Thus, the kinds of production practices that require 'employee voice' (Marsden, 1995: 17), such as those in high-tech and high value-added industries, are less likely to locate in Britain than in other European countries (Casper, 1999). The absence of strong connections between worker groups within the firm not only has production implications, but also widely documented impacts on the cohesion and security of the constituent society that provides the local labour market:

> At the core of the neo-liberal ideal of unfettered capital mobility and flexible labour markets lies an abstract individualism that makes it extremely difficult to keep families intact and communities pulling together.
>
> (Seccombe, 1999: 99)

Overall, then, the British approach to attracting FDI has actively promoted the advertisement of a 'no strings' location for inward investors. In so doing, it has arguably created short-term opportunities at the expense of longer-term objectives. The exposure of British IIFs to the fluctuations and turbulence of international product and financial markets during the period 1997–98 has served to highlight the precarious nature of the FDI beauty contest. In effect, the vicissitudes of globalization are exacerbated by strategies that closely connect everyday social life to the dictates of the world economy.

CONCLUSIONS: THE CONTRADICTIONS AND TENSIONS OF THE FAST BUT FRAGILE APPROACH

Orthodox understandings of the relationship between processes of globalization and strategies of FDI, it has been argued here, tend to overemphasize the economic nature of restructuring, while underemphasizing the political and social underpinnings of this restructuring. In a sense this provides us with a cautionary tale that to be seduced by the imperatives of the globalization mantra is to neglect the complexity and historicity of restructuring for FDI. The analysis here has sought to show that British policy approaches to restructuring to attract FDI are informed by distinctive historical institutions, practices and power relationships. Thus, the British approach does not represent a 'model response' to the challenges of a global era, but rather a specific and particular response with its own inherent tensions and contradictions.

First, British policy debates tend to coalesce around a distinctive set of questions in response to the challenges of globalization. Questions are raised with regard to how government policy can most effectively clear space for a competitive environment for foreign industrial and financial capital. On the one hand, the response to such questions has been to create the image of a 'hands-off' deregulated state attitude to foreign firms. This has been seen, for example, in terms of a deregulated industrial relations system which allows scope for the negotiation of single-union or no-union agreements by incoming firms. On the other hand, a new and 'legitimate' domain for state intervention has been created where the competition state may 'play the game' with subsidies, grants and tax breaks (see Palan and Abbott, 1996). Indeed, new agencies of the state such as, for example, Regional Development Agencies and regional offices in Brussels, are created precisely to implement policies designed to attract FDI. This policy focus, we have demonstrated, finds its distinctive roots in historical institutions and practices. Thus, understandings of global restructuring have tended to be linked to the promotion of Britain as a low cost location for industrial investment and a historically strong centre for financial capital in the City of London.

In some respects the 'low cost' British orientation appears to be more of a 'non-decision'[9] in the sense that the significance lies more in the strategies *not* selected than those supported. The high-tech, high value-added strategies widely ascribed to German state-society, for example, are not seen as congruent with the British context (Streeck, 1997; Casper, 1999). Of course, a central tension here is that the pursuit of 'cost competitiveness' as a priority tends to lock a political economy into a kind of 'race to the bottom'.[10] The adoption of low cost strategies, and the rejection of high skills alternatives, positions Britain in competition with less developed economies and, thus, makes the British political economy vulnerable to company 'exit'. In short, the dominance of the 'how to attract FDI' set of questions has precluded alternative questions such as how to make indigenous firms globally competitive.

Second, the time-frame underlying the restructuring programme in the British context is historically distinctive. The overriding emphasis has tended to be placed on the speed and flexibility of firms' responses to changes in global market conditions. Thus, it is seen as of critical importance that firms have the ability to expand and contract their operations in line with global market trends. For the state, a key policy priority is thus seen as the provision of an environment for firms which allows for this kind of rapid 'just-in-time' adjustment. Within the British state-societal context, the nature of restructuring to attract FDI has been 'fast but fragile', involving few social groups in negotiation with policy makers and corporate actors. This 'instantaneous' conception of time reflects an overall emphasis on equity financing of ventures and the consequent need to secure rapid short-term returns on investment in a 'share-owning democracy' (Graham, 1997: 126). Within such a time-frame, the uncertainties of globalization are exacerbated by acute exposure to the vacillations of world markets so that the collapse of the global semi-conductor market or shocks in the world financial system can be felt almost instantaneously at a local level.

Finally, the debates surrounding restructuring for FDI attractiveness tend to occupy a distinctive set of social domains in the British context. While the British state has actively involved itself in the production and reproduction of a 'low cost' and deregulated competitive political economy, it has tended to remove itself from responsibility for many of the tensions that have emerged as a result. In these instances, responsibility is abdicated to the 'dictates of global markets', and the image of a 'powerless state' is restated (see Weiss, 1998). Thus, the contradictions of the British restructuring programme have tended to be felt most keenly in the branch-plant workplaces where insecurity and uncertainty are intensified (see Rubery, 1993: 17; Seccombe, 1999) and within 'host' regions, where dependency on incoming plants may be acute. This has led some scholars to question the quality of the investment brought to a particular region by the establishment of a plant (see Watson and Hay, 1998).

Overall, then, it is problematic to assume that the British 'FDI focus' represents an archetypal 'best practice' response to globalization. Rather, it is a response that is informed by a distinctive array of historical institutions and social power relations, and which continues to be debated, negotiated and contested as its tensions and contradictions become ever more visible in a period of world economic turbulence.

ACKNOWLEDGEMENTS

This article draws upon research conducted for the PhD thesis 'The Social Roots of Global Change: States, Firms and the Restructuring of Work', December 1998, University of Newcastle-upon-Tyne. The research was funded by the ESRC, award number R00429534005. The author wishes to thank Dr Paul Langley and Professor Philip Garrahan for helpful comments. The usual disclaimers apply.

REFERENCES

Albert, M. (1993) *Capitalism Against Capitalism*. London: Whurr.
Amoore, L., R. Dodgson, B.K. Gills, P. Langley, D. Marshall and I. Watson (1997) 'Overturning Globalisation: Resisting the Teleological, Reclaiming the Political', *New Political Economy*, Vol.2:, No.1, pp.179–95.
Amoore, L. (1998) 'Globalisation, the Industrial Society, and Labour Flexibility: A sense of déja vu?', *Global Society*, Vol.12, No.1, pp.49–76.
Anderson, P. (1991) *English Questions*. London: Verso.
Barrell, R. and N. Pain (1997) 'The Growth of Foreign Direct Investment in Europe', *National Institute Economic Review*, April, 160, pp.63–75.
Beck, U. (1992) *Risk Society*. London: Sage.

Berger, S. and R. Dore (eds) (1996) *National Diversity and Global Capitalism*. Ithaca: Cornell University Press.

Boyer, R. and D. Drache (eds) (1996) *States Against Markets: The Limits of Globalisation*. London: Routledge.

Casper, S. (1999) *National Institutional Frameworks and High-Technology Innovation in Germany: The Case of Biotechnology*, paper presented to the 40th Annual Convention of the International Studies Association, 16–20 February 1999, Washington DC.

Cerny, P.G. (1990) *The Changing Architecture of Politics: Structure, Agency and the Future of the State*. London: Sage.

Cerny, P.G. (1991) 'The Limits of Deregulation, Transnational Interpenetration and Policy Change', *European Journal of Political Research*, Vol.19, No.2, pp.173–96.

Chan, S. (1995) FDI in a Changing Global Political Economy. Basingstoke: Macmillan.

Coates, D. (1999) 'Labour Power and international Competitiveness: A Critique of Ruling Orthodoxies', *The Socialist Register*.

Commission of the European Communities (CEC) (1993) Growth, Competitiveness and Employment – The Challenges and Ways Forward into the 21st Century, White Paper. Brussels.

Cox, A (1986) *The State, Finance and Industry*. Brighton: Harvester Wheatsheaf.

Cox, A., S. Lee and J. Sanderson (eds) (1997) *The Political Economy of Modern Britain*. Cheltenham: Edward Elgar.

Crouch, C. and W. Streeck (eds) (1997) *Political Economy of Modern Capitalism*. London: Sage.

Cumbers, A. (1995) 'Continuity or Change in Employment Relations? Evidence from the UK's Old Industrial Regions', *Capital And Class*, No.58, pp.33–57.

Dore, R. (1973) *British Factory, Japanese Factory: The Origins of National Diversity*. Los Angeles: University of Colorado Press.

Dunning, J. (1993) *The Globalization of Business: The Challenge of the 1990s*. London: Routledge.

Economist Intelligence Unit (EIU) (1998) *Country Report, UK, 2nd quarter*, London.

Elger, T. (1991) 'Task Flexibility and the Intensification of Labour in UK Manufacturing in the 1980s', in A. Pollert (ed.) (1991), *Farewell to Flexibility?* Oxford: Blackwell.

Elger, T. and P. Fairbrother (1992) 'Inflexible Flexibility: A Case Study of Modularisation', in N. Gilbert, R. Burrows and A. Pollert, *Fordism and Flexibility: Divisions and Change*. London: Macmillan.

Gamble, A. (1994) *Britain in Decline: Economic Policy, Political Strategy and the British State* 4th edition. Basingstoke: Macmillan.

Graham, A. (1997) 'The UK 1979–95: Myths and Realities of Conservative Capitalism', in C. Crouch and W. Streeck (eds), *Political Economy of Modern Capitalism*. London: Sage.

Gray, A. (1998) 'New Labour – New Labour Discipline', *Capital and Class*, 65, Summer, pp.1–8.

Harrod, J. (1997) 'Globalisation and Social Policy', paper prepared for 22nd Annual BISA Conference, University of Leeds, 15th–17th December.

Hart, J. (1992) *Rival Capitalists: International Competitiveness in the United States, Japan and Western Europe*, Ithaca: Cornell University Press.

Hirst, P. and G. Thompson (1996) *Globalisation in Question*. Cambridge: Polity Press.

Hollingsworth, J.R. and R. Boyer (eds) (1997) *Contemporary Capitalism: The Embeddedness of Institutions*. Cambridge: Cambridge University Press.

Hutton, W. (1995) *The State We're In*. London: Cape.

Ingham, G. (1984) *Capitalism Divided: The City and Industry in British Social Development*. London: Macmillan.

Jessop, B. (1994) 'Post-Fordism and the State', in A. Amin (ed.), *Post-Fordism: A Reader*. Oxford: Blackwell

Jones, R.J. Barry (1995) *Globalisation and Interdependence in the International Political Economy*. London: Pinter.

Lane, C. (1994) 'Industrial Order and the Transformation of Industrial Relations: Britain,

Germany and France Compared' in R. Hyman and R. Ferner (eds), *New Frontiers in European Industrial Relations*. Oxford: Basil Blackwell.

McCabe, D. (1996) 'The Best Laid Schemes O' TQM: Strategy, Politics and Power', *New Technology, Work and Employment*, Vol.11, No.1, pp.28–38.

Nairn, T. (1993) 'The Sole Survivor', *New Left Review*, 200, pp.40–47.

OECD, (1991) *OECD Observer*, 'Making Labour Markets Work', Vol.173.

OECD, (1994) *'Jobs Study: Facts, Analyses, Strategies'*. Paris.

OECD (1997) *International Direct Investment Statistics Yearbook*. Paris.

OECD (1998) 'Direct Investment Positions', *OECD Observer*, 212, June/July, Paris.

Ohmae, K. (1990) *The Borderless World: Power and Strategy in the Interlinked Economy*. London: Fontana.

Palan, R. and Abbott, J. (1996) *State Strategies in the Global Political Economy*, London: Pinter.

Pickernell, D. (1998) 'FDI in the UK Car Component Industry: Recent Causes and Consequences', *Journal of Economic and Social Geography*, Vol.89, No.3, pp.239–52.

Piore, M. and C. Sabel (1984) *The Second Industrial Divide*. New York: Basic Books.

Rubery, J. (1993) 'The UK Production Regime in Comparative Perspective'. Unpublished conference paper, 'Production Regimes in an Integrating Europe', UMIST, Manchester.

Rubery, J. (1996) 'The Labour Market Outlook and the Outlook for Labour Market Analysis', in R. Crompton, D. Gallie and K. Purcell (eds), *Changing Forms of Employment*. London: Routledge.

Ruigrok, W. and R. Van Tulder (1995) *The Logic of International Restructuring: The Management of Dependencies in Rival Industrial Complexes*. London: Routledge.

Sadler, D. (1992) *The Global Region: Production, State Policies and Uneven Development*. Oxford: Pergamon.

Sally, R. (1994) 'Multinational Enterprises, Political Economy and Institutional Theory: Domestic Embeddedness in the Context of Internationalization'. *Review of International Political Economy*, Vol.1, No.1, pp.163–92.

Sally, R. (1996) 'Public Policy and the Janus Face of the MNE: National Embeddedness and International Production', in P. Gummett (ed.), *Globalization and Public Policy*. Cheltenham: Elgar.

Seccombe, W. (1999) 'Contradictions of Shareholder Capitalism: Downsizing jobs, Enlisting Savings, Destabilizing Families', *Socialist Register*.

Stewart, P. and P. Garrahan (1997) 'Globalization: The Company and the Workplace: Some Interim Evidence from the Auto Industry in Britain', in A. Scott (ed.), *The Limits of Globalization: Cases and Arguments*. London: Routledge.

Stopford, J. and S. Strange (1991) *Rival States, Rival Firms: Competition for World Market Shares*. New York: Cambridge University Press.

Strange, S. (1986) *Casino Capitalism*. London: Blackwell.

Strange, S. (1988) *States and Markets*. London: Pinter.

Strange, S. (1996) *The Retreat of the State: The Diffusion of Power in the World Economy*. Cambridge: Cambridge University Press.

Streeck, W. (1997) 'German Capitalism: Does it Exist? Can It Survive?', *New Political Economy*, Vol.2, No.2, pp.237–56.

Vitols, S. and S. Woolcock (1997) 'Developments in the German and British Corporate Governance Systems', Discussion paper prepared for Workshop on Corporate Governance in Britain and Germany, Wissenschaftszentrum, Berlin, June 1997.

Vogel, S.V. (1996) *Freer Markets, More Rules: Regulatory Reform in Advanced Industrialised Countries,*.Ithaca: Cornell University Press.

Watson, M. and C. Hay (1998) 'In the Dedicated Pursuit of Dedicated Capital: Restoring an Indigenous Investment Ethic to British Capitalism', *New Political Economy*, Vol.3, No.3, pp.407–26.

Weiss, L. (1998) *The Myth of the Powerless State: Governing the Economy in a Global Era*. Cambridge: Polity Press.

Womak, J.P., D. Jones and D. Roos (1990) *The Machine That Changed the World*. New York: MIT Press.

Woolcock, S. (1996) 'Competition Among Rules in the Single European Market' in W.

Bratton (ed.), *International Regulatory Competition and Coordination: Perspectives on Economic Regulation in Europe and the US*. London: Wiley.
World Bank, (1995) 'Workers in an Integrating World', *World Development Report*, Oxford University Press.

NOTES

1. Jeffrey Harrod, for example, argues that the use of the concept 'globalization' effectively reifies and legitimates the concept and that it should be rejected in favour of more precise terms. Insights drawn from discussion following a paper presented by Harrod at the BISA 22nd Annual Conference, 15–17 December 1997, University of Leeds.

2. The 'imperative' interpretation of restructuring under globalization is embodied, for example, in international policy literature that seeks to communicate 'best practice' restructuring to individual nation states: 'The forces of globalisation increase both the benefits of good policies and the costs of failure... Whether a new golden age arrives for all depends mostly on the responses of individual countries to the new opportunities offered by this increasingly global economy' (World Bank, 1995: 54).

3. Barrell and Pain (1997: 63) estimate that between 1975 and 1995 the aggregate stock of FDI in the world economy has risen from 4.5% to 9.5% of world output. The value of sales by foreign affiliates of domestic firms exceeded the value of world exports by one quarter by the mid-1990s.

4. Chan (1995: 1) emphasizes the 'dense networks of cross-holdings of production and financial assets among the industrialised countries of the world', arguing that Western Europe, North America, Japan and a select group of East Asian states accounted for the vast proportion of all FDI flows generated and received in the 1990s. Similarly, Hirst and Thompson argue that the generation and receipt of FDI is almost exclusively the preserve of the 'triadic' countries of the EU, NAFTA, and Japan: 'the Triad countries, while making up only 14% of the world population in 1990, attracted 75% of FDI flows over the 1980s...Adding the ten most important developing countries in terms of FDI... gives a total of 43% of the world's population in receipt of 91.5% of FDI flows' (1996: 67).

5. For contemporary reflections on the 1960s/1970s debate, see Nairn (1993) and Anderson (1991).

6. The author has elsewhere argued that the 'indigenous export'-led strategy tends to be associated with bank-based systems of finance such as that in Germany (see Amoore, 1998).

7. Insights drawn from author's unpublished PhD study, 'The Social Roots of Global Change: States, Firms and the Restructuring of Work', University of Newcastle-upon-Tyne, December 1998.

8. 'Flexibility' in terms of labour markets tends to take on multiple guises. In the main, the concept is used to describe flexibility on three key axes. First, in terms of 'pay flexibility', wherein the employer determines pay levels in individual terms and not as prescribed by group bargains. This form of flexibility may include the ability of the employer to access contract labour on variable levels of pay. Second, 'numerical flexibility' suggests that the employer should be able to determine workforce levels at any given point in time in line with demand for a particular product. As a result, there should be minimal restrictions on the ability of the employer to 'hire and fire'. Finally, 'functional flexibility' suggests that the employer should be able to define and redefine particular working tasks in line with changes in production and demand. In general, this would imply a blurring of traditional demarcations between job specifications.

9. For Strange: 'A change in the locus of authority over the market...can also bring about a key decision... It may be a positive decision – for example to intervene with rules or with resources to influence or restrain the market. Or it may be a negative decision (i.e. a non-decision) to leave the market alone and to allow it more freedom, not less... On the whole, it is probable that non-decisions will be more common than positive decisions' (1986: 26). Strange originally developed this concept in reference to the liberalization of financial markets. However, the concept has resonance with the debates

surrounding regulatory policies that influence FDI. In the main, those states that actively intervene to compete on technology or skills, such as Germany for example, tend to be viewed as making 'positive' market-intervening decisions. Those, such as Britain, that reject such interventions tend, by contrast, to be viewed as acting on 'non-decisions'.

10. The phrase 'race to the bottom' has become common currency in studies in international political economy. Its origin is difficult to determine, though in this instance it is used following the insights of discussions with Dr Barry Gills.

2

The Road from Nissan to Samsung: A Historical Overview of East Asian Investment in a UK Region

MARIE CONTE-HELM

When Peter Wickens' *The Road to Nissan: Flexibility, Quality and Teamwork* was first published in 1987, Nissan Motor Manufacturing (UK) Ltd was being heralded as the largest single investment by a Japanese company in Europe and a major coup for the North East of England, a region hitherto caught in a spiral of industrial decline. As Nissan's Director of Personnel, Wickens wrote of the transferability of Japanese management practices to the UK environment and entered the then flourishing debate on the Japanization of British industry (Wickens, 1987). *The Road to Nissan* was a literally apposite title for the story of Nissan's investment in the UK, but it did not reflect the more long-term relationship between Japan and the North East which began over a century earlier with a mutual interest in coal, ships and armaments.

This contribution charts the various phases of that relationship from the nineteenth century to the present day which can be explored against the backdrop of the rise and fall of the North East's traditional industries and changing national and regional concerns. If the road to Nissan has been marked by economic turmoil in the North East, the road from Nissan to Samsung has seen investments from other parts of East Asia contributing to the diversification of the region's industrial base. While the emphasis necessarily lies with the history and pattern of Japanese investment in the North East, consideration is given to the subsequent influx of firms from South Korea, Taiwan and Hong Kong. The recent Asian economic crisis may now be halting that trend but it is nonetheless an appropriate point at which to pause and reflect upon the history of East Asian investment in the North East and its ongoing social impact. The circumstances of the Japanese, Korean

Marie Conte-Helm, University of Northumbria, Newcastle-upon-Tyne and Chinese communities in the region, the infrastructures generated, and issues of integration and assimilation are raised in this wider context. The essay concludes by highlighting what might be viewed as a reversal in the historic relationship between Japan and the North East, the diversification of that relationship through further East Asian investment, and perspectives on the contemporary significance of this phenomenon.

JAPANESE–BRITISH TECHNOLOGY TRANSFER: THE LEGACY OF THE PAST

The history of technology transfer between Japan and the North East dates back to Victorian times. Britain was then the teacher and Japan the committed pupil, adopting Samuel Smiles' *Self-Help* as the virtual primer for industrialization in the Meiji period (1868–1912). Japan first looked to the North East because of the region's reputation as the centre of Britain's coal trade. An official party, sent by the Tokugawa shogunate to Newcastle-upon-Tyne in May 1862, visited North Seaton Colliery and observed the latest in coal-mining technology at first hand. Ten years later in October 1872, the representatives of Japan's new Meiji government, the Iwakura mission, similarly came to the region and descended the pit at Gosforth Colliery as part of their wider tour of industrial Tyneside.

It was an early British investor in Japan, Jardine Matheson & Co. (acting through their agent, Thomas Glover) who first sold Armstrong guns to the Japanese in 1865 (Sugiyama, 1982: 7). From that point onwards, a lucrative business partnership developed between Newcastle's W.G. Armstrong & Co., later Sir W.G. Armstrong, Mitchell & Co., which strategically contributed to the modernization of the Japanese navy. As Japan determinedly followed a policy of *fukoku kyohei* ('enrich the country, strengthen the army'), Armstrong's became its foremost supplier of ships and guns. When Japan emerged the victor in the Russo-Japanese War of 1904–05, it was the proud boast of Armstrong's Managing Director, Sir Andrew Noble, that 'all the ships engaged in the Battle of the Japan Sea (Tsushima) were armed with guns from Elswick'.[1] On a visit of pilgrimage to Newcastle in July 1911, Admiral Heihachiro Togo, Japan's great naval hero, went further in highlighting the help received from this premier North East shipyard, without which 'the history of the growth of the Japanese

navy might have been written in a different way'.[2] The naval
shipbuilding link between Armstrong's and Japan was of
significance for the state-of-the-art technology which Britain made
available to Japan. It was significant too in its timing. With the
signing of the Anglo-Japanese Alliance in 1902, Britain and Japan
established a bond which would endure beyond the First World
War and which would centre on naval ties and common interests in
the east.

The latter decades of the nineteenth century also saw a lively
trade in merchant ships commissioned by Japan from a variety of
shipyards on the rivers Tyne, Tees and Wear. By 1896
Middlesbrough had forged a particular connection with Japan as
the NYK (Nippon Yusen Kaisha) shipping line began its bi-monthly
European-line service from Yokohama to Antwerp. The Teesside
town became the loading and coaling port for the transport of such
British industrial products as locomotive machinery and spinning
machines to Japan. The importance of the volume of the trade –
which continued through the 1930s, extending to iron, steel and
chemical products – led to Middlesbrough becoming one of the few
port towns in Britain to have its own honorary Japanese consul.
That the succession of consuls from 1899 were also shipping agents
partly accounts for the emergence of a Japanese seafaring
community in Middlesbrough during the inter-war years (Conte-
Helm 1989: 108–24).

Naval shipbuilding links declined in the first decade of the
twentieth century as Japan began to develop her own shipyards.
Business ties with local firms continued, however, through licensing
agreements. Parsons Marine Steam Turbine Company at Wallsend,
for example, supplied turbines to Mitsubishi's Nagasaki shipyard
for both merchant and warships for many years to follow. In Japan,
meanwhile, a joint venture was formed between Armstrong-
Whitworth, Vickers and the Hokkaido Coal and Steamship
Company at Muroran on Hokkaido in 1907. The Japan Steel
Works provided British technical assistance in the development of
an indigenous munitions industry while acting as sole agents for the
armaments and commercial products of Vickers and Armstrong-
Whitworth in Japan. The partnership finally faltered in the 1930s,
against a very different backdrop of declining Anglo–Japanese
relations.

POST-WAR JAPANESE INVESTMENT IN THE UK

The reinstatement of Japan's business interests in Britain in the post-war period is a more familiar story. Following the lifting of the ban on outward investment from Japan in 1951, Japanese banks and trading companies re-established a presence overseas (Mason 1994: 17). The Bank of Tokyo, Fuji Bank and Teikoku Bank opened representative offices in London in 1952. In 1953, Mitsui & Co. re-opened its London branch, the first major trading company to do so. By 1956, Mitsubishi Bank and Sumitomo Bank had also resumed their operations in London. Japanese manufacturing sales and distribution outlets were to follow and contributed to the infrastructure for subsequent Japanese foreign direct investment (FDI) in the UK.

Against the backdrop of Japan's 'economic miracle', Japanese electronics producers and car manufacturers made their first moves into the UK and Europe during the 1960s. Sony had established the first Japanese post-war direct manufacturing investment in Europe with its transistor radio factory, opened in Shannon, Ireland in 1959 (Mason 1994: 20). A pioneer in this respect, Sony products were otherwise handled by local sales agents and then by wholly-owned marketing operations. This was the pattern which other Japanese companies worked to in this period of limited overseas expansion. Between 1951 and 1970, Japan's total FDI to Europe has been calculated at just $636 million (Mason 1994: 21). The relaxation of government restrictions on overseas investment in the early 1970s as well as the rising value of the yen and rising shortages and costs of labour in Japan created a very different environment for Japanese manufacturing industry and one which would witness Japan once again turning to Britain and the North East.

The history of Japanese manufacturing investment in the UK can be traced back to the establishment of YKK Fasteners (UK) Ltd by Yoshida Kogyo KK at Runcorn in Cheshire in 1966 (Conte-Helm 1996: 69). Sony set up its Bridgend colour television factory in mid-Glamorgan in 1973, of considerable importance for the future of Japanese investment in South Wales. In the following year, NSK (Nippon Seiko Kaisha), Japan's leading ball-bearings manufacturer, publicized its decision to build a £7 million bearing factory in the UK. A site at Peterlee in County Durham was subsequently chosen for the NSK factory. From these early beginnings, South Wales and

North East England were marked out as key areas for future investment from Japan.

Japanese Investment in North East England

NSK's decision to invest in the UK, after consideration of a variety of potential European locations, was announced by Christopher Chataway, Britain's Minister for Industrial Development, on the last day of his visit to Japan in January 1974. The UK, as NSK's largest domestic market in Europe, was an obvious choice for the Japanese. The provisos governing the implementation of the NSK project included:

> the establishment of the plant in an 'assisted area', the export of at least one-half of the output, the addition of at least one-half of the value of the product in Britain and 'considerable substitution' of current Japanese imports of bearings resulting from the investment.[3]

In anticipation of criticism at home to the government's promotion of Japanese investment into the UK, Chataway pointed out that it was

> better for Britain that we should have investment in the UK serving the European market, rather than investment in Europe, from where the goods would be exported to Britain.[4]

These sentiments were to be echoed by Norman Tebbit in 1981 when, as Minister of State for Industry, he subsequently countered mounting concerns over Nissan's plans to invest in the UK:

> Surely it is better for the British people to buy Japanese cars made by British workers than to buy German cars assembled by Turks.[5]

The issue of Europe and the formation of the Single Market was clearly central to Japanese companies pursuing investments in Britain. Fears of 'Fortress Europe' on the Japanese side were balanced by the spectre of the Japanese 'Trojan Horse', flooding

Europe with Japanese goods from within its very borders.

After consideration of some 18 sites within development areas in North East England, Scotland and Wales, NSK's decision to establish a base in County Durham was announced in March 1974. The location of a major British ball bearings plant at Annfield Plain not surprisingly produced a backlash from the UK Ball and Roller Bearing Manufacturing Association and the national firm of Ransome, Hoffman, and Pollard, owners of the North East bearings factory which employed some 1300 workers just 15 miles from the chosen NSK site. (RHP's subsequent amalgamation with NSK is an interesting postscript on these early developments.)

This investment in the North East of England, at a time when heavy engineering was in decline, when coalmining and shipbuilding were ceasing to define the region's industrial base and when unemployment was reaching record highs has a deeper resonance. If Victorian values and technology transfer had once set the tone for Japan's relationship with the North East, that sympathetic relationship had been all but severed as the legacy of the Second World War and conflicts over trade heightened sensitivities to Japanese investment. Ships, steel and bearings were problem sectors in the trade dispute with Japan from the late 1960s. For a region that had built its reputation on these 'old' industrial products, the concept of a Japanese sun rising over the new North East was uneasily grasped. This dilemma has been graphically portrayed with respect to Britain's shifting economic base at the time:

> From the flags and elegant strip of landscaped Japanese garden outside to the bonsai tree, calendar, and product exhibition inside by reception, the image is reinforced that the late twentieth century's industrial leader is offering a facelift of the new industrialism to the scarred countenance of the nineteenth century's industrial pioneer (McCormick 1996: 84).

Local concern at the NSK investment was reflected in newspaper headlines proclaiming:
'No Yen for the Japanese Factory', 'Land of Rising Hopes?' and 'Britain Needn't Fear Us, say Japanese' (Conte-Helm 1996: 138). The arrival of the first Japanese managers and the recruitment of

the first British workers put such opinions to the test. By the time production began at the Peterlee factory in April 1976, an initial group of section leaders and charge hands had undergone training in Japan and the focus was shifted to Japanization issues. A sensitively-handled public relations strategy meanwhile charted the positive aspects of working for the Japanese.

NSK's decision to invest in the North East was based on a complex range of factors including the impact of the concerted regional effort made to attract this first company from Japan. The availability of government grants and loans amounting to some £1.4 million coupled with competitive wage levels in the region were highly influential factors. The further attractions of the North East, according to some sources, lay in the suitable factory site on offer, the access to skilled labour, a good communications network and local amenities. Certainly such factors were heavily promoted by the North of England Development Council (NEDC), which opened one of the first UK regional offices in Japan in 1975. The NEDC worked in close collaboration with the Department of Trade and Industry and other local agencies to secure overseas investments and was absorbed into the newly formed Northern Development Company in 1986. Their success in bringing NSK to the region in 1976 was to set a precedent for future overtures to potential investors from Japan and elsewhere in East Asia. The individuals involved in this early effort, working against the odds in a climate of latent anti-Japanese sentiment, must be seen as pioneers in their own right.

The wooing of the Japanese was certainly not confined to the North East during these years. Both European and UK regional bodies operated carefully planned campaigns to distinguish their particular domains from the rest. Regional development grants and other incentives, available in areas of high unemployment, gave the advantage to some over others, though, as the inward investment stakes rose through Japan's 'bubble economy' years, the similar grant status of most UK and European regions created a more level playing field. While Britain's policy on regional assistance has varied over time, most former centres of heavy industry in northern parts of England, Wales, Scotland and Northern Ireland have been designated as 'assisted areas', thus enhancing their attraction for the Japanese (Young, Hood and Hamill 1988: 105).

The successful establishment of NSK at Peterlee in 1976 led

other Japanese companies to look to North East England for a possible foothold in Europe. Hitachi, for example, announced its intention in April 1977 to open a colour television factory at Washington in Tyne and Wear. Protests from the UK television industry and trade unions greeted the announcement and culminated in a Granada television documentary (31 October 1977) highlighting the threat posed by Japanese investment in Britain. The emotive graphics (which portrayed a Japanese businessman swinging a golf club fading into the image of a samurai wielding a sword) played on deeply-held prejudices and feelings and signalled doom for the project (Holly 1983: 49–50). As Hitachi withdrew, steered to South Wales and an ill-fated joint venture with GEC (McCormick 1996: 32–3), the North East development agencies were dealt a public relations blow from which it would take some years to recover. In the late 1970s and early 1980s, there was some further Japanese investment in the North East in the form of sales and distribution outlets. Marubeni-Komatsu, the joint venture company, opened its Washington office in 1979 as did YKK Fasteners (UK) Ltd in 1981. Dainippon Ink and Chemicals Inc. took over Polychrome (Berwick), the previously American-owned printing plate company, in north Northumberland in 1977.

It was in January 1981, however, that the future course of Japanese investment in the North East would be set with the announcement in the House of Commons that Japan's second-largest car manufacturer, Nissan Motor Co. Ltd, was to build a major car production facility on a greenfield site in a development area of Britain. Within months the options were narrowed to three sites in the North East, two in South Humberside and three in Wales, all in 'assisted areas'. Two of the North East sites and one at Shotton in Wales, as 'special development areas', qualified for the highest level of grant available, an automatic 22 per cent payment on all new plant, buildings and permanent machinery.[6]

The North East sites inspected by the Nissan delegation in April 1981 each had their own sad histories of industrial decline. From the once-thriving township of Ingleby Barwick on Teesside, the Japanese moved on to Eaglescliffe and then the Sunderland Airport site, memorably transformed by a freak spring blizzard. The ironic juxtaposition of the region's past and present industrial links with Japan persisted with the prospect of a major Japanese car producer coming to the North East. The North East's only prior foray into the motor industry had been via the manufacture of the Armstrong-Whitworth car from 1906. Armstrong-Siddeley Motors, a subsidiary of Armstrong-Whitworth, moved to Coventry after the First World War and ended this brief episode in Tyneside's automotive history. The mystique of a Japanese car factory bringing new industrial skills to the North East, so many years on, exerted great appeal.

Briefings held for the Nissan executives during their tour were closely coordinated by the local agencies and focused on the 22,000 unemployed engineering workers in the region, the extensive support that would be offered to the Japanese and the successful precedent set by NSK's investment. Direct discussions with the NSK management formed part of this process, providing the opportunity to voice concerns over issues of quality, component sourcing and Anglo–Japanese labour relations. Through the summer and early autumn of 1981, local press headlines reflected the frustrations of the waiting-game and the hopes pinned on the Nissan investment in some quarters as a cure-all for a flagging regional economy. There were, throughout this process, voices of dissent from within the British motor industry and unions, who feared that Nissan would simply mount an assembly operation, using components imported from Japan, undercutting UK car prices while providing little new employment.

Ongoing feasibility studies, postponements and government lobbying took the project through to 1984 before the decision in favour of Washington was announced on 30 March. With so much at stake, feelings were running high on both sides. A leading member of the local negotiating team saw in Nissan, 'one of the last opportunities to revitalize the economic base of the region'.[7] Lord Marsh, senior UK adviser to Nissan, described the investment as giving 'a new lease of life to a part of the country which has had little to cheer it for a long time'.[8] The *Sunderland Echo* expressed local feelings more profoundly with the succinct headline, 'It's like winning the [FA] Cup again'.

Such hyperbolic rhetoric does not belie the fact that, for the North East region, the Nissan investment was a prize well worth winning. It came at a time of crisis for the region's traditional industries. The national miners' strike, begun that same spring, was to accelerate the decline of what had been the region's major employer; the closure of the Consett Steel Works had taken place a few years before; while the region's once-proud shipyards were approaching final closure. Set in this context, Nissan's investment in the North East assumed a symbolic importance as a break with the past and a harbinger of a different future. Its real worth to the region can be measured in more concrete terms. Currently valued at £1.2 billion, NMUK remains the largest single investment by a Japanese manufacturer in the whole of Europe. With planned expansion to 5000, it has become one of the largest employers in the region. Nissan has also brought, in its wake, new investments from Japan, both component suppliers and other firms attracted by the North East's reputation as a European centre for investment from the east.

In terms of regional impact, Japanese investment should be seen in the wider context of North American, Scandinavian and other significant long-term investments from overseas. The value of inward investment projects is quantifiable in diverse ways, from the bringing of new industries and new skills to the region to the direct and indirect employment generated. Despite the overwhelming interest which Japanese investment has invariably generated – perhaps partly a legacy of the deep-rooted fascination with the East in the West – a more measured and objective view demands further analysis of both the regional and national circumstances in which that investment has taken place.

The first Nissan Bluebird rolled off the Washington assembly line in July 1986. In the years that followed, the UK would attract the largest share of manufacturing investment and more than 40 per cent of all Japanese investment into Europe (Mason 1994: 32 and Jetro 1997: 3). Beyond government encouragement and labour and infrastructural factors, historical and cultural affinities (including the importance of the English language to the Japanese) have been highlighted as reasons why Japanese investors most frequently chose Britain over other parts of Europe until a deepening recession and a changing corporate climate in Japan halted this steady flow.

Through the 'bubble economy' years of the 1980s, the North East was to benefit from the pattern of Japanese investment into the UK. The region's Japan profile has been particularly shaped by the presence of Nissan. Where Nissan has led, Japanese automotive suppliers have followed to the extent that, of the 34 Japanese manufacturing companies and R&D facilities in the region to date, more than half operate (either wholly or partly) in the automotive sector (Burge 1997: 17) (See also Ian Stone's contribution). In 1986, the year in which Nissan's official opening took place, three of the company's Japanese suppliers were to locate in Washington. Ikeda-Hoover Ltd, a joint venture between Ikeda-Bussan and the British company, Hoover, provides car seats and interior trim for Nissan. Another UK–Japanese joint venture company, TI Nihon, (later taken over by Calsonic Exhaust Systems (UK) supplies exhaust systems to Nissan in Amsterdam through its Washington-based assembly and distribution operation. SMC Pneumatics (UK) Ltd, a subsidiary of Japan's SMC Corporation, also opened a distribution outlet that same year to supply components to the Nissan factory.

In July 1987, a joint venture between Nissan and Yamato Kogyo, one of its key suppliers in Japan, was announced to the press. The £26.5 million development scheme resulted in the creation of a full-scale manufacturing facility on land adjacent to the Nissan site for the production of steel pressings and associated sub-assemblies. It has been calculated that the employment generated by the company's car plant and technology centre, along with that provided by Nissan Yamato, accounts for just under half of the total jobs directly created by Japanese subsidiaries in the North East (Burge 1997: 17).

Other Japanese automotive suppliers in the region include Llanelli Heater Systems (part of Calsonic Automotive Products), based since 1987 at Shildon in County Durham, which supplies Nissan with heating and air conditioning systems. Hashimoto Ltd, a subsidiary of Hashimoto Forming Industry Company Ltd, opened its factory for the production of plastic and metal automotive trim components at Boldon Business Park, Tyne and Wear, in 1989. It has since invested in a second factory on the same site. The joint venture firms, Marley Kansei in Sunderland and Mi-King in Washington supply plastic and steel components to Nissan and other Japanese firms in the North East. Yazaki UK Ltd similarly set up a base in Washington in 1989 to supply wire harnesses and automotive components to the Nissan factory.

Not all of the Japanese automotive suppliers in the North East arrived on the heels of Nissan. SP Tyres UK Ltd first began production of car tyres at its plant in Washington when under the ownership of the national firm, Dunlop Ltd. The Sumitomo take-over of Dunlop in 1984 and the nearby Nissan investment created a relationship of reciprocal advantage as the re-named SP Tyres went on to supply 60 per cent of the tyres used by the Nissan factory. Similarly, while NSK Bearings Europe Ltd pre-dated Nissan's arrival in the North East by some ten years, it was the opening of NSK's Steering Components Plant at Peterlee by the Automotive Components Division in 1990 which resulted in the supply of advanced technology steering column units to the automotive industry.

Another major Japanese investment within the North East engineering sector was made in 1985 by the international earthmoving equipment manufacturer, Komatsu Ltd Komatsu's move to the region occurred independently of Nissan's but it was the result of the same forces at work. Seeking to expand production into Europe, Komatsu took over the abandoned Caterpillar factory at Birtley near Gateshead, formerly owned by the American firm. Caterpillar's rationalization and restructuring programme had led to the 1983 closure of the Birtley factory which supplied parts and components for the company's main manufacturing plant at Glasgow (Young, Hood and Hamill 1988: 175). With an initial investment of £13 million, Komatsu UK transformed the defunct operation into a full production facility for wheel loaders and excavators.

The theme of the new company brochure – 'A Bright New Dawn in the North' – was in keeping with the revitalization of the old Caterpillar factory though the 270 jobs initially generated were a poor counterweight to the 2000 that had been lost some three years before. At Komatsu's official opening in July 1987, the Prince of Wales expanded upon this analogy, congratulating the company on its contribution to regional regeneration with 'the North East rising like a phoenix from the ashes of an older industrial past' (Conte-Helm: 157). Just four years later, Komatsu UK Ltd was the recipient of the Queen's Award for Export, the first Japanese firm in the region to be so distinguished. It was clear that regional regeneration and Japanese investment would continue to be identified as two sides of the same coin.

Japanese consumer electronics and electronic component manufacturers made further inroads in the North East in the latter half of the 1980s. Tabuchi Electric (UK) Ltd, based at Thornaby-on-Tees, became the European headquarters for the Tabuchi Electric

Co. Ltd of Osaka in 1985. High-quality transformers and power supplies used in consumer electrical appliances and other equipment are produced at and exported from the Teesside plant. Mitsumi UK Electric set up its first European manufacturing base at Jarrow in Tyne and Wear in 1987 for the production of tuners for colour television sets, modulators for video cassette recorders and integrated electric and electronic sub-assemblies for the consumer electronics industry. At the same time, another Japanese electronic component manufacturer, SMK Corporation, invested in a factory site on the Aycliffe Industrial Estate in County Durham. SMK (UK) Ltd produce keyboard switches for computers and fax machines and remote control units for televisions and video cassette recorders. In March 1988, Sanyo Electric Co. Ltd announced its decision to set up two factories at Newton Aycliffe in County Durham for the manufacture of microwave ovens and a third at Thornaby-on-Tees for the production of magnetrons. One of Japan's largest electronic equipment manufacturers was thus added to the roll call of Japanese investors in the North East, nearly half of whom operate within the electrical or electronic component sector.

In 1989, Fujitsu Ltd, Japan's largest computer manufacturer and leading semiconductor firm, announced its plans to build the world's most advanced semi-conductor fabrication plant in the North East. Fujitsu's investment, valued at £500 million, represented – next to Nissan's – one of the biggest Japanese manufacturing investments in Europe. The factory, built on a greenfield site at Newton Aycliffe in County Durham, went into production within 18 months of the start of construction and, like Nissan, has attracted related suppliers from Japan such as Organo (Europe) Ltd and Nippon Silica Glass. While Fujitsu's expansion plans have partially faltered in the light of global competition in the semi-conductor industry, its presence has nonetheless contributed to the diversification of local industry.

Such major investment projects in the North East have also generated support services and research and development facilities like the Nissan European Technology Centre and Ikeda Technology Europe. As elsewhere in Europe, an infrastructure has grown up to support the activities of Japanese firms from the design and construction of factories[9] to freight services, catered for by such companies as Kintetsu World Express UK Ltd, Nippon Express UK

Ltd, MO Air International (UK) Ltd and Hankyu International.[10] The Japanese trading houses which have concurrently opened offices in the North East include Marubeni Corp. and Nissan Trading at Washington, Mitsui & Co. in Sunderland and Bansho Co. Ltd in Newcastle.

SOCIAL CONSEQUENCES OF JAPANESE INVESTMENT IN BRITAIN

In charting infrastructural developments, one must consider too the circumstances of the Japanese company employees and their families who have joined them in the North East over the last two decades. The Japanese community in the UK has grown in direct proportion to the rise in investment from Japan. While the Japanese population was just 13,400 in 1982, by 1994 a total of 54,415 Japanese were living in the UK, with 38,000 Japanese nationals in the greater London area alone (Conte-Helm 1996: 68). The expatriate experience, wherever the country of origin, has its common threads of unfamiliarity, dislocation and necessary adjustment. Despite the often-quoted affinities between the Japanese and the British, there is nevertheless a culture gap to be bridged. For the urban Japanese, a posting to the UK may conjure up certain tourism-based images which do not necessarily relate to the experience of North East regional life. To cope with differences in language, food and other factors, the Japanese have, therefore, generated their own support systems to ease the way.

From a Japanese food delivery van service operating out of the car parks of NSK, Nissan and other local firms, Mr. Mori Akihiko went on, in 1987, to open the first Japanese grocer's shop in the North East, *Setsu Japan*, based in Newcastle-upon-Tyne. The Gateshead restaurant, *Fumi*, followed while more long-established eateries in Newcastle's China Town have broadened their traditional repertoire to include Japanese dishes and *karaoke* to meet the Japanese demand.

The high value attached to education and the competitive and demanding nature of Japan's education system present a particular dilemma for families faced with a posting overseas. A tightly-regulated core curriculum and the Japanese 'examination hell' do not allow for the typical three to five year gap which returnees must fill on re-entry to Japan. This does not only relate to mathematics and science education which are considerably more advanced in Japan but, inevitably, affects the study of the Japanese language itself, with its exacting written system.

Through the 1980s, Japan's Ministry of Education and Japanese companies with overseas subsidiaries sought solutions to the problems faced by the ever-increasing numbers of Japanese children studying abroad. 1985 saw the opening of a Japanese Saturday School at Washington, Tyne and Wear, one of eight in the UK. As the number of pupils reached 100, the Ministry of Education appointed a Head Teacher, thus providing a direct line to educational developments in Japan. While the Japanese children in the North East mainly study at local state schools, the Saturday School has acted as a focal point for the Japanese community while ensuring that the children of employees posted overseas do not forget what it means to be Japanese.

Despite such concerns, or more likely as a result of them, the rising tide of Japanese overseas investment in the 1980s brought about changes in the status of Japanese returnees along with changes in the educational establishment's response to them. In his study of the subject, *Japan's International Youth: The Emergence of a New Class of Schoolchildren*, Roger Goodman has pointed out that, rather than being marginalized,

> they are going to the top universities, they are being preferentially employed, they are proclaiming their 'otherness' (Goodman 1993: 5).

While universities have to some extent adjusted their policies to accommodate returnees, for families posted overseas, as with the many who have been and continue to come to North East England, the time of leaving and returning to Japan is nevertheless perceived as being crucial to their children's educational success.

The Japanese community in the North East has access to a further educational infrastructure for improving English language skills. Special units have been set up in some local schools which focus on the assimilation and integration of Japanese residents. Japanese companies and local authorities have similarly addressed the linguistic needs of employees and their wives with the provision of classes and in-house language resource centres.

In 1990, Teikyo University of Durham was established on the grounds of the University of Durham to provide Japanese undergraduates with a year abroad opportunity in an English-speaking environment. While unrelated to Japanese corporate developments in the region, the Teikyo University investment reflects the North East's increasing identification with things Japanese.

In assessing the impact of the Japanese presence in the North East, the wider social and cultural issues arising from Japanese investment cannot be overlooked. While internationalization and globalization have been specifically defined with respect to the spread of Japanese production facilities overseas and the expanding net of corporate involvements, the temporary relocation of Japanese citizens abroad has had its inevitable consequences in influencing outlooks and attitudes among the Japanese themselves and within the North East community.

Groups like the North of England Anglo–Japanese Society and Ni-Ichi Kai have grown up in response to the mutual interest generated by the location of Japanese companies in the North East. The meetings and activities which they promote provide a focus for that interest and another type of network for socializing and cultural exchange. To some extent, the wooing of Japanese investors and the networks to which that investment has given rise are part of the same process but nevertheless achieve their separate objectives in bringing the Japanese and the British together.

The familiar image of Japanese tourist groups herded at high speed past such London-based cultural totems as the Houses of Parliament and Big Ben is challenged by the experience of the Japanese in a region like the North East. A community of approximately 850 people, spread over four counties, does not have an identity en masse. It is absorbed in different ways into its surroundings. There are significant numbers of Japanese living in and around Washington and in parts of Teesside, County Durham and Newcastle-upon-Tyne. For them, life in Britain revolves around their day-to-day local contacts with colleagues, classmates, neighbours and friends. This is the more mundane reality underpinning the globalization process which has brought Japanese investors to the North East.

OTHER EAST ASIAN INVESTORS IN THE NORTH EAST

The increasing economic strength of the Asia Pacific region over recent years and the consequences of economic growth have led other investors from East Asia to follow the Japanese model. While Japanese investment may have tapered off and changed in character over the last decade, this same period has witnessed a steady influx of companies from South Korea, Taiwan and Hong Kong into the North East, reflecting both national and global trends. As inward investment agencies have shifted their sights to the newly industrializing economies (NIEs), regional competition for investment from the Pacific Rim has accelerated and contributed to a diversification of East Asian investment. Further investments from Thailand, Malaysia and Singapore in the 1990s have expanded the regional profile in this respect beyond the immediate boundaries of East Asia.

Korean Firms

South Korea's total direct investment overseas represents just five per cent of the Japanese figure but the accelerating pace of that investment over recent years has increased its importance to the UK and Europe. Supported by the Korean state, the *chaebol* (or large industrial conglomerates) have been at the forefront of the overseas investment drive. The value of Korean manufacturing investment in Europe by the end of 1995 was calculated at £1.2 billion, reflecting the 126 projects underway (Cambridge Econometrics 1997: 42–3). With 23 of these projects (worth more than £100 million) in place, the UK has registered the highest share.

There are currently six Korean manufacturers in the North East of England which were originally expected to generate some 4300 jobs (Burge 1996: 15). Predictions on the growing significance of Korean investment have rested on the fact that Korean companies generated 47 per cent of the employment created by all new investments in the region in the mid-1990s (Cambridge Econometrics 1997: 42–3). The Asian currency crisis and its backlash in Korea has altered this picture but the early investments made by Korean firms in the North East nevertheless conform to a familiar pattern.

The major *chaebol*, including LG Inc. (formerly Lucky Goldstar) and Samsung are represented among this group. Samsung Electronics was established at Billingham in Cleveland in 1987 for the manufacture of microwave ovens. The company later diversified into other products and now concentrates on printed circuit boards. As the first Korean company to invest in the North

East, it attracted considerable attention and heralded the prospect of a 1990s wave of investment from Korea to replace that emanating from Japan in the previous decade. Indeed, the concentration of Japanese firms in the region and the successful precedent set by their investments first led the Koreans, Taiwanese and other investors to look to this same part of the UK.

Among the Korean manufacturers who have invested in the UK, the electronics sector is most strongly represented. Following Samsung's first venture in the region in 1987, LG Electronics (North of England) Ltd was established at Washington in 1989 with an £8.8 million investment. LG similarly moved into the manufacture of microwave ovens and televisions, both products which were facing trade restrictions and which shared key markets in Europe at the time. LG paved the way for the arrival in 1990 of Inkel UK (now Haitai Electronics) at Cramlington in Northumberland where CD players and car stereos are produced.

In 1994, Samsung Electronics UK Ltd was to build on its initial investment in the North East to become one of the largest Korean investors in Europe. Its decision to establish its main European production base at Wynyard in Cleveland was to mark out the North East as a centre for Korean operations in the UK. The £700 million project, applauded at the time as 'the single biggest foreign manufacturing investment in the UK since Nissan', attracted government assistance amounting to some 20 per cent of the total investment costs.[11] Projected to yield more than 3000 jobs in 'a regional unemployment blackspot', officials viewed the Samsung incentive package as well worth the price.[12] In addition to their original Billingham plant, the company went on to develop two factories on greenfield sites in Wynyard Park, geared to produce a wide range of electronic goods including microwave ovens and computer monitors. A Samsung Training Centre has also been developed at the Wynyard site.

The fortunes of Samsung in the North East, as the implications of the 1997 economic crisis in South Korea set in, make for an intriguing case study. An inevitable deleterious effect on Korean investment abroad has been predicted, given the weakness of the Korean won against foreign currencies and retrenchment measures imposed by the International Monetary Fund.[13] Against assurances made in November 1997 by the Samsung Group that the company would continue to expand overseas, a 'Saving One Million Won' campaign was launched 'in an effort to create a more frugal Samsung'.[14] Construction plans for a £425 million microchip plant in the North East have since been deferred. What this may mean in the long-term for a Korean dawn in the North East is yet to be determined.

At the end of 1997, the value of all Korean investment in the region was estimated at £730 million as compared to £2.8 billion from Japan.[15] Comparisons of scale can most relevantly be made, however, between such global entities as Samsung versus Nissan; with their investments amounting, respectively, to £700 million and £1.2 billion. Like Nissan, Samsung also attracted its supplier firms to the region, accounting for four out of the seven Korean companies in the North East. In 1995, Young Shin UK Ltd established its Billingham factory for the production of plastic injection moulding. Dong Jin Precision (UK) Ltd set up its Peterlee operation in 1996 for the manufacture of microwave oven doors and other components. In that same year, Woo One UK Ltd was to establish a production base for casings for PC computer monitors at Hartlepool in Cleveland.

The North East's Korean community, at 85 people, is just one-tenth of the size of the local Japanese population yet, in terms of cultural background and common concerns, there is a further basis for comparison. This is particularly true of the importance attached to education in both societies. A Korean weekend school, similar in purpose to the Japanese Saturday School, was established in the early days of Korean investment. Organized by the companies themselves, it currently caters for some 23 pupils and allows them to maintain linguistic and cultural ties with their homeland while living in the North East.

Korean investment has also given rise to various exchange activities. A recently-formed region-to-region link between the North East and Kyonggi Province, for example, has led to the staging of Korean cultural displays in the North East while providing the basis for reciprocal events in Korea. The longer history of Japanese investment in the region has seen similar twinnings arranged between Komatsu City and Gateshead and Osaka and the North East. Just as Japanese festivals have followed in the wake of investment from Japan, so too are aspects of Korean culture now entering into the North East frame.

Taiwanese Firms

Following the pattern of first the Japanese and then the Koreans, Taiwanese investment in the UK has been very much a phenomenon of the 1990s. 80 per cent of Taiwan's European manufacturing takes place in Britain with an investment total of £330 million[16] Taiwan's large foreign exchange reserves have left her relatively unscathed by the Asian financial crisis and in pursuit of further sites in the UK. Of the 20 Taiwanese manufacturers currently (1998) operating in the UK, four are based in North East England. All of these are located in Northumberland and employ a total of 650 workers. The value attached to the region's investment from Taiwan has been set at £80 million.[17]

Lite-On (NPE) established its base at Ashington in Northumberland for the design and manufacture of power supplies in 1991. That same year saw the arrival of the penicillin manufacturer, Synpac Pharmaceuticals Ltd, at Bedlington, the first East Asian company to invest in this regional centre for the pharmaceutical industry. In 1993, EMC (Europa Magnetics Corp.) set up a floppy disc production facility at Cramlington. IR Tech followed in 1996 with its sales and marketing office for infra-red security systems, based at Newcastle International Airport.

There are just 20 Taiwanese, including family members, associated with the firms currently in the region, a very small number indeed in relation to the indigenous Hong Kong Chinese population, numbering approximately 11,000.[18] Newcastle's Hong Kong Chinese community, by comparison, has a long history and concentrated business interests in the Stowell Street area of the city.

Hong Kong Firms

In recent years, the Hong Kong Chinese regional presence has been augmented by a range of Hong Kong investors located in various parts of the North East. The first of these to arrive was Tin Lung Knitwear (UK) Ltd which opened its factory at Washington in 1984. Eurasia Knitwear Ltd, based at Middlesbrough in Cleveland, followed in 1990. In 1991, Hutchison Paging UK Ltd and Hutchison Telecom Cellular Services Ltd were established at Darlington for the sales and servicing of pagers and mobile cellular phones. Together, the two firms have generated some 440 jobs.In 1992, H.B. Technologies brought a research, development and testing facility to Newton Aycliffe in County Durham. Then, in

1993, Onwa Electronics established its base at South Shields in Tyne and Wear for the manufacture of colour televisions. A further bicycle manufacturing operation from Hong Kong, Cy-Tech Manufacturing Ltd, came to Hartlepool in Cleveland in 1995. These investments from Hong Kong have been valued at £220 million and have generated 1100 jobs.[19] While distinct in character from the North East's Japanese, Korean and Taiwanese investments, they represent important additions in regional terms to the inward investment base from East Asia.

CONCLUSION

Early ties between Japan and the North East point to a partnership of interests in which the role of teacher and pupil established the flow of technology transfer from Britain to Japan. That relationship underwent a reversal in later years against the backdrop of the decline of the North East's traditional industries and shifting patterns of international trade. The legacy of the past nonetheless forms a part of the intricate tapestry from which the present-day industrial map of the region has been woven.

In tracing the more recent history and spread of East Asian investment in the North East, certain common features have emerged. The value of such investments, including the Japanese at £2.8 billion, the Korean at £730 million, the Taiwanese at £80 million and the Hong Kong Chinese at £220 million, represent a significant contribution overall to the regional economy. Japanese investment led the way from the 1970s, flourished in the 1980s, and has been followed by important investments in the 1990s from Korea and Taiwan. Hong Kong investors have also looked to the region over this same period and have added another dimension to the local Hong Kong Chinese community.

These East Asian companies are spread throughout the North East and directly employ more than 20,000 people. Overseas employees and family members associated with such investments number approximately 1000 and have generated facilities and services relative to the sizes of their respective communities. In the case of the Japanese and Koreans, special part-time schools have been established for the children of company employees while the Hong Kong Chinese community has, over time and separate from the inward investment process, developed its own specialist educational outlets.

Globalization has provided the impetus for East Asian investment in Europe in recent years. This investment still represents, however, a small proportion of the East Asian investment in different parts of Asia and in other parts of the world. In 1995, for example, Korean companies invested more in China than in either Europe or North America (Cambridge Econometrics 1997: 39). Similarly, one must consider East Asian investment in the North East in the broader contexts of Europe, of other regions in the UK and of other locally-based international investments. With the largest concentration of Scandinavian investors in the UK, with over 130 North American and 165 European firms, and with multiple sectoral interests from engineering, automotives and electronics through to plastics and chemicals, pharmaceuticals and consumer goods, the North East's industrial identity may owe much to East Asian investment but, in the final analysis, it is not exclusively defined by it. For the North East, the road both to and from Nissan has been a long and winding one.

ACKNOWLEDGEMENT

The author is grateful to the Northern Development Company for providing recent statistics on East Asian investment in the North East.

NOTES

1. *Newcastle Weekly Chronicle*, 28 April 1906
2. *Newcastle Daily Chronicle*, 20 July 1911
3. *Financial Times*, 24 January 1974
4. Ibid.
5. *Financial Times*, 21 April 1981
6. *Financial Times*, 8 April 1981
7. *Sunderland Echo*, 27 February 1984
8. *Sunderland Echo*, 2 April 1984
9. The Japanese construction company, Kajima UK, now has a Northern branch office based at Tolent Construction in Gateshead, Tyne and Wear.
10. In addition to these companies based at Newcastle International Airport, there is a distribution and storage warehouse for Yamato Transport (UK) Ltd in Washington and warehousing and JIT distribution facilities provided by Autrans Europe Ltd in Sunderland.
11. *Financial Times*, 18 October 1994
12. Ibid.
13. *The Independent*, 27 November 1997
14. Ibid.
15. Figures provided by NDC.
16. *The Sunday Times*, 15 March 1998.

17. Figures provided by NDC.
18. Ibid.
19. Ibid.

REFERENCES

Burge, Keith (1997), 'Japanese Manufacturing Investment in Europe – Recent History and Future Prospects' in *Business Review North*, Vol.8, No.4, Spring.

Burge, Keith (1996), 'Korean Investment in the UK' in *Business Review North*, Vol.8, No.1, Summer.

Cambridge Econometrics (1997), *Regional Economic Prospects (Analysis and Forecasts to the Year 2000 for the Standard Planning Regions of the UK)*. Cambridge: Cambridge Econometrics Ltd.

Conte-Helm, Marie (1989), *Japan and the North East of England: From 1862 to the Present-Day*. London and Atlantic Heights, New Jersey: The Athlone Press.

Conte-Helm, Marie (1996), *The Japanese and Europe: Economic and Cultural Encounters*. London and Atlantic Heights, New Jersey: The Athlone Press.

Goodman, Roger (1993), *Japan's International Youth: the Emergence of a New Class of Schoolchildren*. Oxford: Clarendon Press.

Holly, Stephen (1983), *Washington: Quicker by Quango. The History of Washington New Town 1964–1983*. Washington (Tyne & Wear): Washington Development Corporation.

JETRO (1997), *The 13th Survey of European Operations of Japanese Companies in the Manufacturing Sector*. Tokyo: Japan External Trade Organization (JETRO).

Mason, Mark (1994), 'Historical Perspectives on Japanese Direct Investment in Europe', in Mark Mason and Dennis Encarnation (eds.), *Does Ownership Matter? Japanese Multinationals in Europe*. Oxford: Clarendon Press.

McCormick, Brian and Kevin (1996), *Japanese Companies – British Factories*. Aldershot: Avebury.

Sugiyama, Shinya (1982), 'Glover & Co: A British Merchant in Nagasaki, 1861–1870', in Ian Nish (ed.), *Bakumatsu and Meiji Studies in Japan's Economic and Social History*. London: LSE, International Studies 1981/2.

Wickens, Peter (1987), *The Road to Nissan: Flexibility, Quality and Teamwork*. Basingstoke: The Macmillan Press.

Young, Stephen, Hood, Neil and Hamill, James (1988), *Foreign Multinationals and the British Economy: Impact and Policy*. London: Croom Helm.

3

East Asian FDI and the UK Periphery

IAN STONE

The general expansion of Foreign Direct Investment (FDI)[1] has been a defining characteristic of the process of globalization over recent decades. Japanese and, more recently, other East Asian countries have made an important contribution to this overall flow, and strategies to exploit exogenous growth opportunities through attracting Asian investors have been widely adopted in Europe at both national and regional levels. Numerous agencies have been established and a panoply of incentives and support measures introduced as a means of securing such investment and the jobs, technology, export earnings and spin-off benefits associated with it. The North of England has a record of success in competing for this inward investment, and this article assesses the performance of this peripheral region within the wider context of FDI into the UK.

The article begins by locating FDI from East Asia as an element within increasing overall flows of international investment over the last two decades, especially as it relates to the UK, which is a primary host economy for such investment. It is shown how FDI from the East Asian region is specific in its timing and is also characterized by distinct phases, each of which has conditioned the form of overseas investment undertaken and its spatial pattern. The second section analyses the development and character of the East Asian investment flows in the North of England. The author's database on FDI is used to identify the East Asian contribution to overall regional job generation resulting from overseas direct investment in the region, and to analyse the extent of East Asian FDI in the North relative to other peripheral regions with which it competes for such inward investment. The final section summarizes the findings and considers implications for the region's foreign-owned sector arising out of the current crisis affecting Asia.

Ian Stone, University of Northumbria, Newcastle upon Tyne

EAST ASIAN OUTWARD FDI WITHIN GLOBAL FLOWS

All OECD countries have experienced a rising trend of FDI outflows and inflows over the past three decades, associated with the process of globalization. In fact, flows have grown at an annual rate far above that of either trade or output growth, and the inward FDI stock as a share of GDP consequently rose from 5.5 per cent in 1980 to 12.9 per cent in 1994. FDI tends to fluctuate with the business cycle: the total world flow peaked at $180bn in 1989, fell during the early 1990s, and then, with recovery from recession, rose to $316bn in 1995 and an estimated $349bn in 1996 (United Nations, 1996, 1997).

Some 65 per cent of inward flows went to developed countries in 1995. Western Europe has throughout the last three decades been both the world's largest host *and* source of FDI flows.[2] The EU's share of the world total in 1995 (36 per cent), is down slightly from the early 1990s when, with investors encouraged by the creation of the European Single Market, it was the destination for around half the world total of FDI flows; since the early 1990s, East Asia (at least until 1996) and Central and Eastern Europe (CEE) (up nearly sixfold during 1991–95 to $14bn), have increased in importance as destinations for FDI (United Nations, 1997).

The UK has been by far the main recipient of inward FDI to Western Europe, accounting for 40 per cent of all EU FDI inward *flows* in the 1980s. During the second half of the 1980s it hosted 12 per cent of total world inward FDI and 36 per cent of inflows into the EU. After falling during 1991–94 to around a fifth of the EU total, the UK's share recovered in 1995 and 1996 to 30 per cent ($30bn out of $99bn[3]). In terms of accumulated *stocks*, again the UK share possesses a disproportionately large share within the EU: $314bn out of $1,114bn (United Nations, 1997). Total stocks were equivalent to 21 per cent of GDP in 1994, compared to 13 per cent for the EU overall, and is by some margin proportionately the largest among the G7 countries. East Asian companies, in locating the largest proportion of their European investment in the UK, have been important in maintaining the UK's leading role within the EU as a host for FDI.

Manufacturing investment overseas by Japanese firms, and even more so that from other East Asian countries, was relatively late in developing (Mason, 1994). Until the 1970s, FDI was dominated by US *outward* FDI, and it is only since then that wholesale change has occurred, with the US by the end of the decade becoming also a major host for FDI as other (mainly European) countries dramatically expanded their outward FDI. Only since 1970 has Japan emerged as a major investor overseas. Its share of the world stock of FDI grew to 7 per cent in the early 1980s. During the second half of the 1980s and early 1990s, Japan was the world's largest international investor with around a fifth of the total FDI flows world-wide. This fell back to less than 7 per cent of world flows in 1993–96[4] and the USA and UK resumed their respective positions as the largest and second largest outward investors (United Nations, 1996, 1997).

Japan's emergence as an international investor in the USA and Europe was followed, during the second half of the 1980s and early 1990s, by that of 'Asian Tiger' economies (included within a group of nations hereafter referred to as 'Other East Asian' or OEA); the combined outward flows of South Korea, Taiwan, Singapore and Hong Kong – negligible in 1980 – grew to 3.5 per cent of world flows in 1984–88 (annual average) and reached 11 per cent in both 1995 and 1996 (United Nations, 1996, 1997). While this combined outflow ($39bn) is comfortably above the equivalent figure recorded for Japan, the substantial fall in the value of Japan's FDI outflows since 1990 should be borne in mind.[5]

EAST ASIAN OUTWARD FDI: SUCCESSIVE PHASES

The timing of the outward FDI flows, and the nature of the investment projects themselves, are linked closely to evolving conditions in the countries of origin and certain interactions on an international scale. The local experience of such activity in a region like the North of England is very much conditioned by these factors.

Japan

Japan's economy has evolved especially rapidly in the post-war period. Its has moved, in just a few decades, from 'developing' to 'advanced' country status, with all that implies in terms of changes in markets, product specialization, role of government, cost structures and technological capability. Accordingly, the extent of FDI, its motivation and character has changed radically too. Although some tend to emphasize shorter-term influences, studies which analyse the change in terms of historical phases of overseas investment activity also convey the presence of underlying structural processes (such as Komiya, 1991; Sugitani, 1993; Dunning, 1993; and Mason, 1994). In spite of the complications arising out of the rapidity of Japan's economic evolution, credible explanatory frameworks which can be applied to the succession of phases of outward FDI have been advanced. Prominently, Ozawa (1991a, 1991b) has put forward the hypothesis that Japan's FDI can only be understood as an integral part of the restructuring of Japanese industry. In the same vein, Dent (1997) identifies various 'interactive developments' which link the Japanese economy and outward FDI: (1) the ongoing process of domestic industrial restructuring; (2) systematic up-grading and improvement of ownership specific advantages (including the role played by FDI in acting as a conduit for acquiring information and new technical knowledge); (3) maintaining and extending export markets in developed countries; and (4) the shifting of uncompetitive activities to developing countries. These considerations underpin the following overlapping phases of Japanese outward FDI, each of which is associated with a distinct type of investment:

Phase 1: Japanese Investment in Asia and the Developing World

(a) Relocation of labour-intensive manufacturing. Up to the late 1960s, balance of payments considerations motivated the Japanese government to place restrictions upon outward flows of investment, including the placing of a ceiling on overseas assets held by companies. Controls were relaxed during the early 1970s; a change which effectively marks the start of outward FDI activity.[6] Until this policy liberalization, only service sector activities – mainly engaged in distribution and trading – were operating in Europe (Strange, 1993; Mason, 1994). The government now sought positively to encourage outward FDI by Japanese firms, in response to pressures from the yen's rising value and domestic labour shortages. To maintain competitiveness in overseas markets, firms began shifting labour-intensive activities to production locations within Asia (especially South Korea, Taiwan and Hong Kong) offering investment incentives and competitively waged and relatively skilled labour. They were helped in this process by the enhanced purchasing power of the yen. This overseas investment helped Japan adjust its position within the international division of labour.

(b) Access to and processing of raw materials. Another element of this first significant phase of outward FDI was linked to raw materials rather than labour resources. Structural change during the 1960s and 70s in favour of large-scale heavy industries (chemicals, petrochemicals, metals, synthetic fibres and shipbuilding) subsequently gave rise to problems. Japan is a resource-scarce country, and the 1970s oil crisis made the instability of its position abundantly clear; moreover the clustering of industrial activities heightened the incidence of pollution. A substantial part of FDI during this post-1970s period was thus a response to this situation: Japan restructured its domestic economy towards less resource-intensive and more knowledge-based activities and moved offshore (mainly to Asian neighbours, but also to Canada and Oceania) some resource-intensive processing activities, especially those linked to mining, extraction and timber.[7]

Phase 2: Export-substituting investment in the industrialized economies

The second distinct phase in Japanese outward investment was of an export-substituting nature, in response to growing restrictions faced by Japanese exporters in the US and EC markets. It marks a shift from FDI aimed at achieving vertical integration of production to investment overseas designed to achieve geographical diversification (Froot 1991, cited by Nicolas 1995) – a process in which the Japanese trading companies (*sogo shosha*) have played a vital role in initiating and organizing Japanese overseas FDI. It is also the point when Japanese FDI begins to focus on, in turn, the USA and Europe (and thus the UK).

Japan had responded to the rising price of imported oil by expanding yet more vigorously its export earnings in its developing specialisms of assembly-based mass produced consumer durables (TVs and other electronic products, vehicles, VTRs) and other products (such as electronically controlled machine tools) (Komiya, 1991). Its success in this strategy in the 1970s and early 1980s led to increasing trade frictions with industrialized countries – especially since increasing penetration of OECD country markets coincided with recession and high unemployment in those economies. These frictions led to measures, in both the USA and (nationally and collectively) in Europe to limit the flow of imports of specific items from Japan. Stringent measures have been instituted by the EU since the early 1980s, including 'voluntary restraint' agreements, 'orderly market arrangements' and the imposition of anti-dumping duties (for details and examples, see Belderbos, 1995).

As tariff and non-tariff barriers were successively erected (or threatened) on various products, so the Japanese companies affected planned investment in production facilities inside the borders of the USA and EU. Added pressure for this came from: (1) the appreciation of the yen, which climbed rapidly in the second half of the 1980s, making Japan a high cost manufacturing country (Sargent, 1990); (2) preparations (from 1986 onwards) for the Single European Market, involving the progressive eradication of market fragmentation resulting from non-tariff barriers between EU member states; and (3) 'home content rules' introduced within the EU since 1987, designed to increase the value-added associated with Japanese production in Europe.

Market-related considerations thus dominated decisions to invest in Europe (and the USA) during this period. Of course, investments overseas by companies of various nationalities are often motivated by market-related objectives (Culem, 1988; Christodoulou, 1996). There are practical reasons, to do with gaining new markets and the further penetration of existing ones, why a company might choose actually to produce in a market rather than exporting to it (see Stone, 1998). Advantages include speed of response to orders, aftersales support and responsiveness to local demand patterns. Arguably the main driver in the case of Japanese FDI, however, was protectionism affecting the sectors in which the country had specialized. High customs duties, the threat or actual imposition of anti-dumping duties, pressure to meet local content targets and the fear of 'Fortress Europe' all had the effect of pushing Japanese companies, in one product line after another, to invest in overseas production facilities (Dunning, 1993).

In terms of Dunning's (1988) 'eclectic model' of FDI, Japanese companies originally became competitive in world markets because of their ownership advantages relating to the management and organization of large-scale automated production processes making high quality goods at low cost. These advantages would have ensured continuing export sales growth in both the USA and Europe, but for increasing protectionism. It was location advantages – principally unimpeded access to markets, rather than other factors such as investment subsidies and market advantages from being near to customers – which became the main driving force behind Japanese investment in both the USA and Europe in the 1980s (see, for example, case studies in Strange, 1993). The alternative – producing by means of local firms operating under licence – jeopardized maintenance of product quality, hampered flexibility and entailed high transactions costs in identifying an appropriate licensee and in gearing up its operation for production.

The process was aided by the rapid growth in experience of operating overseas. Even by the early 1980s, Japanese firms had sufficient experience of foreign operations to know that it was possible to transfer firm-specific advantages abroad (Belderbos, 1995). They found, in particular, that the local workforce could adapt well to the Japanese systems of social organization of production (Peck and Stone, 1992a). Also, over time, it was discovered that the sub-contracting network – which in Japan forms an important element of a firm's competitive advantage – could substantially be replicated in overseas contexts, through a combination of transplanting key *keiretsu* firms to the overseas location (via 'follow-on' investments) and developing the supply capability among indigenous firms to the required level (involving their adoption of 'relational contracting' or partnership techniques) (Sachwald, 1995).[8]

Phase 3: Globally-integrated production strategies and efficiency-seeking FDI

While some writers (such as Heitger and Stehn, 1990) have maintained that the Single European Market was the significant influence over the pace of Japanese investment – for example the fear of 'Fortress Europe' and exclusion from the EU market has encouraged Japanese firms to invest inside Europe's borders, thus avoiding the threat to its market access – others contend that this is not the only reason for increased investment activity in Europe. Nicolaides and Thomsen (1991), for example, identify the growing use among Japanese firms since the mid-1980s of ownership-specific advantages on a global strategic scale. From the mid-1980s, a third phase is discernible, in which global objectives have dominated, as the general move towards more knowledge-intensive activities encouraged strategies of global integration of production, linked to what Dunning has described as 'efficiency-seeking' (rather than 'market-seeking') investment decisions (Dunning, 1993). Initially, this related to FDI directed at the USA, with its technological resources and well integrated and freely functioning markets; subsequently it has applied to Europe as well, especially as the business environment became more favourable towards the expansion of overseas investment.

In this latest phase, therefore, the motivation for FDI from East Asia is less the defensive market-oriented and export-substituting type of investment than a form of FDI aimed primarily at accessing specific resources of technology and skills. The ties of some Japanese industrial firms to home production gradually weakened over the 1980s: partly as a result of operating in key overseas markets, firms began to achieve clear technological advantages in new products linked to global rather than home markets (Belderbos, 1995). Related to this is a process whereby shorter product life-cycles and the increasing development costs of new products have been pushing firms towards emphasizing global rather than national markets. While the initial investments of Japanese firms in the EU were country-specific, such cost pressures combined with diminishing market fragmentation have led companies increasingly to adopt pan-European strategies in relation to the organization of production (including R&D centres) and sales/distribution, steadily forming European headquarters to coordinate such activities. Firms have been structuring their production at a European scale in terms of specialized units with increasing intra-EU flows of both components and final goods. This evolving feature of Japanese FDI has undoubtedly been facilitated by the increased number of countries joining the competition for Japanese investment projects, which has occurred partly in recognition of the progressive improvements in the value-added contributions of Japanese firms to the host economies[9] (Hood and Young, 1992).

An important element of this developing strategic phase of Japanese FDI involves the acquisition of a controlling or minority stake in US and European firms – particularly in high technology sectors – specifically to acquire technology and skills needed to upgrade the domestic and overseas operations of major Japanese corporations and to facilitate access to additional markets (Dunning, 1993; and Ohmae, 1985a, 1985b). Most of the Japanese investments up to the 1990s – especially car assembly and electronic products – derived competitiveness from ownership advantages arising out of organizational features internalized within the firm itself (or more usually within the network of firms centred upon the core plant). Such advantages include intangible assets and knowledge which are difficult to trade (and thus pass on to a licensee) and it is not surprising to find that the bulk of manufacturing FDI by Japanese firms in the USA and Europe was for a long time greenfield and wholly Japanese-owned.[10] Japanese firms have not generally favoured acquisitions: indeed, takeovers have been comparatively rare in Japan itself (Dore, 1986). Rather than deal with problems of transforming existing organization, workplace culture and practices, Japanese companies have preferred to hire new labour and establish operations on a greenfield basis.

From the mid-1980s onwards, however, Japanese takeovers of foreign firms have became increasingly common; from 44 projects in 1984 the annual flow rose to 228 in 1987 (*Tokyo Business Today*, 1989); at the end of the 1980s 40 per cent of new Japanese investment into the EU was *via* acquisition or merger (Kirkland, 1990). By late 1992 acquisition was the mode of entry for one in five of the existing stock of Japanese-owned subsidiaries (JETRO, 1992), including Fujitsu's acquisition in 1991 of UK mainframe computer manufacturer ICL. This takeover illustrates the underlying rationale of this latest phase of Japanese FDI. Previously, Fujitsu had only a small presence in the EU market; not only did the acquisition give the company access to a particular technology and allow it to achieve overnight a critical share of the EU market, but ICL's knowledge of European investment opportunities has also been useful. Fujitsu's (and Japan's) very limited presence in CEE, restricted its knowledge of that market; but the company has nonetheless been able to invest in Poland by doing so *via* its ICL subsidiary (United Nations, 1996). Acquisitions of chemicals plants, a sector in which Japanese companies have limited ownership advantages over European and US competitors, should be seen largely as central to a strategy for becoming a global competitor, especially since European and American chemical firms are highly internationalized and many have what Sachwald has called 'de-localised R&D units' with global technological responsibilities (Sachwald, 1995: Ch. 5).

Joint ventures (JVs), which have also grown significantly in the post-1985 period and accounted in 1992 for around 15 per cent of Japanese FDI projects in Europe, are often means by which companies secure market access and a more favourable attitude towards the investment from national governments (Belderbos, 1995). However, there are plenty of examples of JVs which are genuinely motivated by the need to form a broader alliance to develop new products, particularly in situations of considerable risk or where the Japanese company has little experience of international operations; again, these may be alliances which are part of a company strategy to achieve globally integrated production.

Other East Asian Countries

Outward investment flows from city-states Hong Kong and Singapore have been substantially oriented towards trade, hotels, finance and infrastructure and have focused mainly upon the Asian region, especially China (United Nations, 1997). The main outward flows of manufacturing investment have come from the South Korea and Taiwan. Their emergence as significant contributors to global FDI flows is linked to government promotion of outward investment, targeted upon opportunities where investment can secure essential natural resources or technologies, or provide the market-distribution facilities to aid home-country exports. Like Japan, initial outflows from these countries were directed at low-cost Asian countries, but during the 1980s their outward FDI was increasingly directed at OECD countries to circumvent protectionism. Also like Japan, the initial focus of OEA investment in the western economies was the USA, which had 80 per cent of the 'Asian Tiger's' cumulative overseas investment by the end of the 1980s, but subsequently Europe has become increasingly important.

South Korea: Investments overseas by conglomerate firms (*chaebol*), cumulatively valued at just $0.8bn in 1990, rose to $4.2bn by 1996 (*United Nations*, 1997). The strong expansion of South Korea's outward FDI signals a shift from an export to an outward investment-driven phase of internationalization of its economy. Increased competitiveness of its firms reflects state-of-the-art production processes and products in 'middle technology' industries. FDI in developing countries and in CEE (substantially via acquisition of state-owned automobile and engineering plants) has been motivated by the search for lower costs; in developed economies, where the focus is in higher-technology areas, the motives are access to markets and strengthening of existing (or acquisition of new) competitive advantages *via* access to US and European technological knowledge. Pressure from wage costs in Korea itself has been an important factor, especially given that the products are more price sensitive than Japanese ones; while liberalization policies also eased the process of FDI.

Taiwan: With the exception of provisions for outward FDI to secure raw materials, until the second half of the 1980s, such investment was restricted by tight capital controls and difficulties in obtaining foreign exchange; significant relaxation of restrictions on outward investment only really occurred in 1987, followed by active promotion of outward investment, where it is considered to have benefits in terms of restructuring the Taiwanese economy. Thus it is not surprising that until 1989 outflows (excluding those to China) were small indeed, although they subsequently expanded rapidly to average around $1.5bn during 1990–93.[11]

Outward investment was initially impelled by the objective of expanding exports (including establishing facilities in countries with un-used quotas for exporting into the EU, or increasing exports in the form of intra-firm flows of components, as opposed to final products). Taiwan has been shifting towards 'trade replacement' as a means of preserving access to markets, but is increasingly impelled by the aim of improving access to new technology (including *via* joint-ventures and acquisitions) as part of a strategy of technological upgrading of company products with positive feedback to domestic production.

EAST ASIAN FDI IN THE UK

Flows from Japan

In the 1980s, Europe came to be the most important destination for Japanese FDI after the USA,[12] although the value of Japan's cumulative FDI stock in the United States was more than twice that in Europe ($170bn vs $76bn in 1992) and in recent years the level of new investment to Europe has fallen to a greater extent than in the USA.[13] The majority of Japan's outward investment flows have been in the non-manufacturing sector, which accounts for around 70 per cent of total Japanese FDI flows (Japanese Ministry of

Finance).[14] The balance within the total flow has gradually shifted away from primary production, which dominated in the early 1970s, towards financial and other business services and real estate (Matsuoka and Rose, 1994). However, there are large sectoral differences across Europe: in the low-wage economies of Spain, Portugal and Greece, 60 per cent of Japanese investments are in manufacturing, mainly large-scale factories; while only 20 per cent of UK and Netherlands investments fall into this category and the investment projects are far smaller in terms of average employment size. In these latter economies, banking and other financial services are the dominant form of Japanese investment, accounting for around 40 per cent of the total. Within manufacturing, the electrical and electronic equipment sector is predominant, accounting for around a quarter of cumulative flows between 1951 and 1992, followed by chemicals and transportation equipment, with around 14 per cent each (for details of sectoral and spatial distribution of Japanese FDI in Europe, see Kimura, 1996; Mason and Encarnation, 1994).

Within the EU, the UK is the leading destination for Japanese FDI by a significant margin, accounting for than 40 per cent of cumulative flows in 1951–91 (JETRO 1992b; MITI, 1995, quoted in United Nations, 1996), and is the leading country for both manufacturing and services, with the Netherlands, Germany, France and Luxembourg following some way behind. Although mergers and acquisitions have been an important element in the overall inflow of FDI – in 1995 nearly half of the total $50bn mergers and acquisition FDI in the EU was in the UK ($24bn) – Japanese companies, however, have preferred greenfield investments as the main mode of entry. In the late 1980s and early 1990s the UK accounted for around half (59 per cent in 1991) of all Japanese investment into EC member states. In 1993, according to Thiran and Hideki (1996) the UK accounted for 43,600 (33 per cent) of the 134,000 jobs in Japanese-owned plants within the twelve EC member states.

Surveys have shown that Japanese investors seeking a location within Europe favour the UK for a number of reasons, including access to the main European markets, language and culture, government attitude and availability of relatively low cost labour (Strange, 1993; PMG, 1991; see also Darby, 1996). In spite of some earlier 'lapses',[15] the attitude of government towards Japanese investment, as many commentators have observed (for example, Sargent, 1990; Morris, 1989) has been positive, reflecting practical and ideological elements of thinking on how Japanese inward investment might act as a stimulus to industrial change in the UK economy (see Stone, 1998). While other host countries were for many years ambivalent (France) or even hostile (West Germany) to Japanese FDI, the UK, right from the beginning of the 1980s, not only welcomed such investment but gave full backing to such companies in arguing for non-discriminatory treatment in the European market.[16] Japanese investors were, according to Sargent (1990), surprised by the high quality and diligence of the British labour force, finding workers both adaptable and amenable to their systems of work organization. Labour disputes at Japanese-owned plants have been comparatively rare, reflecting structural factors, as well as recruitment strategies, institutional arrangements (including 'no-strike agreements') and effective consultation mechanisms (Peck and Stone, 1992b).

Morris (1988) further distinguishes the fact that the UK was a 'soft' market, given the weakness of its consumer goods production (such as colour TV sets and cars), giving Japanese firms a good initial base in a major national market, prior to expanding production to serve an EU-wide market (see also Kimura, 1996; and Strange, 1993). Other factors include business attitudes and culture (similar to the USA, where the Japanese producers already had operational experience) (Belderbos, 1995).

Flows from the Rest of East Asia

Companies from the OEA economies have been slower to invest in Europe, and most of their FDI is directed towards Asia itself. However, some newly industrialized countries (NICs) are becoming more involved in Europe, as their larger manufacturing firms attempt to transform themselves into global conglomerates. The most notable are as follows:

South Korea: Companies from South Korea have been targeting Europe since the early 1990s to diversify away from existing export markets, reduce market dependence upon the USA, avoid the problems of being an 'outsider' and to take advantage of the Single European Market. South Korean manufacturing companies have in recent years been looking to the EU as a base for high-technology industries, primarily semi-conductors and consumer electronics.

Investment in a number of large single-site production complexes by the main diversified conglomerates (*chaebol*) were announced in the mid-1990s, dramatically underlining the multinational ambitions of these corporate entities. On the basis of these projects (investment have been slowed down or curtailed as a result of the current financial crisis affecting South Korea's economy and individual *chaebol* themselves), the UK was reported to be the destination for over half of the total commitment of Korean investment in the EU (*FT Survey*, 6 Oct. 97). The reasons for the UK being a popular location choice are for the most part similar to those which attracted the Japanese plants, supplemented by the influence on later investment decisions of successful experience of those Japanese plants established in the 1980s. There is an additional influence, however, in that previous phases of FDI by Japanese firms have led to the build-up of networks of reliable subcontractors, which Korean firms have been able to tap into. The ability to borrow (now Korean restrictions on its companies have been lifted) from UK capital markets has also been a consideration (*FT Survey*, 6 Oct. 97).

Taiwan: Some 96 per cent of the total Taiwan's FDI into the EU of $0.72bn was invested after 1990, with the majority (around half) going to the UK.[17] Like Japan and South Korea, there has been in the 1990s a shift in destination away from the Asian region towards, first, its traditional ally USA, and subsequently to Europe, linked to upgrading of activities from labour- to technology-intensive productions. Personal computers and information industries are the main manufacturing products; like earlier experience of Japan, outward investment in services has been growing rapidly, especially in telecommunications, transport and finance/insurance (which accounted in 1993 for 80 per cent of cumulative FDI into Europe, although relatively less for the UK, which has attracted a high proportion of Taiwan's manufacturing FDI in Europe). Some two-thirds of Taiwan's manufacturing investment in Europe in 1993 was in electronics, especially personal computers; the bulk of the rest in textiles.[18] The investors tend to be smaller firms than those from South Korea, although they include significant companies like Acer and Tatung.

The number of Taiwanese companies operating in the UK at the end of 1994 was around 70, with manufacturing units accounting for 15 of these.[19] A pattern of phasing is observable, whereby the

FDI project moves from sales to assembly and on to more complex manufacturing processes, accompanied by shift from focus on the national to EU market. Currently, Taiwanese firms appear more financially sound than the *chaebol* in particular, and this is the one East Asian country which has been maintaining its flow of investments into the UK very recently (for example, investments by Acer and ADI).

DISTRIBUTION OF EAST ASIAN-OWNED PLANTS WITHIN THE UK

FDI from East Asia plays a significant role in some of the UK's peripheral regions,[20] where a disproportionate share of East Asian-owned plants is located. Darby (1996), in his review of the regional distribution of employment in Japanese plants within Europe in 1993, puts the assisted regions of Wales and the North in second and third place respectively on the basis of the share of employment in such plants to total manufacturing employment.[21] There are significant clusters of such plants at some specific locations outside the assisted peripheral regions, notably the New Town environments of Telford and Milton Keynes, which have respectively contributed to the better than average performance of the West Midlands and the South East regions.[22]

Taylor (1993) found that, while he could find no evidence that Japanese investors were influenced by regional differences in labour costs, regional financial incentives such as investment grants were important determinants of location decisions among Japanese manufacturing plants, along with industrial mix. Plainly, the relatively poor performance of Scotland and Northern Ireland (see below; also, Darby, 1996) suggests that the availability of investment grants was insufficient to ensure inward investment from Japan; Darby (1996) argues that the UK 'semi-peripheral' regions such as Wales and the North have attracted Japanese plants because of 'cost minimising and market access reasons', while the peripherality of locations more distant from the main markets has discouraged such investment – a point echoed by Kimura (1996).

The scaling down of regional investment grant payments during the 1980s probably contributed to the wider geographical spread of some of the more recent investment location choices (Pioneer in Wakefield, for example, and Toyota in Derby). Investments which conform to the efficiency-seeking category identified above are likely to be drawn to locations within or nearer to the central core area by the prospect of access to leading indigenous manufacturers, the benefits of which can compensate for higher costs and local competition, compared to a subsidized location (Darby, 1996). This particularly applies in the case of the more sophisticated activities, and is supported by data relating to the distribution of Japanese-owned R&D facilities. In 1994, 38 per cent of Japanese plants with such facilities attached – and over half of the independent R&D facilities – were found in the South East core region. The choice of location for Nissan's European R&D centre in Cranfield (there is only a small test and design facility near to the Sunderland factory itself) and Canon's Science Park R&D site adjacent to the University of Surrey both reflect the primary need to access a pool of specialized skills. The technology-motivated increase in acquisition and joint venture activity by Japanese companies is also leading to a wider geographical dispersal of establishments, since the target plants are, for reasons to do with the spatial distribution of productive functions within the UK, frequently located nearer to the southern core of the national economy.

The major production complexes started by South Korean *chaebol* are all located in assisted areas: LG Electronics in South Wales[23] (semi-conductors and other electronics products, with an original planned outlay of $2.6bn and projected employment of over 6,000); Samsung's North East consumer electronics complex ($0.7bn investment and nearly 3,000 jobs); and Hyundai in Scotland (planned investment of $3.5bn in two semi-conductor plants to eventually employ 2,000). A range of functions was originally planned for each production complex, including higher-order activities such as design. Hyundai's incomplete project was cancelled in early 1998 and the scale of development in the other two has, for the time being at least, been restricted by the current financial crisis in the country of origin.

The spatial distribution of Taiwanese manufacturing plants established during the 1990s has been similar to that of the Japanese ones; apart from a small cluster of such plants in Telford, they are located mainly in peripheral assisted areas. Again, logic dictates that non-manufacturing FDI is more likely to be found in the south, especially finance-related activities, which predictably are focused upon London, but also sales offices; real estate investments are more scattered throughout the UK.

EAST ASIAN FDI IN THE NORTHERN REGION

Growth, Timing and Mode of Entry

The attraction of inward investment was a logical means of responding to the huge job gap left by the collapse of the North's former staples of coal, shipbuilding, heavy engineering and steel. Governments during the 1980s rejected state entrepreneurship, and a policy based upon developing indigenous firms was considered, at best, too slow to meet immediate employment needs. In the event the North, which had lagged behind the other UK peripheral regions in terms of the scale of inward FDI up until the 1980s (Stone and Peck, 1996), became the most successful region in the UK (and possibly Europe) in terms of winning FDI project during the 1980s.[24] The timing was crucial. While macroeconomic and political conditions made the UK the most attractive European location for FDI in general, this East-facing region possessed a number of attractions for inward investors, including a pool of industrial labour made acquiescent by their experience of high unemployment, good access to the continent, numerous industrial sites (including factories vacated by exiting firms) and effective political and institutional arrangements for attracting and supporting investors. The region effectively exploited some early successes in winning flagship plants in promoting the area to OEA investors. Lacking information about operating in the UK, these firms were undoubtedly influenced by the 'demonstration effect' of location decisions by leading firms such as Nissan, Komatsu and (the pathfinder) NSK.

East Asian FDI in the North of England expanded rapidly from the mid-1980s. In the Northern Region in 1986 there were just seven Japanese manufacturing plants (employing 1,650).[25] By 1996 the number had grown to 29, employing 11,550 (see Table 1, right-hand column), which represents 16 per cent of all foreign manufacturing sector employment in the region. In line with the usual means of entry associated with Japanese FDI, these plants have been predominantly established in the region *via* greenfield investments, with only four of the 27 plants being acquired via takeover (refer to Table 2); the three acquisitions since 1986 have accounted for only a small proportion of employment gains over the period 1986–96 (+650 jobs). Database figures indicate that new creations since 1986 and expansions among the surviving

TABLE 1
COMPONENTS OF CHANGE FOR EAST ASIAN ESTABLISHMENTS WITHIN
NORTHERN REGION FDI, 1978–96

	Initial stock	Estab	Closed	Acquis- itions	Divest- ments	In situ change Pos	Neg	Change	Final stock
East Asia (employment)									
Japan	287	9,519	-	1,227	-	512	-	+11,258	11,545
Rest of East Asia	-	2,928	-	575	-	28	88	+3,893	3,893
Rest of World	50,72	8,823	11,22	21,67	6,563	5,163	12,12	+5,287	56,010
Total	51,01	21,27	11,22	23,47	6,563	5,703	12,21	+20,438	71,448
East Asia (no. plants)									
Japan	1	24	-	4	-	1	-	+28	29
Rest of East Asia	-	14	-	3	-	1	1	+19	19
Rest of World	157	69	53	85	20	41	41	+79	236
Total	158	107	53	92	20	43	-42	+126	284

Note: Rest of East Asian entries under in situ change relate to acquisitions of plants existing (under other ownership) in 1978.
Source: NERU, FDI North database

Japanese plants together accounted for 9350 of the 9900 additional jobs in 1996.

Adding the plants belonging to OEA countries to those of Japan, the total number establishments in the North rises to 48 in 1996 with associated employment of 15,450. This is equivalent to just under 22 per cent of the total number of jobs in foreign-owned plants (see Table 1) and 6.5 per cent of the region's total manufacturing workforce. The 3,900 jobs in 19 non-Japanese East Asian plants represents by far the largest total from this source among the three peripheral UK 'regions' (see discussion below).

Figure 1 shows the overall pattern of plant investments over time.[26] The earliest arrival (NSK Bearings), came to the region well over two decades ago, in 1975, but there was only one further Japanese manufacturing investment[27] between then and 1983 (when Sumitomo acquired Dunlop tyres). The take-off began in 1985 – a decade after the 'pathfinder' NKS plant. With momentum given to the process by 'flagship' investments by Nissan and Komatsu, a boom followed which coincided with the world-wide upsurge in FDI in the second half of the 1980s. The recession of the early 1990s dampened down FDI activity, and although flows of new investments into the region resumed from 1993, the number of incoming East Asian plants fell to levels below those of the late 1980s. As can be seen from Figure 1, in the period up to 1990, East Asian investment in new plants (or in acquiring existing

FIGURE 1
DATES OF ESTABLISHMENT (OR ACQUISITION) BY EAST ASIAN MANUFACTURING FIRMS IN
THE NORTHERN REGION

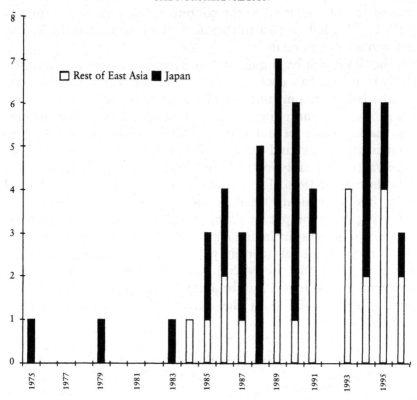

Source: NERU, FDINorth database

plants) was dominated by Japanese companies. From 1991, however, it can be seen how OEA investment came to dominate the inflows (by a ratio of 15 plants to seven).

Sectoral Characteristics

The first manufacturing investment in the region was a factory producing *bearings*. Cost advantages from high volume production led to a steady rise in the share of the European market taken by Japanese companies during the early 1970s, especially in the UK. Japanese bearings exporters have been subject to continual restrictions, including anti-dumping duties, since the mid 1970s (Strange, 1993). Nippon Seiko, anticipating the growing trade frictions, set up NSK Bearings Europe Ltd in Peterlee in 1974. After initially operating as a marketing subsidiary, the facility moved quickly into production (starting in 1976), exporting a large proportion of its output to the continent. Subsequent investments (in 1989-90) led to two further factories making steel balls and automobile components.

The significant beginning of East Asian investment in the region dates from Nissan's decision to locate in the region. By the early 1980s, Japanese companies faced restricted access to every major car producing country in the EC, as governments sought to protect the market share of home firms. Nissan made the decision to establish in Sunderland Europe's first wholly Japanese-owned *car manufacturing* facility in 1984, and began the assembly of kits in a pilot factory in 1986. The Nissan Motor Manufacturing (UK) Ltd plant has subsequently been developed via a number of phases, involving larger output (reaching 230,000 in 1997), an extended range of functions (including engine-building), and a progressively wider range of models (currently the Primera, including diesel and estate versions and the Micra). Over 80 per cent of output is exported. A new model is to be added by the year 2000, taking the employment to 4,800 in the £1.5bn plant (*North East PLC, 1997/98*).

A key feature of Japanese FDI in the region is the build-up of a network of parts suppliers around Nissan's assembly plant. The proportion of *automobile components* produced in-house by Japanese car assemblers is low compared to that in host country competitors and there is substantial reliance upon external suppliers for all parts (often in the form of sub-assemblies) except main components such as engines, transmission systems and large body pressings (Strange, 1993). Other factors contributing to the local build-up of a local cluster of Japanese automobile component firms include: the UK government stipulation that local content after 1990 should reach 80 per cent; production systems at the main assembly plant (that is, synchronized with suppliers to achieve just-in-time delivery); opportunities to supply vehicle plants in Europe other than that of Nissan; and the relatively low production costs *vis-à-vis* those in the home country base.

Within four to five years a cluster of suppliers had been established, led by Japanese firms, but often with a EU partner. Calsonic Exhaust Systems (UK) Ltd began production in Washington in 1986, in a joint venture with TI (TI-Nihon), quickly graduating from welding pipes to imported silencers to the production of full systems. Ikeda-Hoover (UK) Ltd, also established in 1986, was a JV supplying seats and headliners to Nissan, established because the car maker could find no UK manufacturer prepared to supply complete seat units and was reluctant to import the bulky low value items from high cost Japan. Pressure from indigenous industry and the British government led to this being established as a joint enterprise between Ikeda Busan (51 per cent) and Hoover Universal. As with Calsonic – and indeed, with other plants in the auto–related cluster, including the Nissan operation itself – Ikeda-Hoover has steadily developed a more complex production process with a greater degree of involvement with the host economy. Other new Japanese (or part Japanese) plants[28] in the regional supply network include: Nissan Yamato Engineering Ltd (80 per cent owned by Nissan, steel pressings, opened 1988); R-tek Ltd (JV between Kasai-Kogyo and Reydel of France, making interior door panels, opened 1989); Lucas-SEI Wiring Systems Ltd (JV between Sumitomo and Lucas, auto wiring harnesses, opened 1989); Hashimoto Ltd (metal and plastic trim and accessories, opened 1990); and Magna Kansei Ltd (JV with Canadian company, instrument panels, opened in 1990).[29]

Acquisition of appropriate plants has also played a role in the regional build-up of this new industry. Llanelli Radiators (heating systems, formerly owned by Rover) was acquired by Calsonic in 1989. Calsonic has also recently taken over a small local supplier, ARD components. Elta Plastics Ltd, a plastic mouldings firm, was also taken over in 1990. Sumitomo Rubber Industries' 1983 takeover of Dunlop tyre factory in Washington was not specifically related to Nissan's investment decision (announced in 1984), although the plant subsequently became a supplier to the car factory. Sumitomo's involvement in Europe, according to Strange (1993) was involuntary: financial pressures and an overcrowded market forced Dunlop to dispose of its tyre-making capacity and SRI feared that its status as a Dunlop affiliate might be compromised if a competitor acquired these businesses.[30]

Also in the area of engineering is production of *construction equipment*, as represented by the major assembly plant of Komatsu (UK) Ltd. Trade frictions in 1984 when the EC initiated an anti-dumping proceeding relating to hydraulic excavators from Japan, resulting in the imposition of dumping duties in 1985, was undoubtedly a significant factor behind this investment. Komatsu, heavily dependent upon overseas markets and especially the UK within Europe, established production facilities for excavators and wheeled loaders at Birtley on Tyneside which started operations in 1986.

The main products within the East Asian component of the *consumer electronics* industry in the region are microwave ovens (MVOs), colour TVs and computer monitors. Import duties and anti-dumping proceedings and actual or threatened introduction of dumping duties were plainly central to the instigation of these investments (see industry studies in Strange, 1993). Japanese and South Korean MVOs were the subject of EC anti-dumping proceedings in 1986, and it was not long afterwards, in 1988, that Sanyo established a plant in County Durham to manufacture MWOs for European market. In fact, the company is alone among the main Japanese original equipment manufacturers (OEMs) to establish a plant in the North. Colour TV production has been undertaken by Samsung, the first South Korean plant in the region (1987), LG Electric (1989, also South Korean) and Onwa (Hong Kong, 1993). Expansion by Samsung at a major new site on Teesside has recently given rise additionally to production of MWOs and computer monitors.

The OEMs' need to ensure quality of components, and to comply also with 'local content' requirements for inward investor plants, has led to establishment by supplying companies of production facilities inside the EU. Mostly these have been established by specialist *electronics components* firms, and as part of a 'second wave' of investments which followed the original investments by the final product assemblers. In Sanyo's case, the parent company itself established at the outset in 1988 both the main assembly plant and an adjacent factory producing the principal component (magnetrons). Tabuchi's plant in Thornaby was also set up relatively early (in 1985), rather than as a 'second wave' investment. The company made the independent decision to establish itself as a supplier of transformers and power supply units to both EC producers and the Japanese companies in the process of setting up in the UK.

Other Japanese electronics components firms include Mitsumi (UK) Ltd and SMK (UK) Ltd, established in 1987 and 1988 respectively. Anti-dumping proceedings (initiated in relation to dynamic random access memories in 1987) and a growing relationship with the then British computer maker ICL were important factors in the establishment of Fujitsu (UK) Ltd's semi-conductor plant in Newton Aycliffe, which began fabricating, assembly and testing of chips in 1991 (Strange, 1993). In contrast to the car industry investments, the relative absence in the region of the 'brand name' consumer electronics producers from Japan means that supplier plants in this sector are oriented towards a market which is spatially more diverse.

Given the importance of market access considerations in these FDI decisions, the investments correspond to the 'export-substituting' phase or type of outward investment from East Asia. The use of joint ventures by Japanese firms in the automobile sector is arguably motivated by considerations of market access, rather than as a means of accessing technology or innovative production methods (which is largely supplied from Japan). While the degree of sophistication and technical capability of the individual plants has developed steadily since the initial pilot plants were established, production linkages within the region have deepened and the market orientation of some plants has extended within Europe and beyond, the restricted nature of the technical support and skills base in the region limits the extent of efficiency-seeking investment in the region, at least by Japanese companies. It is important in this connection to recognize that in 1992 NSK chose to establish its R&D facility in the East Midlands, and that Nissan has located its main R&D operations in Bedfordshire.

The pattern of East Asian FDI in terms of employment by industrial sector. It reveals a predictable focus on a small number of sectors, with a noticeable difference between Japanese and OEA patterns. Motor vehicles dominates Japanese investment, with Nissan and its satellites accounting for over 6,000 jobs, or over half of the total number of jobs in Japanese-owned plants. In fact, this is a considerable under-estimate of the extent of Japanese FDI involvement in the auto industry, since a number of the Japanese plants included in other sectors (mechanical engineering, electrical engineering, rubber and plastics) are substantial suppliers to the car industry. Allowing for this, the true figure is thus around 7,500. As the figures stand, however, mechanical engineering, and electronic and electrical engineering are the next largest sectors, accounting together for a further 2,800 jobs or nearly a quarter of all

TABLE 2

EAST ASIAN-OWNED MANUFACTURING COMPANIES IN THE NORTH (ACTIVE)

Company	Product	SIC (1980)	Employment sizeband	Estab date	Foreign acq.	Parent	Country
AAF Ltd (1)	Heating & ventilation equip	3284	4		1994	Hong Leong	Malaysia
AAF Ltd (2)	Air filters for industry	3284	2		1994	Hong Leong	Malaysia
Calsonic Exhaust Systems (UK)	Car exhaust assembly	3530	3		1988	Calsonic Corporation/Nihon	Japan
Calsonic Llanelli Heating Systems	Nissan car heating & A/C eqip	3530	4			Calsonic Corporation/Nihon	Japan
Cookson Fukuda	Electrolytic copper foil	2246	3	1989	1990	Fukuda Metal Foil; Nissho Iwai; Cookson	Japan/UK
Cy Tec	Instruments	3710	2	1995		Cy Tec	Hong Kong
Dong Jin Precision UK Ltd	Metal pressers	3120	1	1996		Dong Jin	South Korea
Eastman Chemicals Ectona Ltd	Polyester chips; polyethylene teraphalate (PET)	2514	3	1986		Eastman Chemical Co	USA
Elta Plastics	Plastic injection moulding for cars	4836	3		1990	Nifco Tokyo/Yokohama	Japan
Europa Magnetics Corporation	Floppy disks/CD-ROMS	2599	4	1993		Europa Magnetics Corporation	Taiwan
Fujitsu Microelectronics Ltd	Dynamic random access memories Japan (DRAMS)	3444	5	1991		Fujitsu Co Ltd	Taiwan
Hashimoto Forming Co	Metal & plastic car parts	3740	4	1990		Hashimoto Forming Industry Co Ltd	Japan
Ikeda Hoover Ltd	Car seats & interior trims	3530	4	1986		Ikeda Bussan/Johnsons Controls	Japan/USA
Inkel (UK) Ltd	Home & car audio equip.	3453	2	1990		Inkel Corp	South Korea
International Cuisine Ltd	Chilled meals	4122	3	1987	1995	Singapore Technologies Corp	Singapore
Komatsu (UK) Ltd	Hydraulic excavators	3254	4	1987		Komatsu Ltd	Japan
LG Electric	TVs	3460	5	1989		Lucky Goldstar	South Korea
Lite On	Power supply converters for computers	3302	3	1989	1991	Lite On Corporation	Taiwan
LNP	Plastic granules	4834	1	1994		Kawaski Steel	Japan
Lucas SEI	Manufacture of wiring harnesses for the motor industry	3434	5	1994		Lucas Industries/Sumitomo	Japan/UK
Magna Kansei Ltd	Instrument panels	3740	3	1990		Kansei Corp/Magna Int	Japan/Canada
Mitsumi Electric	TVs/ Electrical components	3453	3	1987		Mitsumi Electric Co.	Japan
Nippon Silica Glass	Components for semiconductors	3453	1	1995		Niipon Silica Glass	Japan
Nissan Motor Manufacturing UK	Car assembly	3510	6	1986		Nissan Motor Co	Japan
Nissan Yamato Engineering Ltd	Press steel components	3530	5	1988		Yamato Kogyo	Japan

TABLE 2 (CONTINUED)

EAST ASIAN-OWNED MANUFACTURING COMPANIES IN THE NORTH (ACTIVE)

Company	Product	SIC (1980)	Employment sizeband	Estab date	Foreign acq.	Parent	Country
NSK Bearings Europe Ltd (1)	Ball bearings	3262	5	1975		NSK RHP (Nippon Seiko Kabushiki)	Japan
NSK Components Division (2)	Automotive components	3530	3	1990		NSK (Nippon Seiko Kabushiki)	Japan
NSK/AKS Precision Ball	Steel balls	3111	2	1989		NSK (Nippon Seiko Kabushik) & AKS	Japan
Onwa (Europe) Ltd (3)	TVs	3454	4	1993		Kong Wah Group	Hong Kong
Organo (Europe) Ltd	Chemical industry machinery	3245	1	1994		Organo	Japan
Oshino Lamps	Miniature lamps, for auto/aerospace industry	3470	1	1995		Oshino Lamps	Japan
Pico (UK) Ltd	Fuses	3420	1	1996		Pico	Japan
R-tek	Interior car door panels	3521	3	1989		Reydel Ind/Kasai-Kyogo	Japan/France
Rose Knitting	Knitwear	4363	2	1993		Rose Knitting	Hong Kong
SammiSound	Loudspeakers	3453	1	1993		SammiSound	South Korea
Samsung Electronics	Electrical equipment; microwaves	3454	5	1995		Samsung Electronics	South Korea
Samsung Electronics (UK) Ltd	TVs	3454	4	1987		Samsung Electronics	South Korea
Sanyo Electric Co Ltd	Magnetrons for MWOs	3460	2	1988		Sanyo Electric Co Ltd (2/2)	Japan
Sanyo Electric Manufacturing UK	Microwave ovens	3460	4	1988		Sanyo Electric Co Ltd (1/2)	Japan
Siam Furniture	Furniture	4671	1	1991		Siam Furniture	Thailand
SMK (UK) Ltd	Computer/TV/CD components	3443	4	1988		SMK Corp	Japan
SP Tyres UK	Tyres	4811	5	1983		Sumitomo Rubber Inds.	Japan
Synpac Pharmaceuticals Ltd	Penicillin	2570	4	1991		China Synthetics Rubber Corporation	Taiwan
Tabuchi Electric UK Ltd	Transformers & power suppliers	4370	3	1985		Tabuchi Electric Co	Japan
Tin Lung Knitwear (UK) Ltd	Knitwear	4363	1	1985		Tin Lung Knits Ltd	Hong Kong
TYK International Ltd	Lances for European steel ind.	2471	1	1989		Tokyo Yogyo Corporation (TYK Ltd)	Japan
Woo One UK	Computer casings	3302	1	1996		Samsung	Japan
Yazaki (UK) Ltd	Motor vehicle parts	3530	1	1994		Yazaki	South Korea
Young Shin	Electrical engineering	3453	2	1995		Young Shin Electronics	South Korea

Employment size bands: 1: 1–49, 2: 50–99, 3: 100–249, 4: 250–499, 5: 500–999, 6: 1000+
Source: NERU, FDI North database

employment in Japanese plants. Some of the sectors which have been prominent in the profile of Japanese plants in the UK – machine tools and electronic office equipment – are not represented in the North.

Investment from OEA countries, amounting to nearly 3,900 jobs, is confined largely to electrical and electronic engineering, which accounts for two-thirds of the employment in OEA plants. Employment resulting from OEA FDI in the electronics sector is larger than that for Japanese companies. Of the other sectors, only mechanical engineering and chemicals are of any significance in terms of employment (for details see list of establishments in Table 2).

EAST ASIAN CONTRIBUTION TO OVERALL UK INWARD INVESTMENT PERFORMANCE

Inward investment is widely considered to have made a crucial contribution to the process of replacing the jobs lost as a result of serious de-industrialization in the 1970s and early 1980s. How important is the East Asian contribution to the inward investment attracted to the Northern economy over the past decade?

The poor performance of UK-owned firms since the 1970s has been the main factor behind the decline of 42 per cent in manufacturing employment in the North between 1978 and 1996 (from 416,000 to 236,000), although significantly improved productivity has also contributed to the substantial fall in the requirement for labour. Over the period 1978–96 employment in the foreign-owned manufacturing sector has risen by 40 per cent, from 51,000 to 71,500 (Table 1). In the context of the decline in overall manufacturing employment, the FDI sector has become relatively more important, rising from 12 per cent to just over 30 per cent of the total for manufacturing in the eighteen year period (associated with a rise in the total number of foreign-owned plants from 158 to 284).

While service sector growth has been important within the restructuring of the regional economy, the rate of job creation in this sector has been below that of the nation as a whole. Moreover, it is a commonplace that many of the new jobs were part-time or taken by women. Manufacturing is thus disproportionately important in the North as a source of employment, particularly full-time for men (the kind of jobs most affected by the de-industrialization process in this region) (Peck and Stone, 1992a).

Table 1 shows how important the East Asian contribution has been to sustaining manufacturing employment within the region. Over the period 1978–96, the Rest of the World (ROW) FDI expanded from 50,700 to 56,000, a gain of 6,400 or 10.5 per cent. Although some 69 surviving new ROW plants had created 8,820 new jobs, these were more than counterbalanced by the heavy losses through closures (53 plants and 11,230 jobs) and net *in situ* contraction among the 82 plants surviving the period (an overall loss of 6,000 jobs). The biggest losses were among US plants, mainly in the first half of the period; as the employment share of US-owned establishments within the North's FDI was reduced from 73 per cent to around a third. The main gains within the ROW group actually came from net acquisitions,[31] which in total (85 plants) exceeded the *overall* gain (+79) in the number of ROW FDI plants over the period, and on balance gave rise to 15,100 'new' jobs. This reflects the extent to which entry by European companies in particular has been through acquisition of UK plants. Whatever its implications for productive efficiency, in terms of simple static comparisons, this process involves a net *transfer* of jobs between the domestic and foreign-owned sector. The ROW sector relied upon this transfer or re-classification of jobs to achieve the positive overall figure of 5,300 jobs gained. Without this contribution arising out of takeover activity, the Rest of the World establishments in the FDI total would have registered a net *fall* in associated employment by nearly one-fifth (some 9,800 jobs) (Table 1).

Given this performance by the ROW plants, the value of the East Asian contribution to the FDI flows is plain, although in making any comparisons, the advantage to the East Asian sector of not having an inheritance of older plants should be borne in mind. While the East Asian sources of investment provided just 37 per cent of the expansion in number of FDI plants over the period 1978–96 (47 out of 126), they accounted for 15,150 (or no less than 74 per cent) of the increase of 20,450 in overall employment in the foreign-owned sector during 1978–96. Moreover, the majority of the East Asian contribution consisted of jobs entirely new to the region. The number of jobs in new East Asian plants was 13,350, while those added as a result of the acquisition of plants amounted to just 1,800. Without the Japanese and OEA contribution, the net job-creating performance of the overseas-owned sector as a whole would have been reduced dramatically.

Comparison with Other UK Peripheral Economies

Has the role of East Asian direct investment been more pronounced in the North than in the other peripheral regions of the UK? The findings (summarized in Table 3) on this indicate that Scotland and Northern Ireland have both been less successful than both the North and Wales in terms of attracting FDI from East Asia, and the proportional contribution to employment in both has been correspondingly lower.

Over the past decade (1986–96) the number of Japanese plants in *Scotland* has increased from 9 to 25, with an associated rise in employment from 1,150 to 9,150, representing 11.2 per cent of the total FDI employment in the latter year (Scottish Office, 1997). However, six of the 18 additional plants which appeared over the period were acquisitions, and these actually account for a substantial proportion of the increase of 8,000 in employment (including making up for the effect of two closures). Compared to the situation in the North, the number of gains through the combined effect of new openings and net expansions *in situ* account for a smaller proportion of the job gain among Japanese plants (4,800 or 56 per cent). Investment by OEA companies in Scotland has been very limited: by 1998 there were only six such plants employing only around 500 people (Scottish Office, CSU data). Total East Asian investment in 1996 amounted to around 30 plants employing some 9,500 workers. At under 3 per cent of Scotland's manufacturing jobs, this well below half the equivalent share found in the North.

The author's FDI data shows that *Northern Ireland's* 13 East Asian plants (eight Japanese, four South Korean and one from Hong Kong), engaged in a mix of activities in the fields of vehicle and electronic component manufacturing, altogether accounted for only 2,150 jobs in Northern Ireland in 1996.[32] All but three of the investment projects existing in 1996 were greenfield investments set up in the very recent period (from 1992 onwards). Two were formerly US plants which had recently become joint venture operations with a Japanese partner. Employment in the thirteen plants is equivalent to only 7 per cent of the total for the foreign-owned sector in Ireland, and barely 2 per cent of all manufacturing jobs in the Province.

The ten existing Japanese plants in *Wales* in 1985 accounted for 3,500 jobs (Welsh Office, 1997). By 1996 this had increased to

TABLE 3
EAST ASIAN FDI WITHIN TOTAL FDI, UK PERIPHERAL REGIONS, 1996

Region	Employment in Japanese plants (no. plants)	Employment in OEA plants (no. plants)	Employment in all EA plants (no. plants)	Employment in East Asian plants as per cent of region's FDI employment
North	11,550 (29)	3,900 (19)	15,400 (48)	22 per cent
Scotland	9,150 (25)	500 (6)*	9,650 (31)	11 per cent
Wales	16,900 (38)	850 (6)	17,750 (44)	22 per cent
N. Ireland	1,050 (8)	1,100 (5)	2,150 (13)	7 per cent
Total (UK Periphery)	37,460 (100)	6,350 (36)	43,810 (136)	–

* Figures relate to 1998

Sources: NERU FDI Databases, Northern Region and N. Ireland; Scottish Office, 1997; Welsh Office, 1997; *Labour Market Trends*

16,900 in 38 plants, a gain of 13,400 over the period and representing 22.4 per cent of all foreign-owned manufacturing employment in the Principality. The gain is made up largely of new openings (24 new plants involving the creation of 5,700 jobs), with net expansions contributing a further 4,200. Compared to the North, acquisitions (of which there were five, involving a gain to the foreign-owned sector of 3,600 jobs), were, as in Scotland, a more important element in the overall increase in employment. In terms of numbers of *new* jobs in Japanese plants (greenfield and expansions) over the period 1986–96, therefore, the expansion was only marginally greater in Wales than in the North.

Moreover, as in the case of Scotland, Wales by 1996 had received only limited FDI from OEA sources. The two plants (and 150 jobs) existing in 1986 had increased only to six plants and 850 employees by 1996 (Welsh Office, EAD data), making a total for all East Asian investment of 17,750 in 44 plants. At 8.6 per cent of all manufacturing jobs in Wales, the East Asian sector is, however, proportionately more prominent within its local economy that its counterpart in the North of England (with just over 6.5 per cent); but the number of new jobs gained from new East Asian investment projects and expansions over the period 1986–96 is actually higher in the North.

CONCLUSIONS AND PROSPECTS

This study has demonstrated how FDI from East Asia has been a crucial source of investment to create new industry and jobs following the collapse in industrial and mining employment in the North during the 1970s and early 1980s. In particular, it has shown how the results of the inward investment strategy would have been drastically diminished in the absence of FDI inflows from East Asia. Indeed, in terms of inward investment the gap in performance of Scotland *vis-à-vis* those of the North and Wales is largely the result of the difference in investment flows from East Asia.

There are numerous aspects to FDI and the way it impacts upon a local area (see Stone, 1998), only some of which have been covered here. Factors such as functional range at plant level, patterns of supply linkage and job types are all linked to the form of investment project and determine the overall impact of FDI upon a local economy. It is not possible to undertake for the North the kind of analysis produced relating to Wales by Munday *et al.* (1996), for want of the kind of survey-derived information they have gathered. However, some general observations on the East Asian FDI sector in the region can be made.

First, the East Asian direct investments in the region are highly cohesive. Unlike American and European FDI, that from East Asia is relatively new, occupies a narrow range of sectors and, for the most part, involves purpose-designed and built facilities rather than acquired ones. At the local level, therefore, these plants are as a group likely to be distinctive in terms of technology, productivity, workforce organization, corporate control, inter-group linkages and pervasiveness of company 'culture'. Other FDI is significantly more diverse given that it embraces more sectors and a wider time span, incorporates different business cultures and has been more affected organizationally and in other ways by change(s) of ownership.

Second, East Asian plants themselves cannot be regarded as static production entities, but rather ones which undergo a process of evolution, changing their character in respect of the complexity of production, range of functions, skill requirements and market orientation. Early plants were often 'pilot' operations which facilitated the learning process for firms lacking experience in operating in European conditions. Many of these achieve their optimal development only over a period of time, and there is additional growth – through further re-investment – yet to come out of the existing group of FDI plants.

The changing business environment – and the pressures to respond in the context of globalization and rapid technological change – will naturally cause companies to respond via investment (perhaps through takeovers and joint ventures) and dis-investment. Where access to modern technology and high-level skills are the motivation for FDI, such investment will often occur outside the peripheral regions (which lack a substantial base of high technology companies). Provided, however, that the appropriate conditions and support exists in regions like the North, there is potential for further development of productive activity within the East Asian plant sector aimed at serving widening markets and integrating production facilities within global networks. Attempts at 'embedding' such investments are a crucial means by which this development can be encouraged, and the base of FDI secured and built upon, although national policies with respect to value of the currency and relationships with Europe will exert an important influence on investment decisions.

The Asian financial crisis has made it unlikely that new East Asian investments will be forthcoming for a period of time. The uncertainty and financial difficulties (both at company level and more generally) will make firms very wary about investments, and the effect of relative currency values will further discourage such activity. Given the importance of East Asian FDI in the growth via investment from exogenous sources in UK peripheral regions over the past decade or so, development agencies, including the new Regional Development Agencies for the English regions, will need to formulate new policies which take account of this. There are good grounds for thinking that the crisis will have a muted impact on current FDI plants, not least because they are an important source of revenue for hard-pressed parent companies, and the recovery in the main European markets (to which they are oriented) will help in generating such revenue. Selling-off of plants and licensing production to raise cash is unlikely (for reasons discussed above), although there is likely to be pressure on some components plants faced with competition from home country or other Asian firms with the advantage of a significantly devalued currency. This is illustrated by the closure in of Fujitsu's semi-conductor plant, announced in September 1998 – within a month of the German company's Siemens decision to shut its recently-opened semi-conductor plant on Tyneside. The collapse in the world market price of memory chips – and the outcome as it has been felt within the North – is an extreme phenomenon linked to the nature of this particular industry, and it should not be inferred that the East Asian-owned sector as a whole is similarly endangered.

ACKNOWLEDGEMENT

The author is grateful to Paul Braidford, Senior Research Assistant in the Northern Economic Research Unit, for his assistance in compiling the tables and preparing the diagram used in this article.

NOTES

1. For the UK, it is conventionally assumed that a shareholding in excess of 20 per cent is needed to acquire control of an enterprise (although OECD and IMF guidelines suggest using a figure of 10 per cent). New creations can be either greenfield investments (entirely new sites) or brownfield ones (reclaimed sites). FDI can also involve inward transfer of capital for purposes of (a) expanding existing productive facilities or (b) collaborating with a company from the home country (or another foreign country) through a joint venture. FDI includes re-invested earnings from operations of previous capital transactions, although this is not captured by statistics on cross-border capital flows. It is important to distinguish between FDI and 'portfolio investment' (in which the UK is also a major world player), which refers to other equity investment (shareholdings of less than 20 per cent) and investment in bonds – investments in which the investor does not have a voice in terms of control. Comparability of FDI data is restricted by variations in data collection methods and definitions used by different countries. Not all countries record every component of FDI flows, and the distinction between direct and indirect investment, in particular, is often unclear (for discussion, see United Nations, 1997, p.44 and Annex). Japanese Ministry of Finance definitions of outward FDI includes all equity shareholding in excess of 10 per cent. For details, see Komiya, 1991 (Ch.3) and Matsuoka and Rose, 1994 (Chs 32, 33).
2. Although, in terms of individual countries, the USA is the largest host for *and* source of FDI.
3. Provisional figures given in United Nations, 1997.
4. FDI outflows from Japan in 1995 amounted to $22bn; although this represents a substantial increase over 1992–94 it was less than half the annual outflow during the high point of 1989–91 (United Nations, 1997).
5. The FDI outflow figure for these four 'Asian Tiger' economies is exaggerated by the fact that 30 per cent of the outward FDI from Hong Kong, which accounts for two-thirds of the total for this group, is made up of indirect FDI by foreign affiliates operating in Hong Kong. It should also be noted that around half of the FDI outflow from Hong Kong is targeted upon mainland China (UNCTAD data quoted in United Nations, 1997).
6. Combined outflows for the years 1972 and 1973 outweighed the total for the previous two decades by 60 per cent (Komiya, 1991). The conditions for outward FDI subsequently deteriorated as a result of the oil crisis, but the outflow resumed in the later part of the decade.
7. Concern over the availability of mineral and forestry resources had in fact led to a number of resource-related FDI projects during the 1950s and 1960s, when overseas investment was otherwise restricted. Most of these involved government participation

(Komiya, 1991)

8. The quality of local suppliers was initially a major concern among Japanese companies establishing pilot plants (Sargent, 1990). A supplier may set up a local plant because it wishes to avoid any threat to its close relationship with the main assembly firm.

9. Notwithstanding the signs of emerging globalization strategies, it should not be forgotten, as Belderbos (1995) is at pains to stress, that in the early 1990s, the EU was still more important as an *export* market than as a production base for Japanese firms. Though 'efficiency-seeking' FDI has become an increasingly important investment for Japanese companies, and foreign production is increasing, its relative importance in total production in the manufacturing sector as a whole is considerably lower than that of firms from Germany and the USA (United Nations, 1996). Japan's overseas industrial production is equivalent only to 4 per cent of the total, compared, for example, to 20 per cent in the case of the USA.

10. In the early 1990s, Japanese companies owned more than half of the capital in FDI projects in the UK in over 90 per cent of the cases (Belderbos, 1995); and were wholly Japanese-owned subsidiaries in 65 per cent of all cases (JETRO, 1992).

11. Taiwan Investment Commission, 1993, 'An Analysis of Outward Investment', Ministry of Economic Affairs, Taipei; the author is grateful to Xian Zhi Wang for his translation of this data. Total outflows, including those to China, totalled $2.7bn in 1995 (United Nations, 1997).

12. More accurately the European Union; CEE has received negligible direct investment from Japan (just 1 per cent of the total flow into Europe according to Darby, 1996), although the NICs, notably South Korea, have been more active in investing in this region.

13. In 1989–91, 23 per cent of the investment total was directed to the EU, compared with 51 per cent to the USA; during 1994–96 the respective proportions were 37 per cent and 13 per cent (United Nations, 1997).

14. Although only accounting for around 57 per cent of the *number* of investments in Europe, and 45 per cent in the US.

15. Most notably the case in the late 1970s of union pressure on government leading to the discouragement of Hitachi's plans for establishing a plant in Washington in the North East (Morris, 1989?).

16. Belderbos (1995) argues that the policy stance of *local* as well as central government is important – presumably on the grounds that local authorities are in a position to influence environmental elements of operational importance (such as transport and training infrastructure) and to offer practical support to companies embarking upon investments in an unfamiliar environment. However, as in the case of investment subsidies, this is often likely to be more influential in affecting inter-regional rather than international location choice (Christodoulou, 1996).

17. Taiwan Investment Commission, 1993 (see footnote 11).

18. Ibid.

19. Taiwanese Trade Representative, 1994, *An Opportunity for the East Asian Economies: an introduction to the investment and manufacturing environment in Britain*, unpublished report, London.

20. Standard UK regions are used throughout, including the 'national' regions of Scotland, Wales and the province of Northern Ireland.

21. Wales was found to have 6.1 per cent of the total workforce in Japanese plants in Europe compared with the region's 0.9 per cent share of total European manufacturing employment, while the respective figures for the North were 4.4 per cent and 0.9 per cent (Darby, 1996).

22. West Midlands had 6.0 per cent of the total workforce in Japanese plants in Europe compared with the region's 1.7 per cent share of European manufacturing employment, while the respective figures for the South East were 3.3 per cent and 1.5 per cent (Darby, 1996).

23. In terms of the original plans, this represented the largest single investment in Europe by a non-European firm (United Nations, 1996).

24. The relative performance of the North and Wales in attracting FDI shifted to slightly

favour Wales in the decade up to 1996 (Stone, 1997).

25. Figures from *Foreign-Owned Manufacturing Sector (FOMS) North of England Database*, Northern Economic Research Unit, University of Northumbria, Newcastle upon Tyne. These are *actual* employment figures, rather than projected figures at the time of establishment which are used by some organizations (for example, Invest in Britain Bureau). (For discussion and details of database, see Stone and Peck, 1996).

26. The Figure shows how plant set-ups (i.e. initial greenfield investments) and acquisitions by East Asian owners are distributed over the relevant time period. Subsequent expansions through *re-investment*, which are a feature of many of the new plants, are not shown in the diagram. Note also that the figure includes only those East Asian plants still operating in 1996. It thus omits the following Northern-based plants: Polychrome Ltd, acquired when DIC Japan bought the US parent Polychrome Corporation in 1979, and which closed in the early 1990s

27. Polychrome Ltd's plant in Berwick (see previous note).

28. Companies from the rest of the East Asia are not represented in this cluster.

29. A number of local companies and non-Japanese foreign ones have also developed as suppliers to Nissan; the most striking case involve the US company TRW, with has established no fewer than five plants near to Nissan's factory.

30. Strange (1993) takes the view that it was unlikely that an alternative bidder would have been found; in which case, the Japanese takeover may have prevented the Washington factory's closure.

31. That is, the number of jobs in 1996 in plants acquired from UK owners by overseas companies during the accounting period 1978–96 (86 acquisitions=22,300), minus the number of jobs in 1978 in overseas-owned plants which were subsequently acquired by UK-based companies (including management buy-outs) (20 divestments=6,550).

32. NERU *FOMS Database, Northern Ireland* (for details, see appendix in Stone and Peck, 1996).

REFERENCES

Belderbos, R. (1995), 'The Role of Investment in Europe in the Globalisation Strategy of Japanese Electronics Firms', in F. Sachwald (ed.), *Japanese Firms in Europe*. Luxembourg: Harwood Academic Publishers.

Burge, K. (1997), 'Japanese Manufacturing Investment in Europe, Recent History and Future Prospects', *Business Review North*, Vol.8, No.4, pp.14–19.

Burge, K. (1996), 'Korean Investment in the UK', *Business Review North*, Vol.8, No.1, pp.13–17.

Christodoulou, P. (1996), *Inward Investment: An Overview and Guide to the Literature*. London: The British Library.

Culem, C. (1988), 'The Locational Determinants of Direct Investment among Industrialised Countries', *European Economic Review*, Vol.32, pp.885–904.

Darby, J. (ed.) (1996), *Japan and the European Periphery*. Basingstoke: Macmillan.

Dent, C. (1997), *The European Economy: The Global Context*. London: Routledge.

Dore, R. (1986), *Flexible Rigidities: Industrial Policy and Structural Adjustment in the Japanese Economy*. London: Athlone.

Dunning, J.H. (1993), *The Globalisation of Business: The Challenge of the 1990s*, London: Routledge.

Dunning, J.H. (1993), *Multinational Enterprises and the Global Economy*. Wokingham: Addison-Wesley.

Dunning, J.H. (1988), 'The Eclectic Paradigm of International Business', *Journal of International Business Studies*, Vol.19, No.1, pp.1–31.

Dunning, J.H. (1986), *Japanese Participation in British Industry*. London: Croom Helm.

Dunning, J.H. and J.A. Cantwell (1990), 'Japanese Manufacturing Direct Investment in the EEC, Post 1992: Some Alternative Scenarios', in B. Burgenmeir and J.L. Mucchielli (eds), *Multinationals and Europe 1992*. London: Routledge.

Haslam, C. and K. Williams *et al.* (1996), 'Learning from Japan: The Yeast for Britain's

Manufacturing Regeneration?', in J. Darby (ed.), *Japan and the European Periphery*. Basingstoke: Macmillan.

Heitger, B. and J. Stehn (1990), 'Japanese Direct Investment in the EC – Response to the Internal Market 1993?', *Journal of Common Market Studies*, Vol.29, pp.1–15.

Japanese External Trade Organisation (JETRO) (1990), *Current Situation of Business Operations of Japanese Manufacturing Enterprises in Europe*, 6th survey report, Tokyo.

JETRO (1992a), *European Operations of Japanese Companies in the Manufacturing Sector*, 8th survey report, Tokyo.

JETRO (1992b), *White Paper on Foreign Direct Investment 1992: The Role of Direct Investment in Filling the Gap between Capital Demand and Supply*, Summary, Tokyo.

Kimura, Y. (1996), 'Japanese Direct Investment in the Peripheral Regions of Europe: An Overview', in J. Darby (ed.), *Japan and the European Periphery*. Basingstoke: Macmillan.

Kirkland, R.I. (1990), 'The Big Japanese Push into Europe', *Fortune*, 2 July, pp.94–8.

Komiya, R. (1991), *The Japanese Economy: Trade, Industry, and Government*. Tokyo: University of Tokyo Press.

Mason, M. (1994), 'Historical Perspectives on Japanese Direct Investment in Europe' in M. Mason and D. Encarnation (eds), *Does Ownership Matter? Japanese Multinationals in Europe*. Oxford: Clarendon Press.

Mason, M. and D. Encarnation (eds) (1994), *Does Ownership Matter? Japanese Multinationals in Europe*. Oxford: Clarendon Press.

Matsuoka, M. and B. Rose (1994), *The DIR Guide to Japanese Economic Statistics*. Oxford: Oxford University Press.

Ministry of International Trade and Industry (MITI) (1995), *Dai 24-kai Wagakuni Kigyo no Jigyo Katsudo*. Tokyo: Ministry of Finance Printing Bureau.

Morris, J. (1988), 'The Who, Why and Where of Japanese Investment in the UK', *Industrial Relations Journal*, Vol.19, No.1, pp.31–40.

Munday, M., J. Morris and B. Wilkinson (1996), 'The Rising Sun? The Japanese Contribution to the Local Economy in Wales', in J. Darby (ed.), *Japan and the European Periphery*. Basingstoke: Macmillan.

Nicolas, F. (1995), 'The Expansion of Foreign Direct Investment', in F. Sachwald (ed.), *Japanese Firms in Europe*. Luxembourg: Harwood Academic Publishers.

Ohmae, K. (1985a), 'Becoming a Triad Power: The New Global Corporation', *The McKinsey Quarterly*, Vol.21, Spring, pp.2–25.

Ohmae, K. (1985b), *Triad Power: The Coming Shape of Global Competition*, New York: Free Press.

Ozawa, T. (1991a), 'Japan in a New Phase of Multinationalism and Industrial Upgrading: Functional Integration of Trade, Growth and FDI', *Journal of World Trade*, pp.43–60.

Ozawa, T. (1991b), 'Japanese Multinationals and 1992', in B. Burgenmeier and J.L. Mucchielli (eds), *Multinationals and Europe 1992*, .London: Routledge.

Peck, F. and I. Stone (1992a), *Inward Investment and the Northern Region Labour Market*, Research Paper No.6. Sheffield : Employment Department, .

Peck, F. and I. Stone (1992b), 'Japanese Inward Investment in the North East of England: Reassessing "Japanisation"', *Environment and Change (C) Government and Policy*, Vol.10, No.4, pp.55–67.

PMG (1991), *Perceptions of England as an Investment Location: A Survey*. London: Report for the DTI.

Sachwald, F. (1995), 'Japanese Chemical Firms: A Limited Internationalization', in F. Sachwald (ed.), *Japanese firms in Europe*. Luxembourg: Harwood Academic Publishers.

Sargent, J. (1990), 'Japan's Manufacturing Investment Overseas: Its Implications for Britain and the European Community', *Japan Digest*, July, pp.32–40.

The Scottish Office (1997), *Overseas Ownership in Scottish Manufacturing Industry, 1996*, Statistical Bulletin (Industry Series), No.Ind/1997/A3.7, July, Edinburgh.

Stone, I. (1998), 'Inward Investment in the UK', *Developments in Economics*, Vol.14, pp.133–56.

Stone, I. (1997), *Overseas-owned Manufacturing in the Northern Region: Growth and Structural Change, 1989–96*, report for Tyneside TEC, Northern Economic Research Unit. Newcastle upon Tyne: University of Northumbria.

Stone, I. and F. Peck (1996), 'The Foreign-owned Manufacturing Sector in UK Peripheral Regions', 1978–93: Restructuring and Comparative Performance', *Regional Studies*, Vol.30, No.1, pp.55–68.
Strange, R. (1993), *Japanese Manufacturing Investment in Europe: Its Impact upon the UK Economy*. London: Routledge.
Sugitani, S. (1993), 'Expansion of Japan's Overseas Direct Investment', *Kwansei Gakuin University Annual Studies*, Vol.42, pp.49–56.
Taylor, J. (1993), 'An Analysis of the Factors Determining the Geographical Distribution of Japanese Manufacturing Investment in the UK 1984–91', *Urban Studies*, Vol.30, No.7, pp.1209–24.
Tokyo Business Today (1989), 'Rapid Increase in Japanese Overseas M&A', anon. January: pp.20–24.
Thomsen, S. and P. Nicolaides (1991), *The Evolution of Japanese Direct Investment in Europe*. Hemel Hempstead: Harvester Wheatsheaf.
Thiran, J-M. and Y. Hideki (1996), 'Patterns of Japanese Manufacturing Employment in the European Regions', in J. Darby (ed.), *Japan and the European Periphery*. Basingstoke: Macmillan.
United Nations (1997), *World Investment Report, 1997: Transnational Corporations, Market Structure and Competition Policy*. New York and Geneva.
United Nations (1996), *World Investment Report, 1966: Investment, Trade and International Policy Arrangements*. New York and Geneva.
The Welsh Office (1997), 'Employment in Overseas Owned Manufacturing Plants in Wales', internal paper No.SDP 29/97, 23 July, Cardiff.
Young, S. and N. Hood (1992), 'European Business Environments in the 1990s', in S. Young and J. Hamill (eds), *Europe and the Multinationals*. Aldershot: Edward Elgar.

4

Working Miracles? Regional Renewal and East Asian Interlinkages

JOHN RITCHIE

As the century ends the traffic in ideas about economic miracles continues apace (Isaak, 1997). Such transmigratory ideas might well follow certain recognizable circuits (Ritchie, 1994). However, until very recently, those concerning East Asia typically upstaged most others, while switching from Japan towards China en route (Ritchie, 1997). As previous economic miracle claims concerning the former Soviet Union (Krugman, 1994) and Latin and South America pass off-circuit, the ruling British state presses similar arguments too. More lately these have switched focus from its core towards semi-peripheral regions with prominent international tie-ups and alliances. The so-called 'New' North East of England is a particular case in point, since state/public narratives about its economic re-emergence often cite growing East Asian interlinkages, as if these bring about transformations without parallel and precedent For example:

> The major successes of development agencies and regenerative bodies...working together to bring into the Great North companies such as Nissan, Komatsu, Gold-star and Fujitsu, have created a highway along which a growing stream of others are now speeding into the North (Northern Development Company/Tyne and Wear Chamber of Commerce, 1990).

> The North is a fantastic success story...the biggest collection of inward investment and Japanese companies bringing the latest technology, a really good living, superb management...a colossal success story (Margaret Thatcher, cited in *the Newcastle Journal*, 5 June 1990).

John Ritchie, Durham University Business School

> I think what has happened over the past 12 or 13 years in
> the North has really been one of the unspoken miracles of
> economic development, really anywhere in Europe (Tony
> Blair, cited in the *Newcastle Journal*, 26 April 1997).

Since growing competition means few national or local states leave
the presentation of these East Asian interlinkages to chance, many
reinvent them instead. However, the way they do so not only
reflects upon East Asia, most notably Japan, but also these states
themselves. State/public narratives about a 'New' North East
economic miracle illustrate this well. In this process of seeking
whatever competitive advantage high profile East Asian
interlinkages might confer, such narratives simultaneously
reconstitute the North East, and how it should be regarded, as if
any 'New' North East particularly depended upon tie-ups and
alliances with others outside. Carefully conceived exemplars like
Nissan's Wearside automobile plant have been deemed
extraordinarily significant thus:

> In the last ten years thousands of business executives have
> visited Nissan in Sunderland looking for a magic formula.
> Every European car manufacturer, virtually every British
> company of significance and hundreds who wish to be of
> significance have joined with visitors from all continents
> in wanting to learn the secrets (Wickens, 1995:xv).

Of itself the underlying idea of a large scale – not necessarily East
Asian capitalized – automobile plant reviving this local economy
was not new, having circulated through North East economic
folklore long before Nissan's much heralded arrival. Any claim that
Nissan has been miraculously transformative has moreover been
strongly debated (Wickens, 1987; Garrahan and Stewart, 1992,
1994; Beale, 1994; Rehder and Thompson, 1994; Crosbie, 1995;
Stephenson, 1995). Despite that leading state/public narratives
about the 'New' North East still seek to capitalize on its high
profile when claiming this region's growing East Asian
interlinkages have been working miracles. In submitting these
claims to more detailed scrutiny this essay adopts a concept-led
social constructionist standpoint which specifically addresses how
such interlinkages have become phenomenally constituted this way,

not least when forcefully backed with high conviction argumentation, almost putting them beyond constructive challenge. To that end it first outlines the genre of economic miracle claims, then specifies a whole range of trajectories the North East economy might alternatively take, assigning East Asian interlinkages different roles within each individual one, before judging how these roles compare, and to where they might lead.

ARGUING ECONOMIC MIRACLE CLAIMS

The very idea of economic miracles first poses major theoretical problems. As an idea this surprises, intrigues and captivates differently from most economic theorizing, while still puzzling and perplexing more too. Given how they appear extraordinary beyond explanation, one should consider both how, as well as what, economic miracle arguments first register. These should not usually be treated like neutral hypotheses testable against the pure facts of the case, as if the method of argument was purely incidental, with little real bearing otherwise.

The kind of high-conviction argumentation behind most miracle claims rather considers them so extraordinary that it would sweep aside any rival claim pursued through more standard methods thus:

TABLE 1
ECONOMIC MIRACLE CLAIMS COMPARED

	Promiracle claims	Nonmiracle claims
Purpose	Claims-leader	Claims-extender
Philosophy	Exceptionalist	Evidentialist
Problematization	Framebreaking	Framebound
Frequency	Rare	Recurrent
Exposition	Phenomenalist	Probabilist
Proof	Transcendant	Measuremental
Explanation	Counter-explanatory	Self-explanatory
Replicability	Nonreplicable	Replicable
Argumentation	High-conviction	High-reliability

On this basis promiracle arguments extend where nonmiracle claims would not. Their exceptionalist philosophy implies that, on the basis that nothing else really compares, alternative ways for appreciating such phenomena should be discounted. Less predictable and measurable than nonmiraculous occurrences, their rarity and uniqueness means they recur less too. Accompanying expositions therefore dramatize and phenomenalize rather than probabilize their existence as if they exhaust other explanations available. As a method of argument which is more framebreaking than framebound, the way this deploys more high-conviction than high-reliability principles thereby makes promiracle claims different in kind as well as content.

Translated into current affairs East Asian economic miracle ideas have worked like masterclaims from which many other subclaims – the 'New' North East for example – have taken public cue. Other promiracle claims elsewhere have since passed off-circuit for these purposes and the timeframe concerned would still appear important. For the most part promiracle claims are timeframed as if extraordinary events arose within aftersight, foresight, or as 'live' occurrences happening still. As well as crossing conventional time boundaries these claims migrate over spatial boundaries as well. For example, the interlinking of East and West, as between East Asia and North East England, appears to cross these boundaries, as if this were a 'live' occurrence without precedent. In actuality this might not be so, however, because there were pioneering mining, iron and steel, shipbuilding, railway and military-related exports and 'technology transfers' from the North East to Japan and China at the turn of the century (Conte-Helm, 1989), when the popular appreciation of the passage of trade went outwards from, rather than inwards into, the North East instead. To summarize, then, economic miracle ideas rise and fall, and follow their own particular circuit, but only form part of a wider repertoire of ways for constituting different economic trajectories in general, which ideally/typically appear thus:

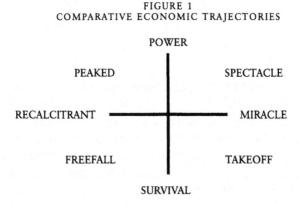

FIGURE 1
COMPARATIVE ECONOMIC TRAJECTORIES

POWER

PEAKED   SPECTACLE

RECALCITRANT ———————— MIRACLE

FREEFALL   TAKEOFF

SURVIVAL

Cutting right across the power–survival continuum depicted here, the miracle and recalcitrant trajectories appear either growth-exciting or growth-defeating, with various crossovers between. The path of development from survival onwards theoretically requires economic takeoff before the prospect and process of further miraculous transformation becomes characteristically all-absorbing thereafter. Such transformations immediately feed upon, and further excite, each other like nothing else possibly compares, despite lacking any real sense of final outcome. Of course, even the most dramatic macro-entrepreneurial upsurges will eventually stabilize, but first they may be made into attentive spectacles outside, as with the one-time Japanese economic miracle for example. More successful outcomes finally materialize into economic power but, should that power peak and growth-defeating recalcitrance set in, further possible downswings might threaten economic freefall, as experience within the former Soviet Union and Eastern European states illustrates well. Upswings and downswings apart, the way this constitutes economic miracles implies nothing else really compares, as prevailing equations about relative economic growth rates continually reiterate. Nevertheless, such miracles only promise, but cannot fully deliver, absolute economic power in its own right, and typically focus upon the processes of economic transformation themselves, as further consideration of the North East case will reveal.

CONSTITUTING NORTH EAST ECONOMIC TRAJECTORIES

From the social constructionist standpoint these trajectories might therefore follow any one of several possible paths, each of which regards any East Asian interlinkages differently too. No such quantum leap from the North East to East Asia is feasible without first appreciating how the rest of Britain and its surrounds intervenes however. The North East might be considered one of Britain's semi-peripheries lately subject of economic miracle claims which, first arising from the centre the decade before, regard it as their final proving ground, and thus ultimate 'test case'. In the first instance the North East appeared economically recalcitrant towards 'the enterprise culture' which supposedly paved the way (Amin and Tomaney, 1991; Ritchie, 1991), but the 'New' North East economy apparently transcends those problems, and imposes itself upon other possible trajectories thus:

FIGURE 2
ALTERNATIVE NORTH EAST ECONOMIC TRAJECTORIES

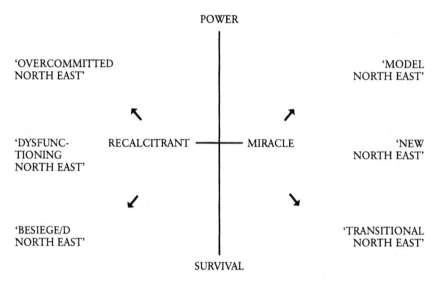

'GLOCALIZED NORTH EAST'

POWER

'OVERCOMMITTED
NORTH EAST'

'MODEL
NORTH EAST'

'DYSFUNC-
TIONING
NORTH EAST'

RECALCITRANT —— MIRACLE

'NEW
NORTH EAST'

'BESIEGE/D
NORTH EAST'

'TRANSITIONAL
NORTH EAST'

SURVIVAL

'ENCLAVE NORTH EAST'

Set against all the different possibilities raised those asserting 'New' North East economic miracle claims first dramatize their arguments in order that they outweigh others. By comparison any advocacy of adjoining takeoff and spectacle claims appears deliberately moderated. In takeoff, for example, the North East economic trajectory comes under 'Transitional' mode, increasingly, though incompletely transformed compared with developments before. Consequently this miracle-in-the-making still anticipates further transformations ahead, whereas 'pure' miracle claims make these appear all-absorbing 'live' occurrences. In spectacle mode these become less vividly 'live' phenomena, and undergo further selective re-representation, so that any 'New Model' North East which thereby emerges captures outside attention. The way all three such trajectories promise uplifting changes ahead necessarily timebounds the North East's recently disinvested coalfields, railways, shipyards, steelworks and accompanying plant, service and social networks as if they represented its fast departing collective past. For state/public purposes these might further represent the 'New' and 'Old' North East respectively, pictures of the latter's wasteland dereliction, for example, being subtly juxtaposed against others which portray newer, carefully sanitized, latter-day workplaces, shopping malls, consumer bastions, urban trafficways and eco-walkways. Such contrasting juxtapositions circulate throughout local 'news' media set-piece reportage, not least when local workforce contractions/'incidents' are pictured against newer inwardly invested and small business related developments, which are now taken to represent 'bad' and 'good' news respectively. But while any differences between takeoff, miracle, and spectacle based claims are more ones of degree than kind, none really considers the North East a sovereign, independent, accomplished regional economic power in its own right, except when possibly invoking older historical myths about 'The Great North' of some imaginary heyday long before. Any such North East would presumably appear 'Glocalized' in a best-of-all-worlds scenario where it managed its own economic destiny, while maintaining its basic character, with an open, growing economy which recycled the benefits of any learning outside.

With neither sovereign economic power nor everyday material survival at stake most arguments dwell upon miracle-recalcitrance issues. But, whereas promiracle arguments distance the past, magnifying present occurrences instead, the more recalcitrant cannot split time this way, for they neither write the past off, nor magnify the present to the same degree. Those imbued with customary local concern over 'raising the working class' particularly question whether, and how beneficially, this region might have changed, sometimes regarding current events as if they only demonstrate how 'Dysfunctioning' the North East economy has become. The more radical formerly considered certain North East localities almost 'Besieged' by forces beyond their control during what was probably the last national coalfield dispute during the 1980's, leaving them possible future economic 'Enclaves' (Beynon, 1985). The general tenor of argument presented by Austrin and Beynon (1979), Hudson (1989), Sadler (1992), and Beynon, Hudson and Sadler (1994) therefore challenges 'New' North East miracle claims. Since they arise across Britain at large these issues are not exclusive to the North East, however, for all this might constitute their ultimate test case. In that respect challenges might range anywhere from how much – and what – has actually changed, into what this has cost, who has benefitted, and what other alternatives have been foregone. Whatever their standpoint, few consider the North East itself regionally powerful, while even those designating this 'Europe's fastest changing region' rarely nominate any final end, thereby making 'change' itself appear all-important. All told, it is apparent that, whatever the economic trajectory concerned, much depends upon the standpoint assumed, purpose intended, and timescale employed. In some respects the idea of a 'New' North East carries particular appeal however, for 'younger' generations for whom detraditionalization might eventually erase other collective memories about the North East economy, which still influence the way its East Asian interlinkages are constituted now.

RE-POSITIONING EAST ASIAN INTERLINKAGES

Since few now believe these interlinkages are not really significant, many state/public agencies position them very carefully, seeking further competitive advantage from the way they are presented, although others might regard them differently. For that reason, it is important to gauge their broad meanings from several different standpoints, acknowledging any tensions and contradictions between. These strains also occur across different state/public agencies, where inter-agency competition over inward investment prospects – like that between Wales, Scotland and the North East for example – has raised questions about respective national/local state standing along the way. Rather than assume such differences arise randomly, one can alternatively propose they have certain predictable bases, as revealed when they are plotted against the whole range of possible economic trajectories outlined before.

This first suggests that, particularly among state/public agencies, these interlinkages front economic miracle claims as if they were transformational par excellence. No longer solely Japanese led, such agencies' networks extend into South Korea, Taiwan, Singapore, Malaysia, India and beyond, while the County Durham Development Company has been locally advertized as a new China business pathfinder for example. The way they use incoming developments like Nissan and Samsung also maximises their East Asian connections. Otherwise, under the 'Transitional' model, these same connections get threaded into 'regional revival' stories portraying the passage to 'better times' ahead, about which 'New Model' North East versions appear more upbeat still. As well as

TABLE 2
ALTERNATIVE REGIONAL EAST ASIAN BUSINESS ROLES COMPARED

Basic economic configuration	Corresponding North East economic trajectory	Projected regional East Asian business role
Power	'Glocalized'	Confirmation
Spectacle	'Model'	Exemplification
Miracle	'New'	Transformation
Takeoff	'Transitional'	Acceleration
Peaked	'Overcommitted'	Attenuation
Recalcitrant	'Dysfunctioning'	Amelioration
Freefall	'Be/sieged'	Refraction
Survival	'Enclave'	Appropriation

appearing altogether beneficial for the North East at large such interlinkages increasingly overshadowed longer standing Western European and North American connections until the recent Asian economic crisis intervened. Whatever angle they take, all these claims would nevertheless carry much less appeal should East Asia lose its special mystique. In terms of time span few extrapolate far ahead, although fears that the rate of inward investment might falter raise doubts about the North East's future generally, not always mitigated by wider consideration of trade, investment, technology transfers and other outgoings from this region.

By contrast, nonmiracle standpoints constitute these interlinkages differently, the 'Overcommitted' model regarding them as timebound attenuations, only partly mitigating the North East's basic political and economic peripheralization, job-dependency and other publicly recognized downsides. In regarding these as more intractable still, the 'Dysfunctioning' model considers these interlinkages more often to reproblematize, rather than solve, existing regional development syndromes, in a 'New North, Old Problems' scenario (Burge, 1994) leaving one-time 'regional policy' behind. Even more critically still, some consider that East Asian interlinkages epitomize the North East's growing capitulation unto more powerful economic forces outside, propelled by self-serving international capitalist manoeuvres, fast and loose global markets, footloose multinationals and other transient forces beyond local control. In this 'Besieged' model such interlinkages further refract the North East economy and re-institutionalize its dependency with little true respite in sight. As we shall now see, given how differently these interlinkages are regarded, often with quite contrasting claims juxtaposed, just finding/weighing the evidence poses problems, and varying interpretations result.

RE-ENVISIONING EAST ASIAN INTERLINKAGES

Being different in kind as well as content economic miracle arguments cannot be fully confirmed or denied by purely empirical means alone. By making them appear phenomenally transformative 'New' North East versions re-envision these interlinkages as if they bear some special significance beyond whatever they alone materially amount to. For that reason purely economic data alone cannot fully convey what meaning East Asian invested plants – irrespective of other regional outgoings – give to the 'New' North East except when suitably embedded within another, larger frame instead. In essence, then, the typical presentation of promiracle claims virtually amounts to a pastiche of nominally 'live' snapshots that superimpose 'New' North East symbolism over 'Old', thereby amplifying specially selected features about inwardly invested plant employment prospects, seemingly far flung exports/technology transfers abroad, further international tie-up possibilities, and glossy images of new style interiors where younger North East workforces pursue other job and career paths ahead. Further 'special effects' stem from stories about other seemingly extraordinary occurrences like the Japanese owned NSK Bearings plant re-exporting products back into China and East Asia in order to avoid redundancies at Peterlee, County Durham, and how certain Wearside built Nissan cars have gained unique prestige among domestic Japanese buyers. While these 'special features' address those within this locality itself others intend impressing different interests outside. A whole stream of apparently region-supportive storylines and symbols that connect with East Asia therefore front economic miracle claims concerning issues which might once have appeared just one-off curiosities without wider import. For example, when the BBC first broadcast their 'Chopsticks, Bulldozers and Newcastle Brown Ale' documentary about Komatsu's partial reoccupation of the former Caterpillar factory in Birtley, Tyne and Wear over the national television network in 1987, this development appeared more like a one-off individual curiosity than something altogether symbolic of 'Europe's fastest changing region' today. Whatever slant most promiracle claims put upon the stories, symbols and data they provide much rests upon prior faith and belief that some economic transformation will transpire. By contrast those less favourably disposed towards that very possibility seek other/further evidence before making/accepting promiracle assertions instead. For example, those who consider they only extenuate regional economic problems set any East Asian interlinkages against the North East's persistent relative economic decline, making them appear much less consequential while, under the 'Dysfunctioning' model, they turn into another developmental syndrome, so that eventually several leading lines of debate become clear.

LEADING LINES OF DEBATE

The very first lines of debate were drawn around why East Asian investors were possibly attracted by/into the North East in the first place, considering how few existed before, and how controversial some – like Hitachi's one-time Washington television component venture proposal – had become since. By comparison outgoing trade and investment into East Asia attracted much less attention both then and now. For that reason it is possible to call this the 'original attraction' debate, since the way incoming ventures were eventually organized and managed was less at issue during the 1980's particularly. Only after more such events transpired, and other claims were made about it, did ongoing organization and management itself become another leading issue, not least when this bore consequences for the way more established plants might possibly reinvest. Since it is only necessary to grasp the broad contours of these debates for these purposes Table 3 only charts respective leading lines of debate without exhausting the possibilities.

This whole sequence of debates together illustrates the course of argument concerning how initial investments were made, plants constructed and operations brought onstream until ventures became more firmly embedded throughout. For example, while the early debates concerned issues 1–3, they later extended towards issues 4–6 once ventures moved onstream, going through several more cycles before becoming fully worked through. At the outset the debate clearly focused upon what mode of capitalism first brought such investment prospects about. The promiracle argument would maintain this was latter-day 'frontier' capitalism obtaining much sought-after East Asian investment under well worked favour amid tight international and interregional

TABLE 3
LEADING LINES OF DEBATE

		Promiracle claims	Counter claims
1	Capitalist mode	Rising crossborder 'frontiership' mode	Incomer 'opportunist' mode
2	Prime movers	Emerging transnational business brokers	Distant business powerbrokers
3	Venture jurisdiction	Self-sustaining 'independent' units	Inbuilt strategic/developmental dependency
4	Management	Lean informated 'professional management' hierarchies	Overbearing production-driven factory regimes
5	Production technology	Uprated multi-tier configurations	Programmatic 'screwdriver plant'/'warehouse assembly' operations
6	Workforce formation	Specially filtered/Resocialized groupings	Part socially exclusionary/wage restricting impositions
7	Operational workflows	Flexibilized interdependencies	Co-restrictive workplace routines
8	Human resource development	Managerially empowering 'new' employment/industrial relations practices	Hidden/downloaded managerial responsibilities
9	Communal outreach	New 'business' bridgebuilders	Persistent local social class/place based barriers
10	Model outcome	Synergistic hub/satellite network transformations	Limited self-dramatizing 'showpiece' developments

competition, while the counterargument considered this incomer 'opportunist' capitalism exploiting national economic subsidies, North East regional dependency and related features. Neither highlighted much about ventures' eventual organization and management until the whole course of debate switched towards what kind of ventures these had become. As regards who held ultimate authority over their development – and also the pinnacle of the regional economy as a whole – the issue of East Asian 'absentee ownership' appeared potentially contentious throughout the course of debate. Once that changed, the promiracle case maintained that new uprated multi-tiered technological configurations would emerge, where synergy between 'hub' and 'satellite' companies like Nissan and its suppliers would beget continuous improvements right down the supply chain. Other counterargued these were largely highly programmatic 'screwdriver plant'/'warehouse assembly' type operations lacking genuine value-adding research and development. Given such diverging standpoints very different interpretations of the implications for North East workforces resulted. While the avowedly optimistic promiracle argument maintained these incoming employers would soon reinvigorate local labour markets, others countered that they could never fully replace, let alone compensate for, outgoing large scale employers before, not least where they also imposed other agebound, gender based, wage and salary restricting strictures upon local labour market workings. For example, while the incoming Samsung's new Teesside plant's employment policy first appeared less agebound than Nissan, for example, its reportedly low wage rates soon brought about local media campaigns against such, before these were subsequently improved. In any case certain greenfield ventures would inevitably disappoint, since their full job-creation potential often appeared exaggerated; individual enquiries and expectations far exceeded actual jobs available; selection processes typically favoured younger workforces above others; many wondered over trade union recognition; and all this arose just when initial production runs raised pointed questions about skills and capabilities. Once onstream, local management autonomy became the crux of much debate thereafter. Whereas the promiracle argument maintained these ventures would enhance managerial autonomy right down the line, others suspected that 'just-in-time', 'continuous improvement' and suchlike were conceptual camouflage for strictly production-driven factory regimes where 'hub' companies exerted overbearing control over their own workforces while further subordinating 'satellite' workforces likewise. Such criticisms have met with the response that, in the case of Nissan for example, this actually constitutes 'lean, people centred, mass production' (Wickens, 1995), largely brought about through enlightened, lean, informated, 'professional' management hierarchies that specifically employ 'new' employment and industrial relations practices which have gained high employee acceptance regardless. Critics like Garrahan and Stewart (op. cit.) clearly disagree, however, seeing this as downloading hierarchical management responsibilities onto shopfloor work groups themselves, whose consequent entrapment might eventually prove difficult. Going outside workplaces into their local surroundings, opinion also divided over how these incoming employers would link into their local community, given other persistent social class/local place based barriers against their integration and acceptance. For some, certain employers are not yet sufficiently locally embedded to be considered of, let alone from, any genuine North East community, although others like NSK Bearings have clearly made progress this way. Finally, having switched from how ventures were once attracted into how plants were actually brought fully onstream, the line of debate turns towards the outcome for the North East itself. Here, what the promiracle argument considers new, highly synergistic, technologically uprated hub/satellite organizational networks quite unlike anything before, others simply deem highly self-dramatizing 'showpiece' developments, less consequential than they appear, which cannot inspire regional economic transformation accordingly.

All such lines of debate, whether 'live' or not, still need to be put into context however, since most concern miracle/recalcitrance issues, without necessarily addressing either the purely power based 'top down', or indeed 'bottom up' survivalist standpoints described before. Certain debates would also benefit from timeshifting, since once the 'original attraction' debate finally recedes, for example, another concerning organizational management could arise, and dwell upon the transition from 'greenfield' towards 'brownfield' status, and passage towards Post-Japanization instead. Beyond that few ever compare East Asian with other, particularly US, German, French and Scandinavian invested ventures, while differences between East Asian invested plants themselves appear similarly underexplored. Above all this analysis emphasizes mutual interlinkages, since too much concern with inwardly invested plants might obscure other forms of ownership arising, as well as any corresponding trade, investment and similar outgoings, from the North East. Although difficult to trace, East Asian backed capital has circulated within local town centre property markets, for example, along with other favoured leisure pursuits, the region's leading golf and hotel complex included. Outward trade and investment from North East affiliated – if no longer wholly owned – businesses should also enter the picture. For example the former ICI's biggest single capital investment during the previous decade was located in Taiwan rather than Teesside before being sold, while other nationally known firms such as Davy, Rolls Royce and Kvaerner, among others, undertake major contracts across East Asia. Within the public sector some like the Northumbria Ambulance Service have specialist technology transfer agreements with East Asia while regional higher educational institutions are developing contacts and exchanges. Meanwhile Tyneside has its own growing Offshore Chinese grouping with its own particular business networks which some believe cannot quite penetrate so-called higher managerial/professional spheres outside (Wei, 1994).

All told, much of this appears relatively, if not completely, new to the North East, without making this the 'New' North East in consequence. Certain debates are not particular to the North East alone, since they clearly circulate elsewhere, however. For some time media accounts have exaggerated what gross East Asian manufacturing investment actually amounts to (Smith and Stone, 1989) and even when, as with Japanese investment in Wales, this has all been considered together, it is usually more limited than first thought. Further issues arise when re-investment takes attention away from diminishing new inward investment inflows, for which other Eastern European states increasingly compete too. Meanwhile regional investment attracting agencies might well switch between different East Asian targets, and more towards others elsewhere, changing priorities in the process. In the end any convergence between local state/regional level economic miracle claims, like those which draw parallels between the inward investment-led transformation of the older US Midwest (Florida, 1996) and that of North East England for example, may prove relatively short-lived. In that respect the North East appears far from unique in its original susceptibility towards such claims' undoubtedly popular appeal.

CONCLUSION

The case that economies at large, and particular subeconomies thereof, can undergo virtually miraculous transformations has been argued across several different fields, while currently being remade at the edges. If they bore any forward momentum East Asian economic miracle claims would not stay constant, but move towards less well charted territories outside, like the British semi-periphery where the North East has been customarily situated. In so doing they have helped remake this into the 'New' North East through high profile East Asian tie-ups and alliances which two decades ago hardly seemed possible. In tracing how this occurred, this contribution has hypothesized not only how economic miracle claims are made, but how differently their trajectories compare with others, before detailing any empirical variations and contrasts the North East case represents. It finds that, as regards the North East, many leading debates have focused upon miracle-recalcitrance issues, thereby limiting both the problems posed and solutions provided. Any idea that East Asian interlinkages alone will transform the North East economy will stay debatable in both principle and practice, so long as its regional development prospects remain modest, with different consequences attached.

REFERENCES

Amin, A. and J. Tomaney (1991), 'Creating an Enterprise Culture in the North East? The Impact of Urban and Regional Policies of the 1980s', *Regional Studies*, Vol.25, No.5, pp.479–87.
Austrin, T. and H. Beynon (1979), *Global Outpost*. Durham: University of Durham Sociology Department, Working Paper.
Beale, D. (1994), *Driven by Nissan?*. London: Lawrence.
Beynon, H., R. Hudson and D. Sadler (1994), *A Place Called Teesside*. Edinburgh: Edinburgh University Press.
Beynon, H. (ed.) (1985), *Digging Deeper: Issues in the Miners' Strike*. London: Verso.
Blair, T. (1997), cited in *Newcastle Journal*, 26 April, pp.6.
Burge, K. (1994), 'New North – Old Problems', *Business Review North*, Vol.5, No.2, pp.43–7.
Conte-Helm, M. (1989), *Japan and the North East of England*. London: Athlone Press.
Crosbie, A. (1995), 'The Japanese Model, Transnational Production and the North East', *Northern Economic Review*, No.24, pp.32–47.
Florida, R. (1996), 'Regional Creative Destruction: Production, Organization, Globalization and the Economic Transformation of the Midwest', *Economic Geography*, Vol.72, No.3, pp.314–34.
Garrahan, P. and P. Stewart (1994), 'Foreign Direct Investment and Local Economic Recovery' in P. Garrahan and P. Stewart (eds) *Urban Change and Renewal: Paradox of Place*. Aldershot: Avebury, pp.143–61.
Garrahan, P. and P. Stewart (1992), *The Nissan Enigma*. London: Mansell.
Hudson, R. (1989), *Wrecking a Region*. London: Pion.
Isaak, A. (1997), 'Making "Economic Miracles": Explaining Extraordinary National Economic Achievement', The *American Economist*, Vol.41, No.1, pp.59–65.
Krugman, P. (1994), 'The Myth of Asia's Miracle', *Foreign Affairs*, Vol.73, No.6, pp.62–78.
Ritchie, J. (1997), 'Arguing Chinese Economic Miracle Claims', *The Journal of Interdisciplinary Economics*, Vol.7, pp.277–90.
Ritchie, J. (1994), 'Theorizing Economic Miracles', *The Journal of Interdisciplinary Economics*, Vol.5, pp.11–22.
Ritchie, J. (1991), 'Enterprise Cultures: A Frame Analysis' in R. Burrows (ed.) *Deciphering the Enterprise Culture*. London: Routledge, pp.17–34.
Sadler, D. (1992), *The Global Region*. Oxford: Pergamon.
Smith, I. and I. Stone (1989), 'Foreign Investment in the North: Distinguishing Fact from Hype', *Northern Economic Review*, No.18, pp.50–61.
Stephenson, C. (1995), 'The Differing Experiences of Trade Unionism in Two Japanese Transplants' in P. Ackers, C. Smith and P. Smith (eds) *The New Workplace and Trade Unionism*. London: Routledge, pp.210–39.
Thatcher, M. (1990), cited in *Newcastle Journal*, 5 June, pp.1.
Wickens, P. (1995), *The Ascendant Organization*. Basingstoke: Macmillan.
Wickens, P. (1987), *The Road to Nissan*. Basingstoke: Macmillan.
Wei, L. (1994), *Three Generations, Two Languages, One Family*. Clevedon: Multilingual Matters.

5

East Asian Investment and Reinvestment in the 1990s: Implications for Regional Development

CAROL BURDIS and FRANK PECK

During the 1990s, changes in the nature of production processes which appear to give rise to superior forms of international investment in regional economies have been the subject of considerable debate (Amin *et al.*, 1994; Burge, 1995, 1997; Cooke and Morgan, 1993; Young *et al.*, 1988; McCann, 1997; Phelps, 1997; Potter, 1995; Sabel, 1994; Turok, 1993, 1997). Some authors have identified examples of externally-owned production locations which are more embedded in their local economies than was evident in previous rounds of multinational investment (see, in particular, Amin *et al.* 1994). This 'embeddedness' relates not only to a shift towards more regionally-based supply chains, but also a possibility that branch plants created by contemporary new inward investment may be more sophisticated in terms of the range of high order functions on site and their responsiveness to changes in markets and technology. These arguments have not only been applied to new inward investment, but also include the possibility of widespread corporate adjustment across existing sites leading to forms of re-investment which raise the technical and decision-making status of existing branch factories.

This debate concerning the character of externally-owned production locations in peripheral economies forms an important element within wider discussions about the changing nature of competitive processes under contemporary capitalism. Indeed, many of the arguments used to support claims for 'quality' investment in branch plant economies can be identified with particular interpretations of industrial restructuring. There is a strong connection between the nature of investment in branch economies and aspects of recent labour process debate which

Carol Burdis and Frank Peck, Department of Geography and Environmental Management, University of Northumbria.

consider the response of corporations to the crisis of Fordist mass-production. In particular, it has been suggested that the 'enhanced quality' of recent inward investment has been induced by organizational changes designed to create greater flexibility and more rapid response to shifts in markets (Schoenberger, 1997). These types of change not only have significance for theoretical debates, but also have important implications for the design of policy and regional development strategies. Development agencies at various levels have begun to see the advantage of moving towards more holistic forms of investor development designed not only to attract further new inward investment, but also to encourage the process of plant upgrading. This contribution examines the theoretical basis of these expectations, reviews some of the evidence and illustrates these processes using case studies of East Asian investments in the North East of England.

CORPORATE CHANGE AND REGIONAL RESTRUCTURING

The forms of competition which characterized the major growth sectors spearheading the long post-war boom have been linked by many authors to forms of technological change and organization associated with 'Fordism' (for a recent overview, see Holly 1996). Explanations of the meaning of Fordism have been given many different emphases at the level of the macro-economy and in terms of the labour processes at factory level. A fundamental feature, however, was the productivity gains (growth in output per worker) which could be achieved by standardizing products, developing semi-automatic conveyor assembly lines and fragmenting the work process in order to de-skill the individual tasks involved in production. In its advanced form, the Fordist system of production led not only to a high degree of fragmentation of production processes, but also to spatial and organizational separation of different parts of production chains which were controlled and co-ordinated by the development of strong vertical managerial hierarchies within planning system firms (for example, see Dunford and Perrons, 1983; Froebel Heinrichs and Kreye, 1980; Massey, 1984). These processes created a particular phase of inward investment, which produced 'branch plant economies' in peripheral regional economies characterized by high levels of external control and relatively low levels of integration within host economies (Watts, 1981).

It is now widely accepted that this system of production entered a crisis point during the 1960s, which contributed to the economic instability experienced during the 1970s (Lash and Urry, 1987; Piore and Sabel, 1984; Schoenberger, 1988). Fordism proved incapable of dealing with production in the context of rapid change and volatility in markets. The emergence of new niche markets and the fragmentation of mass-markets exposed the inflexibilities inherent in dedicated Fordist production lines (Sabel, 1982). Large hierarchical firms with production lines organized in an inflexible manner were incapable of responding to these changes without incurring excessive cost. These difficulties were made worse for mass-production industries, which were subject to intensified competition as a consequence of the penetration of global markets by Japanese producers since the 1970s.

There has been considerable debate about the broader structural characteristics of capitalist development and its impact on regional economies (see, for example, Hudson, 1992; Lovering, 1990; Piore and Sabel, 1984; Sayer, 1989; Storper, 1995). At the level of corporate organization, however, it has been widely observed that large hierarchical firms have tended to disintegrate in favour of more decentralized forms of organization with flatter management structures and a greater emphasis of intra-firm networks (Todtling, 1994; Cooke and Morgan, 1993; Morgan, 1997). There are also widespread experiments in the creation of more flexible forms of technology and organization in situations where competition is increasingly based not only on cost, but also on an ability to respond quickly to demand fluctuations and changes in markets.

These debates concerning shifts in the nature of production have been closely linked to changes in patterns of consumption. David Harvey (1989) argues that competition is increasingly driven not by cost *per se* but by an endless race to seek out new markets and reduce the turnover time of capital (see also, Schoenberger, 1997 and Stalk, 1988). This, he suggests, is being achieved by reducing the time taken to identify, develop, produce and market new products. The shortening of the product cycle is accompanied by processes of globalization whereby products are launched on major market areas simultaneously, a process commonly referred to as *time-space compression*. In order to feed this competitive process, there is a need for capitalism to generate new patterns of consumption involving a move away from standardization in mass markets towards constantly evolving, specialized and fragmented markets. In other words, the corporate sector via advertising and marketing has created a mood of individualism in order to produce new opportunities for competition. Harvey argues that this has led to the creation of a condition of postmodernity which is characterized by the mobilization of fashion in mass-markets (clothing, cars, consumer electronics, ornaments) and the creation of new lifestyles based on recreation, entertainment and various forms of 'distraction'.

There is growing evidence that these changes in the nature of markets and competitive advantage have had important effects upon the spatial structure of large corporations since the early 1980s. As implied above, Fordism generated corporate organization which separated different parts of the production process both functionally and spatially. Typically, research and development (R&D), finance and key corporate decision making were often retained centrally while different elements of the production process were commonly dispersed across different regions and even continents thereby creating a distinctive spatial division of labour. In this system, local production units of the type found in many peripheral regions were often controlled by strong internal hierarchies and local management were simply required to implement plans and directives from head office.

As the requirement for companies to respond to rapid and constant changes in demand has increased, many writers now suggest that this has led to various forms of regional restructuring. These regional changes are fundamentally related to the ways in which firms are developing distinctly different inter-firm and intra-firm relationships (Cooke, 1996; Cooke and Morgan, 1993). Many complex global firms are experimenting with different methods of networking involving the creation of very varied configurations in production and developing flexible co-ordinating processes (Dicken, 1994). Fundamentally, producers have recognized the necessity to re-integrate production chains by finding ways to reconnect research and development of new products, marketing of new products and production. This has involved dismantling hierarchies and creating networks between functions which assist constant innovation and interaction right through the system and the application of the principle of 'reverse engineering' which involves constant feedback of best practice between different parts of the production chain.

The shift away from hierarchies towards corporate organization based on networks can have different outcomes at a regional level. Global reintegration can be facilitated to a high degree by the development of advanced communication systems (Charles, 1996). In some cases, it may be possible for flexible networking arrangements to exist between spatially separated functions, particularly for more specialized high value-added activities. Indeed there is a growing number of global firms which have developed R&D networks which span several continents (Florida and Kenney, 1994). In other situations, however, there may be strategic reasons for global companies to maintain central control over functions which deal with commercially sensitive information, such as corporate investment and basic research, and to supply these services to dispersed production units using the new technologies. Notwithstanding the centralizing and decentralizing effects of modern communications technologies, there is some evidence that on balance, these processes have led to *spatial reintegration* in local economies as former 'screwdriver' branch factories are upgraded in status through the partial reintegration of value chains within local units.

At an operational level, Hayter (1996) has noted the trend towards the development of systems of innovation which require constant interaction between the various elements involving the relocation of R&D professionals to factory sites for extended periods of time. He argues that this innovative process extends right through the system so that experimentation takes place throughout the organization including on the shop floor in the form of learning groups, quality circles and improvement groups. These developments, which are commonly associated with Japanese firms, are now much more pervasive across industry including longer-established firms in the UK (Peck and Stone, 1992). These structures can be used to involve all employees in the process of identifying and solving problems in production, and in their most advanced form this can even extend to product modification.

INVESTMENT QUALITY AND THE 'NEW' BRANCH ECONOMY?

If the process of 'deep integration' is widespread, then the insertions of R&D and marketing functions into existing branch factories may be leading to greater levels of autonomy, sophistication and technical status for existing local units which are owned by large global companies. These arguments imply that upgraded branch factories and new inward investors in the 1990s may create production units which have a more beneficial effect upon host economies in terms of the range of job types, the multipliers generated by supply linkages and long-term employment stability. It also follows that corporate decisions on re-investment and expansion (and its counterpart, closure) may be influenced by managers' perceptions about the ability of different regions to support innovative activity within manufacturing units. Under this scenario, local units will be expected to develop an ability to interpret market information and apply rapid technological solutions in production independently. In other words, they may be required to develop an all-round ability to innovate and learn from experience rather than just follow corporate planning procedures (Lundvall, 1992; Maskell and Malmberg, 1995; Morgan, 1992, 1997).

This line of reasoning implies that the competitiveness of firms is much more dependent than in the past on the particular characteristics of regions in which they operate. Morgan (1997) has developed these ideas using the concept of the 'learning' region. A key element in competitiveness concerns the ability of firms to innovate and respond to change. Morgan argues that innovation is an interactive process which is shaped by institutional routines and customs that involve the exchange of knowledge which is not formalized. He suggests that tacit knowledge of this type is necessarily collective in nature and dependent upon trust relationships which develop between individuals and institutions. As a result, it is possible that the ability to innovate may be more territorially-specific than generally thought and that some important learning processes may necessarily occur in a regional context. Storper (1995) makes the same point with reference to the 'untraded interdependencies' or the collective knowledge that builds up in a regional economy. He suggests that access to these pools of specialized knowledge provide firms with a greater capacity to innovate and change.

Recent case studies of corporate change in regional economies, however, present contradictory evidence of investment quality and levels of embeddedness. Some empirical studies of supply linkages appear to show that local integration of supply chains is little different from previous phases of investment. In a survey of over 200 manufacturing establishments in the Northern region, Phelps (1993) observed an overall decrease in the level of local purchasing between 1979 and 1989. Furthermore, the more recent inward investors did not have higher levels of local purchasing. This has also been noted in surveys of electronics establishments in Scotland. According to Turok (1993) only about 12 per cent of inputs to these establishments are sourced locally within Scotland. These authors conclude that, on the basis of linkage data alone, the recent phase of new inward investment and reinvestment is little different from the branch economy of the 1970s.

However, there are other ways of interpreting 'embeddedness' in terms of the sophistication and integration of on-site production facilities where other studies demonstrate important change. It has been observed, for instance, that corporate reorganization in some key sectors such as electronics and vehicles has been associated with attempts to introduce *single product mandates* into selected sites serving the whole of the European and even global market. Driven by the search for greater economies of scale (Bachtler and Clement, 1990), the sites selected for this purpose become the focus for reinvestment opportunities in regional economies and the technological and decision-making status of such plants is generally greatly enhanced in the process. This has been observed in the electronics sector by Glasmeier (1986) in the United States who refers to these as stand-alone 'technical' branches. In Scotland, Young *et al.* (1988) have identified 'strategic independent' establishments which have the capacity to develop products for end-users. Henderson (1989) has noted the existence of American-owned 'developmental' branches across Europe which have *design authority* for specific types of electronic componentry. The same subtle changes have also been observed in foreign owned subsidiaries in electronics in the South of Spain (Peck and Stone, 1994).

RECENT INWARD INVESTMENT FROM EAST ASIA

In the context of these debates, the quality of recent inward investment from East Asia is of considerable interest. It has been suggested that these investors have pioneered such changes, creating 'demonstration effects' of quality investment in regional economies across the UK. Production sites operated by East Asian investors tend to be the sole outlet for the European market for particular products of these large corporations. As such, these plants are arguably in the vanguard of the trend towards the creation of continental product mandates leading to the insertion of 'high quality' investment within existing branch plant economies. This contribution illustrates this particular aspect of the branch plant debate drawing on recent empirical research based on interviews with senior managers in inward investor plants in the North East of England.

Reinvestment in East Asian Plants in the 1990s

The initial impacts of the flow of East Asian investment which came to the North East of England during the 1980s has been researched extensively (Burge, 1995, 1996, 1997; Garrahan and Stewart, 1992; Morris, 1988; Munday, 1990; Munday et al., 1995; Peck, 1990; Peck and Stone, 1992, 1993; Strange, 1993). This study, in contrast, presents some evidence of change within these plants *subsequent to the set-up period,* obtained through in-depth interviews with senior managers conducted during 1996. The case studies are drawn from a wider survey of investors that came to the region during the 1980s.[1] The analysis focuses on the processes that generate reinvestment using illustration drawn from in-depth interviews with managers of seven large East Asian firms that established production in North East England between 1986 and 1989 (as shown in Table 1). The interviews covered a range of aspects of recent change in the site, including details of phases of reinvestment, decision-making processes and forms of plant up-grading associated with high order functions. In total, the seven plants accounted for 3,033 employees at the time of interview. Individually, these are medium-sized employers ranging from 240 to 530 workers engaged in the production of vehicle components, consumer electronic products and capital goods equipment.

Competitive Processes and the Functional Characteristics of Sites

In relation to the concept of 'deep integration' and the reintegration of value chains within local production units, there are clear examples of this process in these case studies. In five of these plants, the functions on site included sales, marketing, design, product testing as well as procurement and production. In these cases, senior managers linked these characteristics explicitly to

TABLE 1
THE SURVEY ESTABLISHMENTS

Co	Nationality	Set-up Date	Emp	SIC	Reinvestment Phases	Outcome
A	Japanese/ US (JV)	1986	450	3530	1988	New purpose built factory. Expanding workforce.
					1995	Reinvestment in equipment and buildings.
B	Japanese	1987	416	3254	Continual reinvestment – c.£4m per year over last decade	Introduced new 'machine, design and test' facilities. Expanded workforce.
C	S. Korean	1987	490	3454	1992/3 –reinvested £11m	Increased production facilities and expanded product range
					1996 – £600m reinvestment	Development of new plant – fully integrated production unit. Expanded workforce.
D	Japanese (JV)	1988	507	3530	1990 – 'Phase II' – £25m reinvestment	Increased production capacity. Expanded workforce.
E	Japanese	1988	400	3460	Major reinvestment – 1994 (£8m) but also smaller and more constant levels due to nature of product	Introduced new tooling and equipment. Improved productivity and efficiency. Increased turnover. Expanded workforce.
F	Japanese	1988	240	3450	£6m reinvestment	Extension of existing and purchase of new plant facilities. Introduction of new functions and new process technology. Expanded workforce.
G	S. Korean	1989	530	3460	1994 – c.£23m reinvestment	Additional purpose built factory. Increased capacity, product range and workforce. Design facility added. Expanded workforce.

Source: Author's Survey 1996/97

corporate strategies designed to 'accelerate design to manufacture time' and improve responsiveness to customers. All of these plants have European-wide product mandates and it is clear that the localization strategies of these companies has led to enhanced status for these sites. In two cases, this enhancement has involved the relocation of pre-existing sales and marketing functions from continental Europe. This implies that broader strategies to localize production chains within the European market can, in some instances, lead to closer integration of production at a regional level. However, it is important not to overstate these patterns. In most cases, the product development function was focused explicitly on customizing products rather than developing entirely new product ranges. Several managers noted that 'research' was still concentrated in the home country. Even so, the ability to respond rapidly to subtle changes in consumer tastes in terms of colour, design features and styling can have dramatic effects upon sales and may therefore be critical to competitiveness. The characteristics described by these managers are therefore important and they do appear to correspond with the concept of 'deep integration' at the scale of individual production sites.

While the examples described above seem to offer some indication of re-integration, other evidence draws attention to some contradictions in this concept. First, there were two cases where particular firms displayed surprisingly little integration of high order functions. Both of these were suppliers to Nissan where neither of these sites possessed an independent marketing or research facility. Both were highly dependent, commercially and technically, upon Nissan as a major customer. Research and development activities for these firms has remained in Japan as 'the most efficient way to communicate with the main research facility of Nissan'. The downturn in orders from Nissan during the early 1990s caused these suppliers to consider the possibilities of diversification, but recent capital expenditure has primarily been directed towards up-grading equipment and further expansion in buildings.

These two examples draw attention to the need to view the activities of individual firms within the whole supply chain. The 'Nissan complex' clearly displays elements of an integrated production system in which there exists a high degree of flexibility created by interaction between product design, development of production technology and marketing of products. These interactions, however, are controlled centrally and permeate down through the supply chain only in ways that enhance the performance of final assembly. Viewed from the perspective of Nissan, their suppliers are a vital part of their local flexibility and production integration – a significant part of their locally-embedded 'value-chain'. From the perspective of the supplier, however, their ability to diversify is considerably reduced by their involvement in this system which makes no requirement for independent marketing and research. In many cases, therefore, the supply chain may be a more significant structure within which to explore the concept of deep integration than the structures created by the boundaries of individual firms.

There are also dangers in drawing conclusions from particular case studies that reflect sets of circumstances at particular points in time. In at least one instance where the trend towards integration of production chains was observed, the interviewee noted that there may be some 'downsizing' of the plant in future and loss of high level functions from the site. It was suggested that in the next three to four years, competitive pressures may result in some consolidation of management functions across Europe. The company was currently developing a European Management Framework which might involve relocating higher management functions at some central location. This clearly points to the need for caution in making generalizations about the geographical scale at which the advantages of agglomeration can be realized.

Reinvestment Decision-making in East Asian Plants

While the competitive processes that led these firms to invest in the UK are fairly well understood, there are important differences in the way in which these strategies were implemented and in the sequence of events that followed the initial investment. In some prominent cases, the decision to invest was part of a long-term strategy involving re-investment plans after specified periods of time. Three of these investors had explicit plans for reinvestment after a three year period. In one case, the initial investment was specifically identified as 'phase 1' and targets were set for the first three year period. This was followed by the implementation of a phase 2 expansion involving an investment of £25m, the introduction of a new product line and a doubling in the size of employment. In another instance, the investment programme was not divided into discrete phases, but involved a commitment to invest in a gradual expansion over a ten year period.

In other cases, however, management adopted a 'wait and see' strategy as regards subsequent expansion, sometimes involving specific preconditions before further investment would be considered. It has been noted in previous research that many inward investors adopted pragmatic approaches to the introduction of production techniques and personnel practices commonly used by the firm in East Asia. There has been a tendency for local managers to experiment with different ways of working in order to adjust to local customs and expectations in relation to working practices, labour relations and manufacturing methods (Peck and Stone, 1992). It would appear that this kind of experimentation has also been a feature of the overall investment strategies of some firms. In one instance, a Japanese investor that set up in 1988 had no explicit plans to expand, but entered a reinvestment phase after three years once the profitability of the site had been guaranteed. Another example involved a Japanese firm that delayed reinvestment for six years until the plant had proven its viability. Unexpected shifts in economic conditions and particular difficulties in specific markets have also led to changes in plans. In fact, even in those firms which had explicit expansion plans, managers noted that there was considerable pressure on local management to meet targets and achieve success in order to secure further rounds of reinvestment.

Another aspect of the process of reinvestment concerns the influence and ambitions of key senior managers, not only in the local plant but also in East Asia. As far as local managers are concerned, their competence and the relationships that they build with senior managers in East Asia are clearly critical to early success and the medium-term prospects for reinvestment. During interviews, most managers commented on the pressure for local managers to 'earn' further commitment of corporate resources. At another level, however, the reputations of managers in East Asia are also involved in this process. As one example, an electronics company launched a new corporate identity that stressed value for money and high service for customers. As part of this campaign, senior managers committed themselves to a 'localization' policy with regard to its major markets. In this situation, the overall direction of the company and the reputations of senior managers in East Asia clearly depended upon the success in creating a fully-integrated business unit in Europe with local responsibility for design, customer service and marketing as well as production. In these circumstances, board members of major corporations may be prepared to accept short-to-medium term losses in order to secure their reputation with end-users of their products. In another example, a change of senior personnel in a Korean company led to a shift in approach to reinvestment in the UK. This company embarked on a much more ambitious localization strategy involving reinvestment in the North East of England following the appointment of a new company chairman. These examples imply that the influence of key individuals and groups of individuals in the process of corporate change should not be underestimated.

Current Investment Plans in the Late 1990s

The North East of England has undoubtedly benefited not only from the initial decision to invest in the region by firms from East Asia but also from their subsequent reinvestment plans. Evidence from the interviews indicates that most of the plants in the study have recently witnessed the effects of restructuring and that this has led to the upgrading of the existing facilities throughout the early to mid 1990s. Therefore, substantial reinvestment has already occurred within the recent past. However, a number of managers also commented that as a result of the fierce nature of competition particularly within the consumer electronics industry, further measures were currently being implemented as part of a longer-term strategy to 'secure survival into the next century'. The outcome of these measures has the potential to enhance facilities in the region, as reflected in the comments of one production manager who stated that while 'product development is currently in Japan, this is set to transfer to the UK... [as] We need research nearer to the market'.

While the experience of the study firms over the past ten years suggests that localization strategies have generally enhanced the status of production sites in the region, evidence from some firms indicates that this may not necessarily be the case in future. In two cases interviewees stressed the importance of establishing 'flexibility' within the organization of production at a corporate wide level. This allows the firms to 'shift production around European sites' in an effort to maximize efficiency in the production system. As an example of this one interviewee commented that 'putting TVs at the UK plant was a direct reaction to what was happening in Germany'. However, the interviews not only highlighted the importance of creating flexibility within an existing production framework but also the need for 'flexibility' in developing new sites. As the same interviewee commented, 'Factories are shifting locations... this is the name of the game in international competitiveness'. As a strategy this requires the company 'to be very dynamic in terms of new products, designs, new technology.' In terms of regional development, such comments emphasize the need for regional and local development agencies to consider ways of maintaining their existing stock of investors.

For all the firms involved in the study, participation in globally competitive markets in which the pace of consumer-driven change is rapid requires that they develop in ways that allow swift access to knowledge of markets which are continental in scale. The response of one Korean firm to this challenge has been to create headquarters within five major geographic areas of China, North America, Europe, South East Asia and Japan. This restructuring was introduced to allow the company to play an insider role in major markets and also to move much of the decision making from Korea to these local market areas. The company is currently pursuing its long-term goal for this strategy which is to convert all 'regional' headquarters into holding companies. Although the North East has benefited from reinvestment as a result of this, it is significant that the headquarters of the European operation is to be located in the South East of England.

Another Korean firm engaged in the production of electronic goods also indicated the way in which current competitive processes are leading to further restructuring within the firm. In this instance the entire organization of the company is undergoing substantial changes which will allow it to 'respond more quickly to changes within the external business environment'. The existing structure is seen as 'limiting' to this aim and therefore major organizational changes based on the formation of new business divisions centred around investment, R&D, production and sales are being implemented in an attempt to meet current competitive challenges. Although this focus on 'localization' since 1996 has proved favourable for the company's North East plant the region failed to secure a potential reinvestment in this same year. In 1996 the company announced that major investment was to be directed elsewhere in the UK rather than as an addition to its North East facility.

These examples reflect the scale at which reorganization is

occurring within some of the larger multinational organizations. In both instances 're-engineering' within the company is producing positive outcomes for the region but further evidence from the interviews also indicates that recent changes within Eastern Europe are influencing current investment plans. Four companies indicated that production facilities had either already been established or were soon to be established within Eastern bloc countries (the exceptions being those firms which were heavily locked into Nissan's input-output structure as this limited their ability to operate beyond supplying their main customer). One example which illustrates this point is a Japanese firm which located in the North East of England as part of its globalization strategy in 1988. Since then the plant has upgraded from its initial status as an assembler of remote control units through the introduction of facilities and on-site functions which allow it to manufacture more of the product in-house. Although operations at the plant have proved extremely successful the company continues to search out potential new markets which could further expand their opportunities and has recently taken the decision to set up production facilities in Eastern Europe.

The importance and implications of such strategies for existing plants within a multinational organization rests on whether these new developments are intended as an addition to existing production facilities or as a replacement for this. Given the recent emphasis within large multinational organizations on the reintegration of production chains and the requirements of this in relation to available technology and range of skills within the labour market, the impact of Eastern Europe as a production location may depend on how successful it is at marketing itself beyond that of a supplier of cheap labour in the future.

Reinvestment and After-care Support

The initial attraction of foreign direct investment has been a long-term feature within the remit of regional development agencies. The provision of prepared sites, advanced factories, assistance with grant applications and initial training requirements are among the services offered to new investors. However, under the current conditions of intensified competition for a diminishing number of new investment projects, development agencies have now recognized the need to focus more closely on attempting to 'anchor' existing investment in the local economy and assist with upgrading of these projects (Peck and Burdis, 1996). As such, a number of development agencies now provide an 'after-care' or 'investor development' facility for existing investors which includes a range of services to support development and expansion phases. This can incorporate assistance with applications for grants linked to expansion phases (especially regional selective assistance), local supplier development, commercial networking to link common interest groups within industry and service networking to improve links between companies and agencies involved in the development process. The role of the after-care manager is essentially to establish contacts between the investor and organizations which can promote upgrading with the ultimate aim being to nurture the firm while at the same time producing benefits for the region.

Interviews with managers in firms from East Asia revealed that, despite the growing recognition of a need to provide services for existing investors, there was a wide variation in experience of working with support agencies. A number of managers indicated that a tremendous amount of help and assistance had been made available to them during the initial set-up phase and that they had been 'adequately publicised and cared for'; as one interviewee commented 'We got so much help it was brilliant. We weren't just left. For the first couple of years we had regular visits. We were also asked to participate in schemes to help attract other investors'. In these instances the companies worked closely with a range of agencies to secure the services they required, such as regional development agencies, TECs, local councils and English Partnership to provide a 'team based' approach. As such, the role of institutional support was of tremendous importance to the initial stages of development within these plants. The experience of one Korean investor reflects such initial satisfaction with service provision during the establishment of production facilities in the region in 1987 but it also illustrates the crucial role of a range of institutions in securing their £600m reinvestment in the mid 1990s. Management at the plant revealed that co-operation and co-ordination between service providers from both local and regional institutions had been instrumental in the decision to reinvest in the region. This example reflects the importance which investors place on the ability to develop their facilities with minimal bureaucratic hindrance and a 'seamless' provision of services.

In some cases, however, there appeared to be less satisfaction with post set-up, or after-care, support among other investors. Findings revealed that investor experience of after-care ranged from enthusiastic praise for the range and quality of assistance available to frustration and lack of awareness of the existence of these services. This lack of awareness became apparent in interview comments such as, 'it would be helpful if we knew what was available rather than have to go and ask'. Although figures from NDC (Northern Development Company) indicate that 50 per cent of UK investment comes from the expansion of existing investment, managers indicated that expansion phases in some plants has occurred largely without assistance from regional institutions. Additionally, responses from those firms which had received assistance with upgrading indicated that services were not always well co-ordinated between organizations and that very often investors 'became caught up in the agendas of each service provider'. This is partly a consequence of the way in which agencies attempt to promote the region as a 'prime' manufacturing location through the use of successful existing investors. As one manager indicated, agencies can sometimes place 'too many demands' on them in terms of involvement in regional promotion activity. This perhaps also reflects the pressures that are placed upon agencies to perform to national/regional targets that can be inflexible when dealing with particular local needs

CORPORATE CHANGE, SPATIAL DEVELOPMENT AND POLICY

The competitive pressures to localize global production have clearly benefited the economy of North East England over the past ten years. The firms studied here provide effective illustrations of these process which have led to some partial reintegration of production chains within branch factories. Our interviews identified examples of plants with a stronger marketing, design and technical capability than would normally be associated with the branch plant economy. Our research also indicates that the growth of these plants has involved different approaches to decision-making. In some cases, the original plans have been implemented, including phases of subsequent planned expansion. However, in other cases, a more pragmatic approach was adopted whereby subsequent reinvestment decisions were either delayed or altered in response to changes in circumstance. This 'wait and see' approach appears to have had an important effect upon the short-to-medium term future of specific plants. As regards plans for the late 1990s, there are some indications that the enhanced status of these plants could be threatened by new strategies designed to maximize flexibility in the organization of production on a continental scale. These indications imply that the quality of these investments cannot be taken for granted.

While the experience of the survey establishments generally conforms with ideas concerning the nature of competitive processes and the concept of deep integration, the extent to which these characteristics have affected production sites more broadly across the North of England requires further research. As these production sites have often been set up as greenfield developments with single product mandates by these East Asian firms, it is perhaps not surprising that they possess a more integrated range of functions. What is less certain is the extent to which existing European and North American multinationals operating in the North East have restructured their production to mirror these types of changes.

As far as policy is concerned, however, the case studies demonstrate that reinvestment and expansion of new inward investors cannot be taken for granted. If these types of characteristics are viewed as desirable from a regional development perspective, then a more systematic delivery of aftercare services than has been customary in the past might well be justified (Young and Hood, 1994). Decisions to expand a facility and enhance its technical and managerial status are evidently not pre-determined and can presumably be influenced by the regional dynamic created (in part) by the extent to which local management are able to access regional resources to achieve their corporate objectives. Furthermore, the trend towards enhanced status through design authority, technical capability and marketing responsibilities is not necessarily fixed. Some evidence of counter-trends that could lead to reorganization involving loss of key management functions from production units and the development of specialized management centres at more central locations within Europe cannot be discounted. The role of aftercare to embed local production units in the local economy and prevent leakage of high order management functions is therefore a point worthy of attention.

Aftercare, however, can be costly as it requires constant

corporate monitoring both locally and elsewhere. The services offered may also require increasing levels of state resource drawn from local, national and European levels. The problem of a subsidy war in which local development agencies attempt to win new greenfield projects is already a major point of conflict between regions of the UK (*Newcastle Journal*, 9 September 1997). If this process were to be extended to a much wider range of activities under the umbrella of aftercare, then the potential for large firms to make more and more demands on local institutions remains (Peck, 1996; Peck and Burdis, 1996). National and European regulation of these processes is an issue which is likely to be intensified following the creation of the new Regional Development Agencies in the regions of the UK.

ACKNOWLEDGEMENTS

This research was supported by a Research Studentship of the University of Northumbria at Newcastle. The authors extend thanks to the managers of firms who agreed to be interviewed and to Dr Ian Stone (Northern Economic Research Unit) who provided valuable advice throughout the project.

NOTE

1. The interviews reported in this article are drawn from a survey of 60 inward investors in the North East of England as part of a PhD research programme. The in-depth interviews with 25 companies were conducted during 1996–97.

REFERENCES

Amin, A., D. Bradley, J. Howells, J. Tomaney and C. Gentle (1994), 'Regional Incentives and the Quality of Mobile Investment in the Less Favoured Regions of the EC', *Progress in Planning*, Vol.41, No.1, pp.1–112.
Bachtler, J. and K. Clement (1990), 'Inward Investment in the UK and the Single European Market', *Regional Studies*, Vol.24, No.2, pp.173–9.
Burge, K. (1997), 'Japanese Manufacturing Investment in Europe – Recent History and Future Prospects', *Business Review North*, Vol.18, No.4, pp.14–19.
Burge, K. (1996), 'Korean Investment in the UK' *Business Review North*, Vol.18, No.1, pp.13–17.
Burge, K. (1995), 'Japanese Manufacturing Investment in Europe – An update', *Business Review North*, Vol.6, No.4, pp.11–17.
Charles, D. (1996), 'Information Technology and Production Systems' in P. Daniels and W. Lever (eds), *The Global Economy in Transition*. London: Longman.
Cooke, P. (1996), 'Reinventing the Region: Firms, Clusters and Networks in Economic Development' in P. Daniels and W. Lever (eds), *The Global Economy in Transition*. London: Longman. pp.310–27.
Cooke, P. and K. Morgan (1993), 'The Network Paradigm: New Departures in Corporate and Regional Development', *Environment and Planning D: Society and Space*, Vol.11, pp.543–64.

Dicken, P. (1994), 'Global–Local Tensions: Firms and States in the Global Space Economy', *Economic Geography*, Vol.70, No.2, pp.101–28.

Dunford, M. and D. Perrons (1983), *The Arena of Capital*. London: Macmillan Press.

Florida, R. and M. Kenney (1994), 'The Globalisation of Japanese R&D: The Economic Geography of Japanese R&D Investment in the United States', *Economic Geography*, Vol.70, No.2, pp.344–69.

Froebel, F., J. Heinrichs and O. Kreye (1980), *The New International Division of Labour.* Cambridge: Cambridge University Press.

Garrahan, P. and P. Stewart (1992), *The Nissan Enigma: Flexibility at Work in a Local Economy.* London: Mansell.

Glasmeier, A. (1986), 'Factors Governing the Development of High Technology Industry Agglomerations: A Tale of Three Cities', *Regional Studies*, Vol.23, No.4, pp.287–301.

Harvey, D. (1989), *The Condition of Post-Modernity: An Enquiry into the Origins of Cultural Change*, London: Basil Blackwell.

Hayter, R. (1996), 'Research and Development' in P. Daniels and W. Lever (eds), *The Global Economy in Transition.* London: Longman.

Henderson, J. (1989), *The Globalisation of High Technology Production.* London: Routledge.

Holly, B. (1996), 'Restructuring and the Production System' in P. Daniels and W. Lever (eds), *The Global Economy in Transition.* London: Longman.

Hudson, R. (1992), 'Industrial Restructuring and Spatial Change: Myths and Realities in the Changing Geography of Production in the 1980s', *Scottish Geographical Magazine*, Vol.108, No.2, pp.74–81.

Lash, S. and J.Urry (1987), *The End of Organised Capitalism.* Cambridge: Polity Press.

Lovering, J. (1990), 'Fordism's Unknown Successor: A Comment on Scott's Theory of Flexible Accumulation and the Re-emergence of Regional Economies', *International Journal of Urban and Regional Research*, Vol.14, No.1, pp.159–74.

Lundvall, B. (1992), *National Systems of Innovation: Towards a Theory of Innovation and Interactive Learning.* London: Francis Pinter.

Maskell, P and A. Malmberg (1995), 'Localised Learning and Industrial Competitiveness', Paper presented at the Regional Studies Association European Conference on 'Regional Futures', Gothenburg, 6–9 May 1995.

Massey, D. (1984), *Spatial Divisions of Labour.* London: Macmillan.

McCann, P. (1997), 'How Deeply Embedded is Silicon Glen? A Cautionary Note', *Regional Studies*, Vol.31, No.7, pp.695–703.

Morgan, K. (1997), 'The Learning Region: Institutions, Innovation and Regional Renewal', *Regional Studies*, Vol.31, No.5, pp.491–503.

Morgan, K. (1992), 'Innovating by Networking: New Models of Corporate and Regional Development', in Dunford, M. and G. Kafkalas (eds), *Cities and Regions in the New Europe: The Global–Local Interplay and Spatial Development Strategies.* London: Belhaven Press.

Morris, J. (1988), 'The Who, Why and Where of Japanese Manufacturing Investment in the UK', *Industrial Relations Journal*, Vol.19, No.1, pp.31–40.

Munday, M. (1990), *Japanese Manufacturing Investment in Wales.* Cardiff: University of Wales Press.

Munday, M., J. Morris and B. Wilkinson (1995), 'Factories or Warehouses? A Welsh Perspective on Japanese Transplant Manufacturing', *Regional Studies*, Vol.29, No.1, pp.1–17.

Peck, F. (1996), 'Regional Development and the Production of Space: The Role of Infrastructure in the Attraction of New Inward Investment', *Environment and Planning A*, Vol.28, pp.327–39.

Peck, F. (1990), 'Nissan in the North-East: The Multiplier Effects', *Geography*, Vol.75, No.4, pp.354–7.

Peck, F. and C. Burdis (1996), 'After-care for Inward Investors: Implications for Regional Development in the European Union', in C. Collis and F. Peck (eds), *Industrial Restructuring: FDI and Regional Development.* London: Regional Studies Association.

Peck, F. and I. Stone (1994), *Sunrise in the Costa-del Sol? Global Restructuring, State Policies and Local Economic Change in the Electronics Sector in Southern Spain*, Division of Geography and Environmental Management, Occasional Papers New Series No. 6.

Peck, F. and I. Stone (1993), 'Japanese Inward Investment in North-East England: Reassessing Japanisation', *Environment and Planning C*, Vol.11, pp.55–67.

Peck, F. and I. Stone (1992), *New Inward Investment and the Northern Region Labour Market*, Research Series No 6, Employment Department.

Phelps, N. (1997), *Multinationals and European Integration: Trade, Investment and Regional Development*. London: Jessica Kingsley.

Phelps, N. (1993), 'Contemporary Industrial Restructuring and Linkage Change in an Older Industrial Region: Examples from the Northeast of England', *Environment and Planning A*, Vol.25, pp.863–82.

Phelps, N. (1992), 'The Locally Embedded Branch Plant? A Study of Material Linkage Change in the Northern Region of England' *Unpublished thesis*, Department of Geography, Newcastle University.

Piore, M.J. and C.F. Sabel (1984), *The Second Industrial Divide*. New York: Basic Books.

Potter, J. (1995), 'Branch Plant Economies and Flexible Specialisation: Evidence from Devon and Cornwall', *Tijdschrift voor Economische en Sociale Geografie*, Vol.86, No.2, pp.162–76.

Sabel, C.F. (1994), 'Flexible Specialisation and the Re-emergence of Regional Economies', in A. Amin (ed.), *Post Fordism: A Reader*. Oxford: Blackwell.

Sabel, C.F. (1982), *Work and Politics: The Division of Labour in Industry*. Cambridge: Cambridge University Press.

Sayer, A. (1989), 'Post-Fordism in Question', *International Journal of Urban and Regional Research*, Vol.14, No.4, pp.666–954.

Schoenberger, E. (1988), 'From Fordism to Flexible Accumulation: Technology, Competitive Strategies and International Location', *Environment & Planning D: Society & Space*, Vol.6, pp.245–62.

Schoenberger, E. (1997), *The Cultural Crisis of the Firm*. Oxford: Blackwell Publishers.

Stalk, G.R. (1988), 'Time – The Next Source of Competitive Advantage', *Harvard Business Review*, Vol.4 (July/Aug), pp.41–51.

Strange, R. (1993), *Japanese Manufacturing Investment in Europe: Its Impact on the UK Economy*. London: Routledge.

Storper, M. (1995), 'The Resurgence of Regional Economies, Ten Years Later: The Region as a Nexus of Untraded Interdependencies', *European Urban and Regional Studies*, Vol.2, No.3, pp.191–221.

Turok, I. (1997), 'Linkages in the Scottish Electronics Industry: Further Evidence', *Regional Studies*, Vol.31, No.7, pp.705–11.

Turok, I. (1993), 'Inward Investment and Local Linkages: How Deeply Embedded is 'Silicon Glen'?', *Regional Studies*, Vol.27, No.5, pp.401–17.

Todting, F. (1994), 'The Uneven Landscape of Innovation Poles: Local Embeddedness and Global Networks', in A. Amin and N. Thrift (eds), *Globalisation, Institutions and Regional Development in Europe*. Oxford: Oxford University Press.

Watts, H.D. (1981), *The Branch Plant Economy*. London: Longmans.

Young, S. and N. Hood (1994), 'Designing Developmental After-care Programmes for Foreign Direct Investors in the European Union', *Transnational Corporations*, Vol.3, No.2, pp.45–72.

Young, S., N. Hood and S. Dunlop (1988), 'Global Strategies, Multinational Subsidiary Roles and Economic Impacts in Scotland', *Regional Studies*, Vol.22, No.6, pp.487–98.

6

East Asian FDI and the Political Economy of Local Development

ANDREW PIKE and JOHN TOMANEY

The attraction of Foreign Direct Investment (FDI), particularly of the East Asian variety, has been an integral part of the UK's industrial regeneration strategy in the last decade. In addition to the jobs and investment, the more cost efficient 'lean' production techniques employed by East Asian (particularly Japanese) investors have been alleged to generate a 'transformative' effect upon local economic development prospects both through their own development and their 'demonstration effect' on the activities of existing firms. In particular, recent vintages of East Asian FDI are seen as the vanguard of a new type of 'networked' branch plant, more 'embedded' in local networks, and providing better 'quality' employment and more local supply spin-offs than their predecessors. New East Asian factories have been utilized as potent symbols of regeneration for localized business support networks in their battles to capture future rounds of FDI and have become focal points in local economic strategy making.

This essay situates the experience of the North East region within the context of these debates concerning East Asian FDI and the political economy of local development.[1] The analysis looks in detail and reflects upon the Sedgefield Borough economy to offer a more critical reading of the role of East Asian FDI in local economic development. Sedgefield is typical of the North East region's recent experience in attracting substantial East Asian FDI. The locality has been portrayed as having successfully undergone the transformation from rationalization, associated with closures among the formerly nationalized industries and earlier waves of (predominantly) US and UK investment, to a situation in which the role of FDI, often from Japan but also from Hong Kong, is seen as

Andrew Pike and John Tomaney, Centre for Urban and Regional Development Studies, University of Newcastle upon Tyne integral to future prosperity. Indeed, Sedgefield is promoted as a 'manufacturing district' by its own local development institutions and as a 'flagship' locality among partner institutions within the North East. The evidence from Sedgefield suggests that the character of East Asian FDI and its influence on local institutions has fallen short of an outright transformation in the fortunes of the local economy. Changes are evident but they appear to reflect an uneven and partial set of shifts which do not always have positive implications for local economic development. The essay concludes that East Asian FDI is a small but significant segment of the Sedgefield Borough economy which reveals evidence of some 'leading edge' developments in particular areas in tandem with a recurrence of some of the structural characteristics reminiscent of previous 'branch plant' investments. The conclusions for the business support network concern the need to change the focus and apparent control over the local economic development strategy and to make links to the agenda of more active regional institutions and policy being promoted by the current Labour government.

EAST ASIAN FDI AND LOCAL DEVELOPMENT IN THE UK

The attraction of FDI, particularly of the East Asian variety, has been an integral part of the UK's national industrial regeneration strategy in the last decade. Through the jobs, investment and (often export oriented) output, the more cost efficient 'lean' production techniques employed by East Asian (particularly Japanese) investors have been expected to generate a 'transformative' effect upon local economic development prospects both through their own efforts and their 'demonstration effect' on the activities of existing firms (Coopers & Lybrand Deloitte, 1991; Economists Advisory Group/IWG, 1994; Florida and Kenney, 1988). As the previous Conservative government's Competitiveness White Paper claimed, 'inward investment brings world class production techniques, technical innovation and managerial skills, which can be transferred to local companies' (HM Government, 1994: 94).

This industrial renewal strategy and the promotion of the UK as a destination for mobile capital have changed somewhat with the incoming New Labour administration. The previous emphasis upon low labour and social costs and the 'opt-out' of the UK from the Social Chapter of the European Union's Maastricht Treaty has been altered. The incoming government signed the Social Chapter

TABLE 1

LOCAL ECONOMIC DEVELOPMENT IMPLICATIONS BY TYPE OF PLANT (SUMMARY)

	'Branch Plant'	'Performance/Networked Branch Plant'
Role and autonomy	External ownership and control; structured position and constrained autonomy; truncated and narrow functional structure involved in part-process production and/or assembly; cloned capacity and vertically integrated with limited nodes capable of external local linkage (e.g. suppliers, technology); state-policy subsidized establishment via automatic grants to broadly designated areas.	External ownership and control but possible enhanced strategic and operating autonomy as well as responsibility for performance increased within a 'flattened' hierarchical structure; wider functional structure involved in full process production tilted toward manufacturing rather than solely assembly; sole capacity with product (range), division or market mandate at the expense of rationalization elsewhere; increased nodes capable of linkage (e.g. R&D with technology support, human resources with training); state-policy support for establishment on selective and regulated basis (e.g. job creation, local content).
Labour process	Labour-intensive, semi- and unskilled work; 'routinized' and specific tasks within refined technical division of labour; high volume production of low to medium technology products; standardized process technology; short-term, task-specific, 'on-the-job' training integrated with production.	Capital and technology intensive, semi- and skilled work with increased need for diagnostic and cognitive skills; recombined job tasks and individual/team responsibility for performance; low to high technology and low to high volume production flexibility; flexible and re-programmable process technology; longer term, co-ordinated with investment, 'on-' and 'off-the-job' training.
Labour-management relations	Organized and unionized labour; job classifications, task assignments and work/supervision rules linked to seniority-based pay scales; formalized and collective negotiation and bargaining tied to employment contract; personnel management with administrative focus.	Business unionism; reduction and streamlining of grading, job titles and meritocratic salary structure; shift to company-based non-(traditional) union arenas, individualized negotiation and bargaining tied to 'enabling' agreements; Human Resource Management techniques.
Labour market strategies	Employees considered interchangeable, replaceable and in need of constant supervision; limited screening and high labour turnover and absenteeism; reliance on external labour market.	Rigorous scrutiny and increased selectivity in recruitment; employees as human resources needing investment; teamworking to reduce labour turnover and identify employee with the goals of the company; development of core internal labour market and peripheral (part-time, temporary) segments.
Supplier linkages	Limited since integration with broader corporate structures of production and supply chains; intra-firm linkages substituted for local ties; limited local supply chain knowledge and greater awareness of potential suppliers in headquarters region.	Outsourcing increase with JIT and synchronous suppliers; increased potential for local procurement and supplier agglomeration; 1st and 2nd tier supply chain management; increased global sourcing and partnership relations; growth in dependence in the local supply network; geographically distributed production networks and JIT operated over (inter-)national distances.
Local economic development implications	Externally-owned and controlled plants with limited decision-making powers locally ('dependent development', 'branch plant economy'); vulnerable to closure or relocation ('footloose', 'runaway industries', 'hyper-mobile capital'); limited growth rates in employment and output; low technology and skills ('screwdriver plants'); few local linkages ('enclave development', 'dual economy', 'industrialization without growth', 'cathedrals in the desert'); diversified industries not building upon or modernizing existing regional industrial strengths; limited innovation potential and technology transfer from dedicated production processes and suppliers.	New concepts of externally-owned and controlled plant with increased decision-making autonomy for strategic and operational issues, more rooted and anchored in the local economy ('embedded firm'), higher levels of technology and skills, higher innovative potential, more local linkages and increased technology transfer through research and technological development functions; supplier links upgrading process technology improvement and partnership development with suppliers; potential for the plant to be a 'propulsive local growth pole', 'vehicle/catalyst for local economic development' and capable of setting in train 'sustainable development'.

and has sought to emphasize the UK as a centre of 'quality, added-value, high technology and market leadership' (Margaret Beckett, President of the Board of Trade, quoted in the *Financial Times*, 24 July 1997). However, despite this change of tack, many of the other benefits that were touted to inward investors during the 1980s and the first half of the 1990s remain, including: the competitive labour and social costs allied with sufficient levels of workforce skills and education to provide acceptable quality and productivity levels; low corporate taxation; the deregulated environment and relatively easy exit in case of rationalization (particularly with regard to labour recruitment and redundancy); and the English language.

The UK attracted substantial inward investment, particularly from East Asia, during the 1980s and 1990s (House of Commons, 1994). Indeed, the UK is a globally significant destination and source of FDI flows. The latter has occurred through the activities of UK transnational firms 'hollowing out' their UK-based productive capacity (Williams *et al.*, 1990). The gross figures for all sectors reveal negative net effect on the productive base in the UK. Between 1984 and 1994, inflows increased from $241m (–0.06% of GDP) to $11,066 (1.1% of GDP) while outflows increased from $8,039m (1.86% of GDP) to $29,721 (2.93% of GDP) (current prices) (OECD, 1996). Debates developed around the impacts and significance of these FDI inflows initially concerned the theme of the 'Japanization' of industry in Britain during the 1980s (Oliver and Wilkinson, 1990) but more recently have scrutinized the significant growth in FDI from other East Asian countries with somewhat different national strategies and practices, notably South Korea, Taiwan, and Hong Kong (see, for example, Jung, 1997). Critical questions have been recurrent within these accounts, including: industrial strategy and the reinforcement of 'branch plant economies' in the UK regions; the extent to which the higher productivity among foreign-owned firms is attributable to their greater innovativeness than indigenous firms; the amount and nature of jobs created; new labour processes and the intensification of working practices; reconfigured labour–management relations and the emergence of a 'new realism' in British industrial relations; new localized supplier linkages allied to the level and nature of component sourcing; and the 'transformative effect' of such 'greenfield' investments on existing 'brownfield' plants and on local and regional economic development prospects (Beardwell,

1992; Garrahan and Stewart, 1992; Mair, 1993; Munday et al., 1995; Stone and Peck, 1996; Pike, 1996; Williams and Haslam, 1991).

One significant strand of recent debate has situated East Asian FDI at the vanguard of the development of a new type of 'networked' or 'performance' branch plant, more 'embedded' in local networks, and providing better 'quality' employment and more local supply spin-offs than their predecessors (Amin et al., 1994; Morgan, 1995, Phelps, 1993; Young et al., 1994) (Table 1). This revisionist work has emphasized the reorganization of the forms of corporate economic co-ordination incorporating 'branch plants', and the potential for enhanced local economic development prospects. Central to the changes are 'flattened' corporate hierarchies devolving autonomy to individual plants, their porous nature increasing the capability of heightened local linkages (for example to suppliers and the technology support infrastructure), and the capacity of local institutions to exploit these developments. A division still exists, however, between more progressive developments associated with the 'networked' or 'performance' plant, and the 'cost/price-based' plant which exhibits more continuities with previous branch plants (Pike, 1998).

The impact of inward investment, especially from East Asia, has been stressed in debates concerning economic development institutions and policy (Dicken and Tickell, 1992). Local institutions have been keen to utilize positive images of new factories as symbols of regeneration in the competition to attract further inward investment projects and to promote re-investment projects to further anchor their stock of existing plants. East Asian investors, in particular, have often been used to illustrate the 'global' and 'modern' nature of the success of local partnerships in securing the benefits of 'globalization' for their local economies. Critically, the influence of inward investors in shaping the local economic development agenda along lines favourable for their own development has also emerged as an issue (Garrahan and Stewart, 1992).

FDI IN THE NORTH EAST

The Northern region, comprising the North East and Cumbria, has received a disproportionate share of inward investment among the English regions, reflected in the jobs created during the 1980s, although Northern Ireland, Scotland and Wales have a higher relative share of their regional manufacturing accounted for by foreign-owned firms (Table 2). Within the Northern region, the North East has accounted for the larger relative share (Peck and Stone, 1992). The record of the North East has been attributed to the benefits it adds to the general UK attractions noted above, including infrastructure, sites, relatively flexible incentive regime, targeted marketing from dedicated investment promotion agencies (such as Northern Development Company (NDC) and County Durham Development Company (CDDC)), and labour surplus due to levels of unemployment persistently above the national average. Wage costs relative to value-added per employee in manufacturing were initially touted as an advantage but these have become less 'competitive' than several other regions throughout the 1980s (Table 3). Indeed, labour costs have become a poor guide to developments due to the higher capital intensity of some of the

TABLE 2
NEW JOBS PROMOTED BY FOREIGN FIRMS INVESTING IN THE UK 1981–90

	Jobs Promoted[1]		Relative	Estimated Jobs Created[2]	
	Total ('000s)	Share of UK Total	Concentration Index[3] (UK=100)	Total of Region's Mfg.Empl. ('000s)	As %
South East and E. Anglia	21.5	9.8	39.1	16.1	1.2
South West	11.2	5.1	69.4	8.6	2.1
West Midlands	29.6	13.6	104.8	19.4	2.7
East Midlands	10.5	4.8	51.3	6.9	1.4
Yorks and Humberside	9.2	4.2	43.1	6.2	1.2
North West	15.5	7.1	57.6	10.6	1.6
North	23.5	10.8	205.1	17.0	5.9
Wales	30.1	13.8	298.5	22.2	8.8
Scotland	52.2	23.9	308.1	36.1	8.5
Northern Ireland	14.8	6.8	343.8	8.0	7.5
United Kingdom	218.7	100.0	100.0	151.4	2.9

Notes:
1 Jobs promoted are those promised by the firm. Normally, 100% of jobs approved do not materialize as actual jobs. Also, those jobs that are created will not all appear in the same year as they are approved.
2 Estimated jobs are computed by assuming that 75% of approvals in each year convert to actual jobs over the following three year period. The estimates use approvals data back to 1979. For Northern Ireland the conversion rate is 40%.
3 Estimated jobs are computed by assuming that 75% of approvals in each year convert to actual jobs over the following three year period. The estimates use approvals data back to 1979. For Northern Ireland the conversion rate is 40%.
Source: Department of Trade and Industry, cited in House of Commons (1995).

TABLE 3
WAGE COSTS RELATIVE TO VALUE ADDED PER EMPLOYEE IN
MANUFACTURING (UK=100)

Region	1980	1986	1990
South East	99	101	101
East Anglia	102	96	100
South West	117	102	109
East Midlands	105	101	102
West Midlands	108	101	104
Yorkshire-Humberside	99	100	99
North West	98	98	95
North	97	104	102
Wales	106	92	92
Scotland	99	96	94
Northern Ireland	115 (100)	101 (97)	99 (92)

Sources: BSO Census of Production cited in House of Commons (1995:155).
Note: Wages per employee divided by Gross Value Added per employee
adjusted for the composition of industry at four digit level of the SIC.
Northern Ireland figures in parentheses exclude state-owned companies.
Low values indicate favourable cost competitiveness.

more recent FDI projects and are increasingly being questioned as
the basis for attracting mobile investment in competition with even
lower cost localities in Central and Eastern Europe and South East
Asia.

Direct employment in foreign-owned manufacturing (FOM)
firms in the Northern region, including other non-East Asian
inward investors, reached 55,700 in 1993, and its share of
manufacturing employment rose from 12% in 1979 to 23% in
1993 (Stone 1993). However, net employment change in FOM
firms was only 6,455 between 1979 and 1993. Major East Asian
investors in the North East include Nissan, NSK, LG, Lucas SEI and
Samsung. Typically, despite its small size relative to manufacturing
as a whole, East Asian FDI is seen as significant since it is often
considered to embody 'leading edge' practices. To some extent, the
relatively modest net employment growth in the foreign-owned
manufacturing sector reflects both the final assembly orientation of
much of the investment and its linkage to the vagaries of trading
conditions in export markets. Inward investors have tended to
create full-time, male and female employment, although recently
projects in the North East have been in the form of tele-service 'call
centres' with relative higher proportions of female and part-time
jobs (Richardson and Marshall, 1996).

For regional institutions, economic development prospects in the North East have been transformed by the recent history of inward investment projects. The rhetoric of regional officials seeks constantly to counter claims of the reinforcement of the region as a 'branch plant economy'. According to such as John Bridge, Chief Executive of NDC (which covers Cumbria and the North East): 'Inward investment has revolutionized the North's industrial base. It's not a bolt on. Ministers must understand that it's a highly integrated part of the UK economy' (quoted in the *Financial Times*, 18 July 1997). The response to the North East's attraction of FDI has not all been positive. Sceptics have highlighted the dominance of such investors exercising power within local and regional economies, their nature as easily rationalized 'global outposts' that reinforce the North East's position a 'branch plant economy', and the exploitative nature of jobs available within such factories where 'multi-tasking' and the garnering of employees' knowledge of the labour process are the norm, and the weakening of established structures of trade union recognition and representation (Amin and Tomaney, 1991; Garrahan and Stewart, 1992; Hudson, 1995).

THE CASE OF EAST ASIAN FDI IN SEDGEFIELD BOROUGH

In the context of developments within the UK and the North East region, the case of Sedgefield Borough is instructive. Sedgefield has typified the North East's recent experience in attracting substantial East Asian FDI. The locality has been held up as an example of successful transformation. Earlier rationalization among the formerly nationalized industries and earlier US and UK inward investments has been countered by successful regeneration based upon the attraction of successive rounds of East Asian FDI in the manufacturing sector. Indeed, Sedgefield is promoted as a 'manufacturing district' by its own local development institutions and as a 'flagship' locality among partner institutions within the North East. The public profile and significance of Sedgefield has also grown since the local MP was elected, first, Leader of the Labour Party and, following the May 1997 election, the Prime Minister.

'De-industrialization' and the Emergence of a 'Manufacturing Borough'

The historical development of Sedgefield Borough has closely followed the trajectory of the North East region. The local economy was predominantly agricultural prior to the development of the 'carboniferous capitalism' that propelled the region in the late nineteenth century. Coal extraction and processing as well as the railway industry provided substantial growth and employment throughout the early to mid-twentieth century. Post-war nationalization shaped the National Coal Board's activity, including the Coke Works in Fishburn, and the establishment of the British Rail Engineering Limited (BREL) Wagon Works in Shildon. Newton Aycliffe, in particular, developed from a munitions manufacturing base to an important industrial centre with its designation as a New Town in 1947. Throughout this period, state management marked the development of the local economy.

Contraction among the Borough's traditional employers coupled with the long-run rationalization in the North East's coal industry underpinned rising unemployment in the 1960s. Guided by early regional policy measures, the Borough became an early recipient of inward investment both from relocations within the UK, including Courtaulds and Thorn, and from the US, including Black and Decker. These investments marked the opening up of the local economy and were concentrated in the Newton Aycliffe and Spennymoor industrial estates.

Sedgefield Borough witnessed substantial deindustrialization in the traditional sectors and among some of the earlier wave of inward investors in the 1970s and early 1980s. Both the Shildon Wagon Works (2,600 jobs) and Fishburn Coke Works (260 jobs) were rationalized after vigorous local anti-closure campaigns (Durham County Council and Sedgefield District Council, 1983). The loss of jobs concentrated in specific localities decimated the prosperity of their surrounding communities. The further closures of Courtaulds, GEC and STC at the time were evidence of the ephemeral 'branch plant' industrialization in the locality.

In the latter part of the 1980s and early 1990s, the Borough witnessed the growth of East Asian investment, particularly from Japan, including Fujitsu and Oshino Lamps. Indeed, the Borough has been held up as a symbol of industrial transformation in the North East due to these 'flagship' investments in often 'higher tech' sectors, such as electronics, relatively new to the locality. These inward investors employed cost efficient manufacturing techniques and embodied single or non-union employment deals alien to both the region and the Borough's industrial relations tradition.

Re-investment among the existing stock of plants has also safeguarded and contributed to employment growth. Major branch plant closures occurred in the early 1990s including GPT, Moores International, and Tootals. Even more recently in the late 1990s, the Electrolux fridge factory has been closed and Black and Decker's plant has been reprieved after questions were raised over its role in the corporation's new 'global' investment strategy. However, the solution to the employment problems caused by these closures invariably focuses on attracting further mobile investment.

The background of economic decline and the struggle to generate sustainable growth in Sedgefield Borough has precipitated a marginal fall in population (nearly 4% between 1981–91 to 89,500), often among more mobile skilled and qualified labour, leaving an older and more dependent population (SBC, 1994). Total employment declined by nearly 13% between 1984 and 1995 to 28,000 largely due to the job losses during the 1980s. Similar to the whole of the UK, male full-time employment experienced the sharpest declines, while, in contrast, female part-time employment declined in general but illustrated a mixed picture of stasis, growth and decline relative to national levels in services. Unemployment in the Borough has been divided between the higher levels in the Bishop Auckland part (9.8 in 1994), remaining stubbornly above the national average (8.5 in 1994), and the relatively more prosperous Durham area[2] (7.9 in 1994). Pockets of acute youth and long term unemployment have become entrenched, despite being lower than County Durham levels. The local labour market has also been increasingly opened up to inward and outward flows through the Borough into the regional labour market.

Sectoral employment change has emphasized Sedgefield's 'manufacturing borough' traditions and aspirations. Despite the national decline in manufacturing's share of total employment in the UK, Sedgefield held its own – nearly half of the total jobs in the Borough remain in the manufacturing sector which is twice the rate both for the UK and the Northern region (Table 4). These jobs are increasingly concentrated in the Newton Aycliffe and Spennymoor industrial estates. Service sector employment has not grown as fast as national levels, except in distribution, hotels and restaurants, or it has contracted faster in the shadow of private services development in telephone call centres in Tyne and Wear and nearby

Darlington, as well as the financial services and public sector developments in Leeds. Sedgefield's public sector has contracted and this is set to continue with the run down of the Winterton Hospital in Sedgefield village. The rationalization of the traditional industries has largely concluded and, in the context of the relatively sluggish net service sector growth, the fortunes of the resilient manufacturing sector, and in particular the existing and potential inward (re)investors, are increasingly crucial to the Borough's future prosperity.

TABLE 4
SHARE OF TOTAL EMPLOYMENT CHANGE BY SECTOR, UK AND SEDGEFIELD, 1984–95*

| Sector | 1984 | | | | 1995 | | | |
| | UK | | Sedgefield | | UK | | Sedgefield | |
	No.	%	No.	%	No.	%	No.	%
Agriculture and Fishing	348,200	1.7	200	0.6	280,000	1.3	0	0
Energy and Water	1,400,100	6.7	2,300	7.2	228,700	1.1	100	0.4
Manufacturing	4,529,900	21.7	15,700	48.9	3,944,600	18.4	13,700	48.9
Construction	1,025,800	4.9	1,900	5.9	808,800	3.8	1,500	5.4
Distribution, hotels and restaurants	4,195,300	20.1	3,800	11.8	4,827,900	22.5	4,600	16.4
Transport and communications	1,327,600	6.4	1,200	3.7	1,279,900	6.0	900	3.2
Banking, finance insurance	1,988,200	9.5	700	2.2	3,656,300	17.1	1,100	3.9
Other services	6,030,800	28.9	6,200	19.3	6,410,900	29.9	5,800	20.7
Total	20,846,000	100	32,100	100	21,437,300	100	28,000	100

* Sedgefield figures rounded to nearest 100
Source: NOMIS (1997)

Despite over 30 years of various policy initiatives, the current state of Sedgefield Borough's economy has meant it retains Assisted Area status, although this was challenged in the early 1990s by recession in the South East and the redrawing of the assisted area designation map (Sedgefield Borough Council, 1994).[3] The eastern segment is a Development Area and remains disadvantaged a decade after the Wagon Works closure, most recently attracting funds through the Single Regeneration Budget (SRB) to Shildon. The western part retains Intermediate Area designation but recently lost Rural Development Area status. Sedgefield is situated within the North East Objective 2 region for EU regional policy support for declining industrial regions that is set to be reduced substantially at the end of the current programme period in 1999, and, again, over a decade after the demise of its Coke Works, Fishburn has additional support through the RECHAR II Community Initiative.

East Asian FDI in Sedgefield Borough

In the context of the local economic development trajectory of Sedgefield Borough, East Asian FDI accounts for a small but increasingly significant part of the stock of inward investors. These include operations from global concerns, some in sectors new to the Borough's economy. While only accounting for 1,166 jobs in total – approximately 4.2% of the total 28,000 employed in the Borough in 1995 – the East Asian investors have been highly visible additions to the stock of FDI due to their high profile and allegedly 'leading edge' nature. The following sections analyse the extent and nature of changes in the East Asian FDI factories and their transformative impact upon the local economy. The analysis utilizes some of the dimensions of change in plant type and local economic development prospects noted above, and draws on in-depth interviews with key informants within a sub-set of the East Asian FDI projects and the local business support institutions (Table 6).

In general, the explanations for investment in Sedgefield Borough among the East Asian inward investors comprised: securing access and security of supply within the EU Single European Market; increasing capacity; 'nearness' to market (for interpretation and incorporation of regulatory developments, such as telecommunications standards); proximity to sister organizations in Continental Europe; availability of skilled and low cost labour; grants for sites and services as well as training; infrastructure; the presence of other Japanese companies and a supporting local social infrastructure; other companies from the same sector already located locally; potential for supplier network development; regional universities; and 'lifestyle': 'the Japanese like living here'.

Role and Autonomy

The role of most of the East Asian FDI in Sedgefield reflects the motivations behind the investments. Largely, these plants are 'state of the art' duplicate capacity, established with often substantial investment. Each plant was closely integrated into mainly national and European but sometimes global product and component

TABLE 5
CASE STUDY EAST ASIAN INWARD INVESTORS IN SEDGEFIELD BOROUGH, 1996

Firm	Employ-ment	Ownership and Headquarters	Established	Activity	Stated Investments	Grant Support (£m)	Estimated Annual Wage Bill (£m)	Trade Union Deal	Annual Training Budget (£ '000)
SemiconductorCo	509	Japan, Tokyo	1991	Wafer Fab	£800m	£30 –35m Regional Selective Assistance and Undisclosed training funds from Borough and Durham County Councils	–	Non Union, 'Factory Forum'	Over £1m
Electronics1Co	309	Japan, Osaka	1988	Microwave ovens	–	Undisclosed, training part-funded by Durham TEC	£5m	AEEU Single Union deal, 55% Density	£33k
Electronics2Co	191	Japan, Tokyo	1988	Remote control units (TV, Audio, Satellite)	–	–	£2m	Non-union, Employee, Council	£27k
AutosupplierCo	88	Japan, Tokyo	1989 Take-over of Llanelli Radiator	Heat exchange systems	£3m	–	–	Non-union, Works Council	£50k
TechSMECo	15	Hong Kong (70%), SDC (25%), Local (5%)	1992	Design, engineering, testing and maintenance of electronics and tele-communications products	–	Undisclosed training grants	–	Unionized but low levels, small enough to consult with those concerned	–

Source: Pike and Tomaney (1996)

sourcing markets. This has caused some problems. *Semi-conductorCo* recently delayed a reinvestment due to fluctuations in the global semiconductor market, but gave the following assurance: 'It's not a question of if we will make the second phase investment, it's a question of when. It reflects the cyclical nature of the industry. We are saying 'Let's give ourselves another period of time to see how the market shapes up' (quoted in *Financial Times*, 8 June, 1996). Indeed, despite *SemiconductorCo's* claims that 'profits made here are invested here' (*SemiconductorCo*, authors' interview, 1996), reinvestment was often tied into broader, sometimes global strategies, and subject to market development. Price was integral to plant strategies and quality was becoming increasingly important. Each plant had achieved the latest internationally recognized ISO accreditation. Where heightened autonomy did exist, the importance of developing new features, responsiveness, flexibility, and closeness to market were emphasized. The plants contained a broad range of decision-making functions, but these tended to emphasize budgeting and meeting financial targets. Crucially for longer term development, however, R&D and technological development activity was mostly conducted outside the region. *SemiconductorCo's* recently established research centre in London, for example, was intended to 'give [us] access to very talented researchers in the UK and the rest of Europe' (quoted in the *Financial Times*, 9 January 1996). Some engineering and design change staff were evident in some of the plants, suggesting the bolstering of capability in this area. Only *TechSMECo* actually conducted R&D under contract as part of its core business. *AutosupplierCo* illustrated a degree of change from purely assembly-related activity. This shift was an attempt to diversify from their monopsonistic relationship with their main buyer, reduce their dependence upon Japan and their exposure to fluctuations in the Sterling:Yen exchange rate, and to develop new products. Formerly, *AutosupplierCo* made components to specification but had sought to upgrade their own technological capability to develop 'concept solutions' to client problems, and become more of a manufacturing operation (for example, using Computer Numeric Controlled bending and injection moulding equipment).

Autonomy had increased among the plants in terms of heightened responsibility for performance. Decisions for investment, however, were often referred to parent companies or majority shareholders. *Electronics1Co*, for example, operated within a £10,000 threshold, above which they had to refer to their parent company in Japan. Sterling:¥en exchange rates could often vary this level. Higher levels of investment were often part of intra-corporate competitions for investment where plant autonomy and responsibility was heightened in making the case for winning investments. While *SemiconductorCo* stressed 'it is not a race', *AutosupplierCo* stressed how they secured a recent investment project ahead of their sister plant in Spain due to their size, cost advantage, and the experience of their management team. Generally, the plants were mostly stable or expanding but remained characterized by the parameters of external control.

Level and Nature of Employment

Employment among the East Asian plants was either stable or expanding. However, the structural character of the plants and their dependence upon imports had led to employment fluctuation in the past. In 1992 *Electronics1Co* shed 95 jobs – one third of their workforce – due to the weakness of sterling against the ¥en and high interest rates. Most jobs in the East Asian plants were 'permanent' and there was only limited utilization of temporary contracts. This may have reflected the need to offer 'permanent' jobs in the face of labour competition due to the widespread use of temporary contracts at other larger employers in the Borough including Flymo, and Black and Decker. Simplified grading structures and the utilization of teamworking within the plants meant that occupational stratification was not pronounced. The common panoply of techniques associated with East Asian 'best practice' was evident within each of the plants. These included flexibility and teamworking which served to intensify work rates among employees and reduce the demarcation and idle time associated with previous forms of factory work. There was some evidence of workforce 'feminization', particularly at *Electronics2Co* where 95% of the 70 operators were female, and at the other plants where up to one third of employees were female but again these were concentrated in the operator grades. *AutosupplierCo* even claimed that in some cases the operatives grades were 'women's jobs' in that women performed them more productively since they had 'a higher boredom threshold' (authors' interview, 1996). Among the plants there was a mixture of non-unionized set-ups and single union deals. Those companies without unions had alternative arenas, including 'factory forums' and 'company councils' (Table 5). The unionized plants had single union deals often made with the preferred craft union, AEEU, and established typical 'enabling' agreements that were effectively 'no strike' (Williams, 1997). Generally, wage levels were pegged to average levels within the Borough and the broader region, to ensure firms avoided either paying above the perceived 'going rates' and contributing to wage inflation or having retention problems for particular jobs. Employment turnover was under 5% in all the plants. Elsewhere in the Borough, smaller firms complained that labour retention problems were caused by the larger firms, including the East Asian investors, being both willing and able to 'cream off' the best labour locally by paying sufficiently above local market rates to encourage labour mobility. Absenteeism was generally low, but where high it was emphasized by the firms that this was among production operators, particularly females.

Recruitment and Labour Market Strategies

While recruitment among the East Asian plants has been relatively limited, the potential and actual number of applicants have often been high given the unemployment levels in the Borough and North East. The type of labour sought and methods employed were new to Sedgefield. Recruitment strategy was described as 'skills and qualification driven', and the attributes of the labour sought were 'compliant attitude', 'hard working', 'reliable', 'flexible', 'team player' and 'experience'. In addition, the specific skills sought ranged from unskilled process operators to toolmakers, press setters, designers, engineers and electricians. The willingness of firms to recruit from the unemployed and disabled was also noted. In numerical terms, there is evidence of local labour market segmentation since recruitment was largely from the Borough or County Durham, although more specialized skills required national recruitment. Each plant had relatively limited levels of East Asian personnel, for instance *Electronics1Co* had only 12 Japanese working there (4% of the total workforce). Methods of recruitment followed the common hierarchy, from local press for lower level skills up to specialist trade press for senior engineers. A significant development in local labour market co-ordination was the firm's

TABLE 6
ORGANIZATIONAL CONTEXT OF ECONOMIC DEVELOPMENT IN
SEDGEFIELD BOROUGH

	Local	County	Regional
Public Sector	Sedgefield Borough Council	Durham County Council County Durham Co-operative Development Association	Government Office North East North of England Assembly
			English Partnerships#
	Further Education Colleges		Universities and HESIN (Higher Education Support for Industry in the North) Employment Service#
			Rural Development Commission#
Public-Private Partnerships	SASDA	County Durham TEC	
	Trimdon 2000	County Durham Development Company	Northern Development Company (NDC)
	Shildon Partnership (SRB)	Business Link	Regional Technology Centre (RTC) North
	South West Durham Training	County Durham EconomicI Development Partnership*	North East Innovation Centre
			CADCAM Centre
			Northern Informatics Centre for Achievement in Manufacturing Management (CAMM)
Private Sector and Trade Unions	Personnel Managers Group	Durham Business Club**	North East Chamber of Commerce
			CBI Northern Region
			Northern Business Forum (CBI/ Chamber) Manufacturing Challenge
			British Coal Enterprise#
			Northern Region TUC

* Comprises the County and Borough Councils, Durham TEC, County Durham Development Company, and the North East Chamber of Commerce
** Organized and supported by the North East Chamber of Commerce
# Northern region branches of national organizations

use of the local development agency SASDA (formerly the Shildon and Sedgefield District Development Agency) which notified local employers when groups of temporary contractors more readily used at the other larger firms in the Borough were being released. Psychometric testing was utilized to screen recruits and assess the suitability of individuals for particular jobs. The limited level and increased scrutiny of the recruitment mechanisms was not lost on some segments of the local labour market, and it was noted in relation to inward investment that: 'it doesn't do a great lot for us, like individually. There might be a few jobs coming for X amount of people but unless you are one of those X amount, it doesn't improve life for you does it?' (Social Issues, group interview, 1996).[4]

Competition for labour for the East Asian plants tended to come from elsewhere in the region, including earlier inward investments, from East Asia, the US and Europe, such as Siemens, Samsung, and from firms within the Borough such Flymo, Black and Decker, Rothmans, Thorn Lighting, and Electrolux. This pressure may have been exacerbated by the coincidental expansion of FDI projects within the region, as well as the upturn in the business cycle. East Asian firms in the Borough were both perpetrators and victims of labour poaching. On the one hand, *AutosupplierCo* 'attracted' two people from their main customer in the region and were promptly told 'enough is enough' (authors' interview, 1996). On the other hand, *SemiconductorCo* had a labour retention problem. This had been exacerbated by claims that a recent FDI project had been engaged in 'poaching' staff, which, significantly, had upset the consensus to contain wage inflation within the local economy assisted by networking within a personnel managers group in the Borough. This localized co-operation between personnel managers had worked closely together to co-ordinate pay scales, dampen local wage inflation, and contain poaching, particularly for technician and supervisory grades due to the expansion in regional demand. In particular, the shortages and/or recruitment difficulties were the lack of specific GNVQs for the industry at the lower end, and some specialist problems elsewhere (such as engineers, purchasing, production control and logistics).

Skills and Training

Skills needs and development have been reshaped in the East Asian plants. In the context of flatter organizational hierarchies and shorter lines of command, occupational structures have been simplified and increasingly polarized between an upper echelon or core of professional and technical grades, fewer supervisory posts, and a lower mass or periphery of 'un-', 'semi-' and skilled operatives sub-divided into teams and regulated by team leaders. All of these groups are supported by a smaller band of increasingly 'multi-skilled' support and maintenance technicians. Entry level recruitment requirements have risen, with modularized apprentice-ships tailored to company needs increasing in importance. It is difficult to depict the East Asian factories as 'screwdriver' plants with 'de-skilled' workforces given the investment involved and the particular mixes of qualifications, experience and attitudes sought among the workforce. However, claims of 'multi-skilling' were perhaps inaccurate since the most of the additional skills tacked onto individuals' work loads were of roughly equivalent skill levels. 'Multi-tasking' appears a more appropriate description.

Most of the plants revealed the existence of moderately resourced training policies and departments, and some emphasized the importance of training as part of 'Japanese industrial culture' (*SemiconductorCo*, authors' interview, 1996). Each utilized a mixture of in-house and external delivery mechanisms as well as 'on-' and 'off-the-job' methods. Professional development, for example, was conducted through the regional universities which were also targeted to help solve the problems for the future need for design engineers. Only limited involvement in youth training schemes was evident. The main training providers were local or County-based, including Durham TEC, and SASDA. Some of the plants had achieved the nationally recognized 'Investors in People' (IIP) accreditation. South West Durham Training emerged as an increasingly specialized provider, capable of developing tailored courses in conjunction with firms (for example, a Supervisory Technician course was developed with *AutosupplierCo*) and delivering them more broadly. *AutosupplierCo* was also closely linked with its main customer as part of their supplier development activity, with initiatives based on project management, team leader training, and line balancing.

General constraints on training effort were noted, including the poaching problem, cost and the ability to fit training to the time available in the context of performance targets. Problems were also evident in the training infrastructure. In particular, a need was articulated for more specialized courses (for example, for benchmarking and market analysis), links into schools to emphasize the potential of 'manufacturing jobs' to build on the common work placement schemes utilized currently, and problems with 'understanding who is responsible for what' among the myriad of local provider institutions.

Supplier Linkages

Sourcing strategies among the East Asian plants represent a relatively advanced set of developments. Each plant is subject to such initiatives from their own customers, and are promoting these techniques with their own suppliers. Strategies are evident based upon partnership, long term links, supply chain management, supply base rationalization particularly due to the tooling costs, the search for increasingly specialized suppliers (for example, for plastic injection moulding), and working closely with suppliers on quality and pricing. Indeed, supplier support is well developed, including the utilization of development teams, quality assurance, vendor rating, performance audits, plus technical support and collaboration. The search for quality, cost and delivery underpins these techniques, and accreditation at the relevant current level (for example, ISO9002) is 'not seen as a cost, it is seen as essential' (*Electronics2Co*, authors' interview, 1996).

Component procurement is internationalized, especially in relation to East Asia, with substantial proportions of sourcing occurring at the national and European elements, supplemented by regional sources. Local sourcing at the Borough and County Durham level is limited, although some linkages are evident to other foreign-owned and indigenous firms. Significantly, the East Asian plants had initially developed EU sources to meet local content regulations but stated a preference to increase the proportion of local, national and regional firms in their supply bases to reduce their communication and logistical management problems. Such linkages have been hampered by problems with gaps in the region's manufacturing base which have undermined this intention to source locally (for example, plastic injection moulding tools).

The nature of component sourcing was mixed. Some of the procurement from within the local economy is for cost sensitive components which is liable to change following the emergence of new, even lower cost sources outside the Borough. But commodity parts are also sourced from continental Europe and worldwide (for example, PCBs from Belgium, rubber sheeting from Malaysia) and more specialized commodities come from both international and more national sources (for example, Scotland and Italy for specialist gases). Subcontracting has been utilized more locally, particularly for ancillary services, including security, catering, and site maintenance. Some manufacturing subcontracting is sourced locally, and there is evidence of dependent relations being established between the East Asian firms and smaller subcontractors within the Borough. Although, significantly, *TechSMECo* sub-contracted PCB layout and modification, at least partly due to their size.

Demonstration Effect on Existing Firms

There is evidence of 'best practice' among other FDI and indigenous companies in the local economy but these appear to be more clearly explained as part of broader trends rather than the effect of greenfield developments nearby. It appears that techniques, such as JIT, Total Quality Management, continuous improvement, and teamworking, have become somewhat distanced from their East Asian origins and subsumed into an international set of 'best practice' techniques, often under the emblem of 'lean production', which are mediated by national institutional structures (for example, trade union laws) and the labour–management relations within firms. These practices may be represented by East Asian firms within the Borough but it is unclear how the practices are demonstrated and diffused to other local firms. More pronounced and clearer linkage are evident in trading relationships with East Asian investors outside the Borough but sometimes within the region. Tallent Engineering utilized 'lean production' techniques but this had more to do with links to its main customer, Nissan, than with proximity to East Asian plants in Sedgefield. Firms in Sedgefield Borough have been most influenced in changes to their working practices and types of labour recruited, and changing relations with suppliers. Some areas remain unchanged, however, including the typically multi-union industrial relations structures within the existing firms in the Borough.

East Asian FDI and the Business Support Network

The centre of business support activity in the Borough is occupied by the relationship between Sedgefield Borough Council's (SBC) economic development unit and SASDA and their inter-relation with the regional partner institutions (Table 6). Indeed, SBC and SASDA recently 'co-located', alongside Business Link, in the centre of Newton Aycliffe industrial estate to encourage a closer working relationship and 'to get closer to client firms' (SBC Economic Development Unit, authors' interview, 1996). Given the industrial structure of the Borough's economy, business support strategy has focused on attracting inward investment from East Asia and elsewhere and servicing the needs of the existing stock of large, often foreign-owned, firms in the main Newton Aycliffe and Spennymoor industrial estates. Indeed, further rounds of FDI are seen as integral to promoting the 'manufacturing borough' agenda. The approach has evolved from securing the initial site and services and then 'dropping' the investor to a more sophisticated and integrated 'package' approach that seeks to provide site and service as well as grant support and training links for new investment, complemented by an ongoing 'after care' service to capture reinvestments, expansions and relocations.[5] The new approach is increasingly operated in partnership with Durham County Council, North East Chamber of Commerce, Durham TEC, English Partnerships and the private sector. Increasingly, the onus is being placed on the business development cases for (re)investment projects rather than the formerly subsidized 'site and service' strategy. For example, some progress has been made with the local contact of the Regional Supply Office and 'Project Locus', run from NDC, worked to build up regional sourcing, particularly among SMEs and overcame sourcing difficulties for 3M, Black and Decker, Flymo, *Electronics1Co*, and Thorn Lighting in the Borough.

Past projects have been utilized as potent symbols of regeneration and to serve notice of the effectiveness of the local partnership in bidding in the increasingly competitive market for FDI. The 'flagship' investments, especially the East Asian plants, have been crucial in attracting 'greenfield' and reinvestment projects from East Asia as well as from the US and Europe. Attracting and maintaining the stock of FDI is interpreted as evidence that the Borough has a past record of meeting the demands and terms set by inward investors. SBC has enjoyed first mover advantages of attracting and dealing with the specialized client needs of FDI over a relatively long period. Recent 'Heart of the Park' and Aycliffe Partnership regeneration initiatives have recognized the problem of expanding early and running out of premium sites, however, heightened by the growing competition from the Enterprise Zone established at nearby Easington in response to coal industry rationalization.

The development of more porous factories with nodes capable of linkage with the local and regional technology support infrastructure has been exploited to a limited degree with the East Asian investors in Sedgefield Borough. All the plants had at least considered links with regional universities, and the majority had established relations, for initiatives such as joint ventures, and student placements. *TechSMECo* had developed links with RTC North and the local FE sector. Linkages between the East Asian plants with a range of local, regional and national institutions, especially regional players on arrival, NDC and English Partnerships, were evident. The deepest linkages were with the most local institutions, SBC and SASDA, followed by the lead agencies, particularly for training service provision, including Durham TEC. Networking was evident and a sense of regional identification between the goals of the company and the region was mentioned. Links into the Anglo–Japanese Society had also been established by some of the firms. Community links with local schools and registered charities were evident but were supported by somewhat modest budgets.

The East Asian firms claimed they received an effective business service from the regional network. Suggested improvements were upgrading the image to attract further industry, upgrading the transport infrastructure and parking provision outside of the main Aycliffe and Spennymoor industrial estates, increasing links to regional universities, and reducing the overlap between organizations. *TechSMECo* also claimed that the image was not 'high tech' but industrial which might put other 'high tech' companies off locating in the Borough. In the broader North East region, SBC and SASDA are seen as a 'best practice generator' and 'flagship' operation in economic development terms by regional agencies.

There are signs that the emergent local economic development strategy may become problematic in the future. The increasing focus on client needs and concern with 'after-care', particularly among new and existing FDI and the larger firms in the main Aycliffe and Spennymoor industrial sites, has attracted criticism. In particular, the argument is that SMEs and indigenous firms have been relatively neglected, especially elsewhere in the Borough. Criticism has also been levelled at the local institutions concerning the influence of inward investors in indirectly setting the local economic development agenda. The lengths to which local institutions will go to secure FDI projects was illustrated by the naming of a road 'SemiconductorCo Way' adjacent to the plant which, it was noted, would preclude other FDI projects wanting their address on the same byway. However, some criticisms by the firms concerning local practice were perhaps outside of the control of local institutions and/or were a problem of communication anyway, such as the politicization of local economic development, timing of the infrastructure investments of regional utilities, the opaqueness of the planning system, and, keeping the costs of operating in the Borough down. Also, contradictory signals emerged, with firms simultaneously claiming they were being ignored with regard to the availability of grants once their initial investments were made, and that the intelligence gathering activities of local institutions were occupying too much time.

LOCAL ECONOMIC DEVELOPMENT: IMPLICATIONS AND CONCLUSIONS

The evidence from Sedgefield Borough suggests that the character of East Asian FDI and its influence on local institutions has fallen short of an outright transformation in the fortunes of the local economy. Changes are evident but they appear to reflect an uneven and partial set of shifts. There has been substantial investment in 'state of the art' plants which are currently stable or expanding in output and employment terms. Decision making autonomy has been increased, especially regarding the responsibility for performance and bidding within increasingly competitive intra-corporate investment battles. The hallmarks of foreign-ownership and external control remain evident. The functional range of each plant was relatively broad but with a clear emphasis on financial control and performance. Limited evidence existed of the bolstering of engineering activities, and the bulk of research and technological development functions for the plants took place outside the region. The structural character of the plants has also reinforced the openness of the local economy by tying its fortunes more closely into the increasingly internationalized component supply and product markets. By virtue of their dependence upon imports, the plants are often subject to fluctuating fortunes due to the Sterling:Yen exchange rate.

Much needed employment has been created in the relatively depressed Sedgefield economy by the East Asian FDI, although the total levels are modest in relation to other sources of jobs in the Borough. The workforce is 'feminized', especially at the operator levels, and works within streamlined occupational structures. The common panoply of techniques associated with East Asian 'best practice' is evident with teamworking and flexibility underpinned by the framework of non- or single union plants with mechanisms of trade union recognition and representation different from the Borough's industrial relations traditions. Generally low levels of recruitment now utilize sophisticated screening processes and particular types of labour are sought with the right mixes of skills and experience as well as attitudes. Local and regional sources of labour are significant, despite the increasing regional competition, and investors have participated in networking among local employer-led institutions to exchange labour market information. Skills have expanded horizontally and training has increased with a growing element of specialization. Supplier linkages have incorporated 'leading edge' practices and have internationalized sourcing with mixed implications for the nature of local, regional and international procurement. There is evidence of East Asian 'best practice' among other FDI and indigenous companies in the Borough but these are more clearly explained by broader trends than the effect of greenfield developments nearby. The local business support network has been influenced by the value of East Asian FDI as 'flagships', capable of enticing other FDI of whichever variety to look closely at the District as an investment location. Crucially, the presence of other Japanese companies in the locality has been a stimulus to further East Asian FDI for both greenfield and reinvestment projects. Local economic strategy has become increasingly client-focused and concerned with 'after-care', particularly among FDI and larger firms on the main Aycliffe and Spennymoor industrial sites, to the relative neglect of indigenous firms and SMEs elsewhere in the District.

Developments in Sedgefield Borough appear to suggest that the impact of East Asian FDI on the local economy has been rather less than transformative. Indeed, it can perhaps been seen as naive to expect relatively low levels of investment of a particular national character to promote radical changes in the fortunes of local economies conditioned by enduring historical and social forces that constrain attempts to develop the agency of coalitions of local economic development interest groups. Changes are evident but they represent a partial and uneven mixture which does not always have unproblematic implications for local economic development. Indeed, the latter stages of 1998 witnessed the closure announcement of *SemiconductorCo*. This closure was driven by the collapse of the market for the wafers produced at the plant due to over capacity and the alleged state subsidy to Asian-based manufacturers recycled from the World Bank and IMF loans to these countries due to the Asian financial crisis. *SemiconductorsCo*'s parent company initiated a reorganization plan to reduce capacity, stem losses and restore profitability. The closure of the Newton Aycliffe plant was an explicit part of this strategy. The news of *SemiconductorCo*'s closure represented a grave development for the Sedgefield and North East economies. This 'flagship' plant was considered emblematic of the region's successful record in attracting inward investment and symbolic of the transformation and the industrial future of the region. Once again, however, the legacy of external control and foreign ownership at the heart of the 'branch plant economy' problem returned to haunt the region.

For the Sedgefield Borough economy, East Asian FDI is a small but significant segment. There is evidence of some 'leading edge' characteristics in parallel with traits more reminiscent of previous 'branch plant' industrialization. Problems have become marked due to the closer integration of the local economy into increasingly internationalized product, currency and component sourcing markets, the intensification of work and shifts in the nature of labour sought through recruitment, and reorganized forms of industrial relations which appear alien to the traditions of the Borough. The conclusions for the business support network concern the need to change the focus and apparent control over the local economic development agenda. The evidence suggests that there has been an over-emphasis in the Borough on a sub-set containing large firms and inward investors in the main industrial sites. This focus may become increasingly difficult to sustain due to increased international competition for FDI projects, the feeling that the larger firms and inward investors are influencing the local economic development agenda, and the failure adequately to address other emergent questions in the Borough. These issues comprise: the need to maintain and develop the stock of existing firms – both indigenous and foreign-owned – through promoting inter-firm trading and collaborative linkages; to address the diverse and fragmented needs of SMEs throughout the Borough; and, to encourage employment creation in the smaller and disparate often former mining communities outside the main settlements of Newton Aycliffe and Spennymoor. Given that the experience of Sedgefield Borough has typified the recent experience of the broader North East region in attracting East Asian FDI, the economic development questions faced by the Borough may provide lessons for other localities and the North East region as a whole. If such challenges are confronted sooner rather than later in conjunction with building strong linkages to the emergent agenda and strategy-making of Regional Development Agencies then there is potential for a more balanced local economic development strategy for Sedgefield Borough and the North East region.

ACKNOWLEDGEMENTS

The research upon which this contribution is based was supported by Sedgefield Borough Council (SBC), and forms part of a larger report (Healey *et al*. 1997). We acknowledge the help and advice of Janet Johnson, John Litherland and Richard Prisk from SBC. We would also like to thank Paul Benneworth, Scott Greenwood, Tim Norwood, Damian Thomas, Diccon Whittingham and Michelle Wood for their work on the research underpinning this essay. An earlier version of this paper benefited from comments from colleagues the Centre for Urban and Regional Development Studies (CURDS). We would also like to thank all the firms and business support institutions that participated in the study. The usual disclaimers, as always, apply.

NOTES

1. This paper reports on policy-oriented work conducted for Sedgefield Borough Council (SBC), formerly Sedgefield District Council (SDC) (Pike and Tomaney, 1996) which focused on economic development questions and formed part of a larger project that looked at institutional, social and environmental issues (Healey *et al*., 1997).
2. Sedgefield Borough is divided between the Bishop Auckland and Durham Travel to Work Areas.
3. John Litherland, Planning Director for SBC, commented on the proposed designation of localities in the South East at the time: 'the move out of recession is likely to evaporate

their problems. In our case it's going to be a continuing battle to attempt to achieve self sustaining growth' (quoted in the *Financial Times*, 22 July, 1993).
4. Group interviews were utilized in the broader study (Healey *et al.*, 1997).
5. In 1989, for example, SemiconductorCo's £600m initial investment received £30m Regional Selective Assistance plus an additional £2m through SBC for services and infrastructure channelled through the European Regional Development Fund allocation. Further support is expected when the current reinvestment project comes on stream.

REFERENCES

Amin, A. and J. Tomaney (1991) 'Creating an Enterprise Culture in the North East? The Impact of Urban and Regional Policies of the 1980s', *Regional Studies*, Vol.25, No.5, pp.479–87.

Amin, A., D. Bradley, J. Howells, J. Tomaney and C. Gentle, 1994, 'Regional Incentives and the Quality of Mobile Investment in the Less Favoured Regions of the EC', *Progress in Planning*, Vol.41, No.1, pp.1–112.

Beardwell, I. (1992) 'The "New Industrial Relations"? A Review of the Debate', *Human Resource Management Journal*, Vol.2, No.2, pp.1–7.

Coopers & Lybrand Deloitte (1991) *A Study into the Knock-on Effects of Inward Investment in the English Regions*. HMSO: London.

Dicken, P. and A. Tickell (1992) 'Competitors or Collaborators? The Structure of Inward Investment Promotion in Northern England', *Regional Studies*, Vol.26, No.1, pp.99–105.

Durham County Council and Sedgefield District Council (1983) *The Case Against Closure: Shildon Wagon Works*.

Economists Advisory Group Ltd./IWG, Bonn (1994) *Inward Investment as an Instrument of Regional Industrial Regeneration*, Report for the Anglo-German Foundation for the Study of the Industrial Society. London: Anglo-German Foundation.

Garrahan, P. and P. Stewart (1992) *The Nissan Enigma: Flexibility at Work in the Local Economy*. London: Mansell.

Garrahan, P. and P. Stewart (1994) (Eds) *Urban Change and Renewal: The Paradox of Place*. Aldershot: Avebury.

Healey, P. *et al.* (1997) *The State of the Borough: Main Report*, Report for Sedgefield Borough Council. Sedgefield, Co. Durham: CREUE and CURDS.

HM Government (1994) *Competitiveness – Helping Business to Win*, White Paper, Cm 2563. London: HMSO.

House of Commons (1994a) *The Import and Export of Jobs: The Future for Manufacturing*, Trade and Industry Committee, Session 1993–94, HC 160-I. London: HMSO.

Hudson, R. (1995) 'The Role of Inward Investment' in R. Evans *et al* (Eds.) *The Northern Region Economy*. London: Routledge.

Jung, S-H. (1997) *The Global–Local Interplay of Korean Foreign Direct Investment in the European Union*, Paper for the Regional Frontiers Conference, Frankfurt Oder, 20–23 September (Copy available from the author at Sussex European Institute, University of Sussex, Falmer, Brighton BN1 9QN).

Kenney, M. and R. Florida (1988) 'Beyond Mass Production: Production and the Labour Process in Japan', *Politics and Society*, Vol.16, No.1, pp.121–58.

Mair, A. (1993) 'New Growth Poles? Just-in-time Manufacturing and Local Economic Development Strategy', *Regional Studies*, Vol.27, No.3, pp.207–21.

Morgan K., 1995, 'Institutions, Innovation and Regional Renewal: The Development Agency as Animateur', Paper for Regional Studies Association Conference, Gothenburg, 6–9 May.

Munday, M. *et al.*, (1995) *Working for the Japanese : The Economic and Social Consequences of Japanese Investment in Wales*. London: Athlone Press.

OECD (1996) *OECD in Figures: Statistics on the Member Countries*. Paris: OECD.

Oliver, N. and B. Wilkinson (1988) *The Japanization of British Industry*. Oxford: Blackwell.

Peck, F. and I. Stone (1992) *New Inward Investment and the Northern Region Labour Market*, Research Series No.6, Employment Department, Sheffield.

Peck, F. and I. Stone (1993) 'Japanese Inward Investment in the Northeast of England: Reassessing "Japanisation"', *Environment and Planning C: Government and Policy*, Vol.11, pp.55–67.

Phelps, N. (1993b) 'Branch Plants and the Evolving Spatial Division of Labour: A Study of Material Linkage Change in the Northern Region of England', *Regional Studies*, Vol.27, No.2, pp.87–101.

Pike A, 1996, 'Greenfields, Brownfields and Industrial Policy for the Automobile Industry in the UK' *Regional Studies*, Vol.30, No.1, pp.69–77.

Pike, A. (1998) 'Making Performance Plants from Branch Plants? In-situ Restructuring in the Automobile Industry in UK Region', *Environment and Planning A*, 30, 881–900.

Pike, A. and J. Tomaney (1996) *The State of the Economy in Sedgefield Borough*, Report for Sedgefield Borough Council. Newcastle Upon Tyne: CURDS.

Richardson, R. and J.N. Marshall (1996) 'The Growth of Telephone Call Centres in Peripheral Areas of Britain – Evidence from Tyne and Wear', *Area*, Vol.28, No.3, pp.308–17.

Sedgefield Borough Council (1994) *Continuing the Progress: The Case for the Retention of Assisted Area Status*.

Sedgefield District Council (1996) *Economic Development Strategy, 1995–96*.

Stone, I. (1993) 'Remaking It on Wearside: De-industrialisation and Re-industrialisation', *Northern Economic Review*, Vol.20, pp.6–22.

Stone, I. and F. Peck (1996) 'The Foreign-Owned Manufacturing Sector in UK Peripheral Regions, 1978–1993: Restructuring and Comparative Performance', *Regional Studies*, Vol.30, No.1, pp.55–68.

Williams, K. and C. Haslam (1991) *Factories or Warehouses? Japanese Foreign Manufacturing Investment in Britain and the US*, Occasional Papers on Business, Economy and Society 6. London: Polytechnic of East London.

Williams, K., J. Williams and C. Haslam (1990) 'The Hollowing Out of British Manufacturing and Its Implications for Policy', *Economy and Society*, Vol.19, pp.456–90.

Williams, S. (1997) 'Trade Unionism in the North East', *Northern Economic Review*, Autumn, No.26, pp.86–101.

Young S, N. Hood and E. Peters (1994), 'Multinational Enterprises and Regional Economic Development' *Regional Studies*, Vol.28, No.7, pp.657–77.

7

Managing Culture and the Manipulation of Difference: A Case Study of Second-Generation Transplant

IAN ROBERTS and TIM STRANGLEMAN

This essay explores some of the processes and tensions involved in the introduction and development of management techniques, largely inspired by the Japanese example, into a non-Japanese manufacturing firm in the North East of England. The case is an interesting one from a number of aspects. The enterprise is an established firm in which a radical change in both working practices and culture was consciously engineered by management, primarily inspired by the arrival of a new head of HRM who previously had worked for a Japanese firm in the region. This then represents an attempted case of second-generation cultural diffusion and as such is an interesting development of the question of the generality of Japanese management techniques. Not only is there the perennial question of the relevance and transferability of such techniques into a 'foreign' macro culture but also added to this is the non-Japanese origin of the firm itself. Also unlike the most famous case of Japanese direct investment in the region, namely the Nissan plant (Garrahan and Stewart, 1992; Stephenson, 1996), this firm was not establishing its operation on a greenfield site with a new workforce freshly recruited to meet the specific requirements of the existing organization.

Clearly in the face of such a context an important question must be whether legitimacy of the managerial initiative can be established in this case and does the Japanese connection pose any specific opportunities or difficulties for management or workers? That management should seek to engineer the culture of their firms and employees is hardly a novel aim. Managerial interest in the culture of the firm, and by implication that of its workforce, can perhaps be traced back to the work of F.W. Taylor (1947). His

Ian Roberts, Department of Sociology, University of Durham, Tim Strangleman, International Centre for Labour Studies/Department of Sociology, University of Manchester discussion and study of work practices and the subsequent advocacy of scientific management could be interpreted as a precursor to late twentieth-century writings on the subject. Most famous of these later writings is the work of Peters and Waterman, *In Search of Excellence* (1982), the organizing theme of the book being that the truly successful organization possessed the 'right' culture. The implication is that this culture was something that could, and should, be managed. The present revitalization of a concern with organizational culture is in some senses rather different from its inception in the work of Taylor. His notion of scientific management was built on what he saw as the universalizing potential of the scientific approach, which would indicate the one best way to manage. More recent approaches, while stressing the need for a strong culture, have rather hollowed out universal prescription. Thus James Champy in his book *Reengineering Management: The Mandate for New Leadership* (1995) asks the question 'What kind of culture do we want?' Such a palpably voluntaristic approach to managing culture could be expected to bring with it problems of legitimation. This is exactly what Susan Wright (1994) was alluding to when she critically remarked that culture is being transformed from something an organization *is* to something an organization *has*.

Such a problem suggests why the Japanese example of company culture has achieved a greater imaginative impact than the managerial approach of the last wave of direct foreign investment into the region, overwhelmingly from the USA (Hudson, 1995). It certainly has been greater than the prescriptions of management 'gurus', again overwhelmingly American in origin. The power of the Japanese example perhaps stems from several factors. First, the emergence of the Japanese economy as an economic miracle in the post-war period. Unlike the dominance of the USA, which appeared as a more drawn out evolution of a large country with huge resource endowments, the rise of post-war Japan appeared to occur at a rapid velocity and from the very low base of massive destruction at the end of the Second World War. While evidentially nothing succeeds like success, the perceptual impact of the Japanese miracle was further enhanced by the apparently exotic nature of Japanese culture, combined with a neglect of the material factors behind the 'miracle' (Armstrong, Glyn and Harrison, 1991; Bello, 1992). It was precisely the unlikely combination of the veneration of tradition, inspired by Confucian roots, with obsession for modernization which appeared to offer what US prescriptions could not (Morishima, 1985). Where the latter offered permanent change driven through by strong management, the former appeared to deliver the flexibility of change as the practice of harmony between management and workers. Ultimately what the Japanese example appeared to provide was a grounded account of how workplace culture should be. The enigmatic nature of the cultural exotic would provide the flexibility for management to innovate without the susceptibility and necessity of continual relativistic reinvention and the associated problems of legitimacy apparent in Anglo-Saxon traditions. The combination of a strong legitimate culture with the ability for management to make almost any innovations in the name of that culture (Crosbie, 1995) has proved particularly attractive and provided an elective affinity with the context of the 'new realism' evident in the last decade and a half in Britain in general and 'the Great North' in particular. Such arguably is the meso-context of Japanese emulation, and we now examine whether such a context is realized practically at the level of the organization itself.

CULTURAL CLEANSING AT WORK

The Study

The focus of this article now shifts to research carried out by the authors in the period 1993–96. Examples drawn on form part of a wider study into workplace culture in the engineering and construction industries in the North East of England. This case study is based on an engineering company in the region, here called Engco. The company is a niche supplier of finished equipment in a basically duopolistic product market. Its main competitor is a European manufacturer which has a slightly larger share of the market. The firm employs approximately 400 production staff on one site. The workforce is predominately male and skilled but with a growing female presence.

The fieldwork that forms the basis for this study was carried out in 1995–96 with a number of visits made to the site. In addition to an analysis of company documentation, and a small element of non-participant observation, the main focus of the research was a series of semi-structured interviews with employees. This included talking to respondents from management, supervisory and shopfloor levels. In the case of the latter two groups a selection of workers differentiated along axes of gender, skill and age was obtained. These workers were all chosen by management, although a cross section of views was requested and seems to have been provided. In addition, another highly critical older craft worker had been interviewed as part of the project some time before, outside the factory. While some of the language critical of the company's policy may have been toned down in the 'official' interviews the substantive content was quite similar to that obtained outside.

Changing the Engco Culture

The company has undergone a process of extensive organizational and cultural change over a period of several years. Part of that change has involved sending workers to Japanese firms within the region. Several workers talked of visiting Nissan and Komatsu and even working on projects in these plants. Although the changes at Engco consist of discrete schemes they are seen by the management as a total package aimed at achieving 'World Class' status. Demarcation lines have been removed, with the company moving towards a single status on the shopfloor. In order to achieve this aim work traditionally undertaken by skilled, time served craftsmen using static build methods is now routinely done by semi-skilled workers trained to specific competencies. This latter change is located within a constant flow cellular structure. Interestingly the NVQ route of competence based training and assessment has not been taken. Instead the organization has created a system of internal 'job scopes', a phenomenon identified in several other case studies within the wider research project (Roberts, 1995, 1997). These are sets of descriptions which specify the necessary competencies of a particular role in any of the areas on the shopfloor, described as cells.

The company has put in place a sophisticated Human Resource strategy which records individual workers' competencies with the aim of these job scopes matching those demanded by the cell job scope. The HRM strategy also includes a monthly meeting between an individual worker and their Team Leader who marks their performance against a set of seven categories, collectively described as the 'Philosophy of Work'. These include the more usual requirements, such as total flexibility and continuous improvement, but also workers are marked on the extent to which they 'Share the Vision'. This vision is defined as:

> Where staff participate in helping the company achieve key corporate objectives...and where all share a common vision and a common purpose (Engco document, 1994).

As part of the culture change in the company employees were offered support:

> As a company all...employees will be involved in this new process and training is being provided. Part of the training involves helping people to 'open up' their mind and get rid of any 'mind sets' which they may have, e.g. 'that's not my job' or 'I'm not paid to do that'. This new approach is not welcomed by all employees and the percentage of people who could not foresee themselves accepting change and being trained in new concepts of thinking, decided to leave through the 'window of opportunity' (ibid.).

A Team Leader explained:

> So people who'd worked for a long time, the company chose to open what they called a 'window of opportunity', it wasn't a redundancy situation as such because they had to recruit new people to follow in their jobs....about 42 people chose to take the 'window' and that was there for people who could just not accept that these changes were going to occur (Tape 104: 5).

The Team Leader went on to talk about those that had left:

> So 42 people left, a lot of 'jurassics', that's what we call them, they're like dinosaurs, because they would go extinct...you can have the best machinery or the best factory, but if you're not investing money in the right people you're just putting money down the drain (ibid.).

For both the Team Leader and a manager in the HRM department of the firm the 'jurassics' were more likely to be found among the older, skilled, workers:

> They're the ones you tend to find the trouble with, the
> older ones. That's not something I could statistically back
> up, it's just an observation. They're the ones that can
> remember the good old days, when you built it from start
> to finish, you worked on your own or with your mate, all
> of this. They do tend to be the ones you have trouble with
> because in a way they've lost status, I think that's what the
> problem is – they've lost status (Manager, Tape 102: 5).

What seems to be occurring at Engco is that the management
have attempted to colonize the space within the organization that
hitherto had been an autonomous setting in which the workforce
carved out their own set of practices and understandings. In the
process of changing the culture of the organization management
had invaded such a space and were now defining its content. This
was being carried out under the guise of formal rationality. The
redesign of the labour process and the attitude of the workers who
were to carry it out were both seen to be legitimate areas for
management definition.

The Management of Difference: Gender, Age and Skill

Importantly, however, the workforce was not a homogeneous mass.
They were, as was established above, a mixture of skilled and
unskilled workers who were further differentiated by gender and
age. The issue of gender arose from the move to single status.
Previously all the skilled workers in the factory had been male and
the first level supervisors had been drawn from this pool. After the
change women began to be employed on jobs which had previously
been designated 'skilled'. In addition several of the newly
appointed Team Leaders in the factory, supervising both skilled and
unskilled workers, were female. The Team Leader quoted above
was a member of this newly created grade. Her comments about
the 'jurassics' must also be read with the knowledge of the
opposition she and some of the other women she worked with had
experienced. She explained the response to her promotion to Team
Leader:

> They had one view when I got my £6,000 pay rise, you
> know: 'I'm time-served and you're actually on more
> money'. I try and be positive back, if I can't I've got to

ignore them. If I retaliate I'm just digging my own grave, because I'm just going to get shot down. As I say it's not so much like that now, but very much so getting goaded at the coffee machine and things like that about money, because that's what it boils down to at the end of the day. You want to say 'I'm paid for the responsibility, I've got a lot more responsibility than you for organisational skills, people, products, materials' but you've got to get the coffee and go away (Tape 104: 19).

Change for women in the factory was not necessarily felt negatively, indeed objectively it was advantageous in several respects. First, it allowed them to take higher paid, more responsible jobs such as team leaders. Second, the 'new culture' allowed them the possibility of training up to the highest skill levels practised in the factory without having to go through, or having gone through, a formal apprenticeship. In both cases high, real wage levels were now obtainable.

The women and unskilled workers generally now were able to ask for additional training in new areas so that they could apply for other jobs. One female worker explained:

If you feel you want more training in some areas you go to your team leader and say 'Look, I wouldn't mind some more training in that' to get the beach ball filled in [this refers to the job scope device that is coloured in as new competencies are acquired]. If you go into a new cell, new role, it all contributes towards your training (Tape 106: 15).

The same worker went on to describe her immediate aspirations:

Now I want to go into the test house...I would like to learn the test house. I mean I've never had the chance yet but Val [the team leader] knows that the first opportunity she'll get us in there to train. That's like another string to my bow (ibid.: 16).

But this was not to say that the women had been completely accepted or felt entirely at ease with the new organization. The female worker (Karen) was interviewed with a skilled male colleague who was just out of his apprenticeship and was nearly 20 years her junior. She made a point of emphasizing that the negative attitudes towards the positions women were now occupying were based on a mixture of age as well as gender:

> I think some of the men in here just don't like women working here, that's my point of view, they've got a thing about women coming into their area (ibid.: 23).

Her male colleague then asked her if she felt he thought like that:

> No, but you're like the younger generation. A lot of men don't like women working with them, they'd rather just be a pack of men. There was, in the old factory – they don't like women sort of trying to do the same job (ibid.).

The male colleague, called Rob here, was clearly in a contradictory position. His training with the firm had been a traditional four-year apprenticeship. It had taken the form of both on the job and college experience. Rob was a member of the last cohort of apprentices to be taken on by the firm, and in the future it was indicated that training would take the form of internal promotion based on the job scope system mentioned above. The culture change at Engco was clearly contradictory for Rob as he could see new opportunities had opened up for him, but at the same time he was a product of a system that he respected and he obviously lamented its passing:

> I mean, four apprentices, when I came up there was me and three others and that was it. I haven't seen any more apprentices. It's all things like YT and temporary, all of that. I honestly do think that's a shame. I feel I've learnt a lot and I know a lot about this company (Tape 106: 9).

He went on to define why the apprenticeship had been so valuable:

> It is, I honestly think it's a shame because I know so much about, not the way the company works but the way the machines come together and the way I know how to bring it all together (ibid.).

This would seem to mirror Penn's (1986) understanding of the process by which informal training takes place during the apprenticeship. Rob also sympathized with the older skilled workers who had trained him:

> I talked to a lot of the people and most of them, well many older people...I think they just cannot get used to the new way the factory's going...and I think it's just because of the setting, they will get on with the work and they can do it but I think they just, they probably want it their way. Everyone can probably see their point of view and they see a lot of unskilled people coming in and they maybe would take it as a threat because of their age group. I mean I probably would as well (Tape 106: 7).

At the same time Rob was a beneficiary of the new system and because of his youth in combination with his skilled background he was able to gain promotion and status more quickly. Here again there was an interesting interaction between Karen and Rob over being able to take advantage of this new 'open' culture. Rob described the change in supervision:

> Now everything has been brought down to eye to eye basis and I feel I could go to Chris (production manager) and say exactly what I want to say rather than going through me team leader. I feel really comfortable going and seeing the zone manager and things like that (ibid.: 10).

Karen however did not feel happy doing this and expressed her problem in terms of age:

> I would go through Val to see him, I wouldn't go directly on the shopfloor to see him. I'm 20-odd years older than you but I've got an attitude where my boss is on the pedestal, old-fashioned, non-approachable. It *has* changed but my views haven't changed (ibid.).

It is clear then that even for the beneficiaries of the new culture the results were not entirely positive. Management could defuse adverse comment by appealing to the formal scientific, and hence un-challengeable, methods they were adopting. To oppose such progress was effectively to label oneself a Luddite, or in this case a dinosaur. While most who violently disagreed with the new culture had 'taken the window' there were still voices raised privately in opposition, akin to Casey's (1995) defensive selves.

The Management of Difference: Skill, Age and Gender

This latter group of workers articulated the changes seen at Engco by prioritizing difference in a more traditional sense. One skilled fitter who worked for the company disputed the idea that the company was up-skilling, or multi-skilling its workforce:

> No, it's not multi-skilling, all the people that go around now, they don't have any skills, they just do one menial task, there isn't any skill attached to it at all.... There's two lads who've been brought into one of these cells just the other week, they had a problem, they couldn't line up...these two holes...and a fitter had to point out to them that there was such a thing as a reamer that you put through to line the holes up. They didn't know that. But they can do the job as well as us, according to the management (Tape 6: 29–30).

Interestingly the same worker seemed to resent the position that the semi and unskilled workers were being put in by management – thus demarcation disputes are not necessarily experienced as between workers, rather management were seen as policing areas of skill and demarcation:

> Well you cannot blame them, they're only trying to improve theirselves...it's the management. But they're dropping theirselves in it...because these people are not going to be able to cope...putting pressure on them, I know they're under stress (Tape 6: 35–36).

Another older skilled worker talked of the change in supervision:

> You tend to get very young people being Team Leaders, that was probably the biggest change. I mean in the old days the foremen were always usually the older

people...they would be time-served and probably never been made foreman until they were probably about 45 to 50, whereas then you've suddenly got 21 year olds, possibly taking the job, I could be wrong in this, but basically taking jobs to pay mortgages...That was the snag, it wasn't the job they wanted, they're taking the job for the money and it doesn't really work, they didn't really want the job but they knew if they took the job they get maybe an extra £40...but it doesn't really work like that. It might work in places like Nissan where everyone's young to start with, but I don't think it works too well here (Tape 108: 6).

This same worker linked the changes in supervision with the changes to the organization of the work itself:

Well they brought the Team Leaders in overnight but then they changed to line systems instead of (static build), 'cause a lot of the Team Leaders didn't know the job they were doing. The job had to be broken down into very small components in a lot of areas so, I mean some of us in the previous factory...there was times when I probably never touched the same job again for three months, you know, working each day on something different...But eventually it got down they were trying to get you only to work for an hour and then start and do the same hour's work... (Tape 108: 7).

While it may be true that the two skilled workers quoted above are lamenting a lost status, they are also questioning the management's decision to abandon craft status and adopt a system of training based upon the individual learning a fixed set of fragmented routinized competencies. Those who did voice criticisms of the inflexibility that was apparent under the new culture were marginalized. Part of the power of the new culture was its ability to mediate the interpretation of the past. This is exemplified in a manager's rationalization of terminating recruiting of apprenticed labour:

We haven't taken on apprentices as such for the last few years. Number of reasons for that: One: With the cross training we didn't see the necessity to pay thousands of pounds to train somebody up when we can get somebody in to do the job and they will receive all the training an apprentice would get, effectively, without the cost. Two: The whole apprentice system, if you like, had become discredited. You take somebody in, the first year they're away in college, their second year they are making the coffee and photocopying, their third year they're looking for double headed hammers and the fourth year they actually do a bit of work, at the end of which they get sacked (Tape 102: 10).

When this characterization of the traditional apprenticeship was put to those who had undertaken one it was clear that the description was flawed in several respects. One of the older skilled workers organized his objection to it around the inference that a craft worker, even an apprentice, would be engaged in the performance of menial tasks:

No, you didn't, not the sweeping up – in those days you had labourers that did all the cleaning up and sweeping up and emptying bins, you had none of that, you do more of that now than what you did, housekeeping, that wasn't, you had people employed to do that sort of work them days. You employed people to do certain jobs and that was it (Tape 108: 3).

A time served turner's account of his experience of apprenticeship would also seem to contradict the 'official' characterization:

Did a year's intensive training at their own training centre there and I think there was about a hundred of us started that year. I mean.... R....... is a massive place, had its own internal bus service, big company. We did block release and then after the first year went up to the main factory, the big factory and all split into different departments. Spent so many months doing module system, EITB system [Engineering Industry Training Board], and doing college work at Hebburn Tech...After four years of that you were on the factory floor and on your own (Tape 109: 1).

The traditional apprentice was expected to make a growing contribution to productive work and hence to the cost of his training:

I mean we were on production right from the start really; after about the second year we were actually doing production work (ibid.: 1–2).

This productive aspect is seen to explain the persistence of the apprenticeship in the engineering industry in the post-war era. The decline in the system had more to do with the decline in the British engineering sector and the fact that training was increasingly seen as a cost to be minimized rather than an investment (Elbaum, 1991; Gospel, 1994; Roberts, 1993). The workers interviewed here stressed the formal nature of the scheme, both in terms of the structured training off the job and the contribution they were expected to make in the workplace. This contribution was not simply 'sweeping up'.

What is of importance is the way the past is reinterpreted by management to fit more easily into the present. Thus the 'new culture' is seen to be based on economically rational and thoroughly modern principles as opposed to the traditional 'time served', 'rule of thumb' structure. Perhaps one of the most important differences between the two approaches is the pluralism of the former system. Training seen as a collective practice with input from government, employer, trade union and the skilled workers themselves is replaced by an effectively unitarist structure based on management dictat.

The Quality of Commitment

In spite of the amount of management time and effort spent on the culture change in Engco the resultant new culture was brittle. While a certain, critical, section of the workforce who refused the 'window' may have been marginalized they remain in the factory. Rather than seeing the management style as emphasizing harmony they experience it as dictatorial and authoritarian, often deploying an alternative 'cultural exotic' to frame the experience. As one worker suggested:

> they've decorated the factory with this, what I call Engco confetti, it's posters, labels, booklets, pamphlets, leaflets, flags, banners, things they call spiders webs and they're pasted all over the place. ...You know you've seen them on communist banners...Oh they're right up the factory, right across. Big banners, like communist, Chinese communists. (Tape 6: 33–34)

and at another point:

> It's like they're having a Japanese factory, you know it's ...indoctrination and brainwashing (Tape 6 : 35).

The same worker went on to outline the way in which the authoritarian atmosphere undermined communication between the shopfloor and management:

> they started introducing these team leaders. See – these are the inexperienced, ignorant, insensitive, incompetent people who've been put in charge of these cells, not because of their skills, abilities or experience but just because they're condescending and patronising 'yes-men'. They say what the company wants to hear. They (management) come round but they're totally out of touch, these team leaders will only tell them what they want to (Tape 6: 41–42).

There are of course others who have accepted the changes and replicate what Casey (1995) described as colluding characteristics, but this type of 'self' may well be *less* committed to the organization than the defensive selves were to the older one. This paradox is highlighted in a recent Fabian Society report, '*Changing Work*' (1996). Here the need for ever greater worker commitment in the short term is contrasted to the view that long-term commitment is indicative of a lack of ambition, and therefore perceived negatively by employers.

The quality of this brittleness was illustrated at Engco when the authors returned to the site after a round of redundancies. Interestingly, what had annoyed the workforce was not the fact of redundancies per se, but the way these were implemented and that there had been no prior consultation. The experience was described by a number of interviewees:

> We didn't even know there was one on, but they only started calling names out over the tannoy and somebody said they're paying them off (Tape 108: 8).

Another worker went on:

> Yes, calling people to go to Human Resources. It's like 'I'm going to the firing squad'...'cause there was 30 people in all, and they come and get you, escort you off the premises – they take you to the locker, collect your coat and that and escort, and actually see them off the premises. You know, at a moment's notice. I mean I don't know if they really think somebody would be capable of 'oh they're going to pay us off, I'll go and sabotage something'. I don't think anybody would do it... It's not a nice way to go is it? (Tape 109: 19).

The effect on morale on one of the workers who had been positive about the changes was telling:

> I've been here 21 years now and I've seen them go through all sorts of strange things like that. In the old factory, and we come here and things are improving, they seem to be trying to do things right now. I mean since we've come here there's no doubt about conditions and everything have improved immensely but then something like this happens and you think 'oh what's going on here' (ibid.: 20).

The same worker continued:

> It was just because there was apparently no consultation about it, that was the biggest shock, I'm still not sure whether they were right in what they were doing. I mean I know at the end of the day they're the bosses and it's their factory, but I think the workforce deserves more than a moment's notice. I think no matter who you are you deserve a bit more than that... I'll trust them no

more. It gets everybody's backs up and so what they've been working towards the past few years they've destroyed it all straight away (Tape 109: 20).

Discussion and Conclusion

In analysing the changes to work processes and culture in this case study, we have stressed the unevenness of the effect upon shopfloor workers. In the factory setting, culture change had undoubtedly produced beneficial results for some actors. These were the semi or unskilled workers, some of them women, who gained promotion or extra pay under the new system. For them the management's rhetoric about single status workforce had validity. For others in the organization the result was a loss of status and paralleled diminution of autonomy over their ability to organize work. They were placed in the position of having to train the semi and unskilled workers into their own jobs, simultaneously coping with the problems when these same workers couldn't cope with the full range of problems that were inherent in the task. The new culture therefore effectively marginalized this second set of views by neutralizing them, characterizing them as the last gasps of creatures near extinction.

The result of these processes is to reify the subjective elements of work-based culture. These elements are effectively sequestrated or colonized by management. Workplace culture and organization are then effectively objectified and claimed by management to be formally rational and presented back to the workforce as being a formally scientific process. Collective resistance to such development is made difficult by the changes to the labour process, external labour market conditions, in particular the appeal to Japanese models and the new culture itself, which tend towards individuation of the workers.

There are then several, at first sight contradictory, elements involved in the shift in culture attempted in an extreme way in the engineering case study referred to in this article. First it would seem that the introduction of Japanese, or wider 'Asian' solution on a brownfield site is problematic in several senses. Workplace traditions and culture embedded in the labour process and wider regional economy are the result of decades of autonomous creation by the workforce coupled with market necessity. They are eradicated with difficulty.

Second, the Japanese/East Asian model is itself increasingly viewed as problematic within the Pacific Rim (Berggren, 1995; Bello and Rosenfeld, 1992). Therefore its transfer to a very different political economy must be seen as difficult. The managerial attempt to supplant one 'older' culture with a newer 'realistic' culture involves issues of universalism and individuation, cultural invasion and generational change.

At the most general level it can be suggested that what management have sought to do is replace the postfigurative culture of autonomous craft inspired collective sectionalism with elements of an individuated cofigurative culture. Postfigurative and cofigurative culture are concepts developed by Margaret Mead (1978) to indicate differing ways in which culture is communicated. A postfigurative culture is one in which there is an orderly reproduction between generations where experiential learning is valued as a way of coming to know technique and values. It is arguable that such a postfigurative culture characterized the position of skilled workers in the past where the stable status of the journeyman was valued and communicated to a younger generation by, among other things, forms of anticipatory socialization outlined by Penn (1986).

A cofigurative culture is one that is subversive in respect to the experience of previous generations. As Mead suggests, in such cultures:

> The essential mark of the postfigurative culture – the reversal in an individual's relationship to his own parents – disappears. The past once represented by living people, becomes shadowy, easier to abandon and to falsify in retrospect (Mead, 1978: 49).

It is hopefully not too over-conspiratorial to suggest that where such culture change is being managed, as in the Engco case study, the denigration of the traditional apprenticeship could be seen in these terms. In such cofigurative cultures the past is compressed, a sense of history is lost and the 'young' become the reference group of the younger.

> Adolescents enact their limited and labelled role, with the next younger group as their audience, and full

cofiguration is established in which those who provide the models are only a few years older than those who are learning (Mead, 1978: 49).

Mead suggests that in this sense a cofigurative culture is less 'deep' than a postfigurative culture and may be more easily manipulated. For some organizational members it is more likely to envelop them in a 'culture of silence' (Freire, 1972) than to convert them towards organizational committment.

In dealing with organizations however we must not forget that generational reproduction remains a metaphor, the situation is perhaps more complex than in the reproduction of families. The example of Engco from the engineering industry illustrates that it is not solely the omniscience of the new culture which facilitates the changes undertaken but also the material changes in the division of labour. The move to break down the gender and age proscriptions around the axis of craft have been packaged by the management as representing a triumph for universalism and as thereby liberating individual potential. Clearly such moves have been experienced this way by young team leaders and women workers who occupy positions that would have been unavailable to them with the craft administration of labour.

Such material changes have effectively been legitimized by the appeal to the cultural exotic that 'Japanization' represents. In one register the package is deliberately vague, mystical and beyond scrutiny. Success here is predicated on the intangible nature of the image. But in another register Japanization filtered through a managerialist optic presents itself as a set of ready made prescriptions. Management (in the case of Engco, the HRM manager especially) are seen as white collar anthropologists who have braved the field in order to bring back the solution to the problems of the indigenous culture.

The changes in the labour process and the attempted cultural transformation have been orchestrated around the axes of difference stemming from age and gender. The attack upon the craft administration of labour and the autonomous forms of worker culture therein appears from one perspective as an attack upon an exclusivity based on patriarchal inheritance. Moreover it is true that the position of women has been enhanced, in terms of their very presence in the workplace. However it can be argued that the significance of the deployment of women generally and as Team Leaders in particular, insofar as these changes are allied to an emphasis on youthfulness, is the contribution that they make to a culture of cofiguration. The greater the plasticity of the collective worker and the less embedded any autonomous culture, then the more successful will be management's attempts to define behaviour and beliefs. Ironically what this suggests is not the transcendence of patriarchy but rather the internalization of the perceived passivity of a female and young workforce in the face of managerial patriarchal sponsorship and power.

Moreover the move towards universalism, canonized as formal equality of opportunity accompanied by the decline of collective sectional organization, and the rise of individuated workers (Beale, 1994) have, at best, ambiguous results. As Abercrombie, Hill and Turner have observed:

> We should see such processes as essentially double edged and paradoxical, since individuation means both freedom from particular constraints but also greater opportunities for surveillance and control on the part of a centralised state. (Abercrombie, Hill and Turner, 1986: 155)

So too in relation to complex organizations built on structural inequalities of power accruing from the employment relationship. Such ambiguity allied to the enduring paradox of the commodity status of labour ensures that the coherence and legitimacy of the cofigurative culture cannot be primarily established and unproblematically reproduced, material developments such as the redundancy issue will see to that. In the face of objective events that problematize the viability of unequivocal loyalty, autonomous (that is, non managerially scripted) interpretations will occur. Management attempts at sustaining unitary cofigurative culture are bedevilled – on the one hand by objective material change not always within their control, and on the other hand by a workforce which in generational reproduction, after the first tranche of women workers mature and the young team leaders grow old, will perhaps tend to generate elements of postfigurative culture. Clearly responses which perpetuate a permanent revolution in the age structure of the workforce would incur increased training cost and tend to towards what others have described as organizational amnesia (Strangleman and Roberts, 1997).

One aspect of the managerial response to these tensions has been to attempt to legitimate the changes in the name of formally instrumental rationality as was mentioned above. However, what is really going on here is the substitution of managerial substantive rationality for that of the workers. The appeal is made to the legitimization of formal rationality insofar as it disarms potential critics of the changes, precisely because it is seen as formally rational and therefore beyond debate. Such an explanation facilitates an understanding of the increasing reliance on control systems and 'bench marking' devices which again introduce a formally rational gloss to what is essentially a substantively rational process.

Thus companies will wear the badge of 'Investors in People', as Engco did, at the same time as their personnel policies and work practices deskill the labour process and degrade the experience of work for many in the organization. Any allusion to the latter experience will instantly be marginalized by the appeal to the logic of the company's possession of the badge of 'Investors'. The circle is closed.

There would appear to be several issues that flow from such an understanding of this use of culture. First it would seem that by its very nature the new culture has to attack that of the older.

> Any theory that assumes that culture is the internalisation
> of dominant norms and values, must also assume that all
> members must hold the dominant value system or else be
> 'outside culture'. (Lynn-Meek, 1988: 458)

In the engineering company described above this marginalization took several forms. There was the 'opening the window of opportunity', the reorganization and fragmentation of work tasks which broke down established patterns of social relations; and finally there was the intellectual assault on the workforce to simultaneously build up the new culture and denigrate that of the past.

Such an approach, buttressed by a sophisticated HRM strategy, would seem to erode an older collective, and essentially spontaneous work culture. That is the culture of lived experience in E.P. Thompson's (1968) sense of the phrase, and in Wright and Lynn-Meek's understanding of culture as a living thing, that which a company *is*. While management's understanding and conceptualization of 'how culture works' may be wrong, their actions in attempting culture change are potentially extremely damaging to the autonomous culture. In this sense, as Guest (1992) has suggested in another context, the managerial understanding of culture may be 'right enough to be dangerously wrong'. It would also seem that while management may be able to marginalize the older culture this is only a temporary phase. For those that remain within the organization are active elements of a living culture that is the product of lived experience. Thus collusion in the new corporate culture lasts only as long as the next 'opening of the window'.

ACKNOWLEDGEMENTS

We would like to thank the Economic and Social Research Council for supporting the project from which this case study is drawn. Thanks also to Professor Richard K. Brown for commenting upon an earlier draft of this paper.

REFERENCES

Abercrombie. N., S. Hill. and B.S. Turner (1986), *Sovereign Individuals of Capitalism*. London: Allen & Unwin.

Armstrong, P., A. Glyn, and J. Harrison, (1991), *Capitalism Since 1945*. Oxford: Blackwell.

Beale, D. (1994), *Driven by Nissan? A Critical Guide to New Management Techniques*. London: Lawrence & Wishart.

Bello. W. (1992), *People and Power in the Pacific*. London: Pluto.

Bello. W. and S. Rosenfeld (1992), *Dragons in Distress*. London: Penguin.

Berggren, C. (1995). 'Japan As Number Two: Competitive Problems and the Failure of Alliance Capitalism After the Burst of the Bubble Boom', in *Work, Employment and Society*, Vol.9, No.1 (March), pp.53–95.

Casey, C. (1995), *Work, Self and Society After Industrialism*. London: Routledge.

Champy, J. (1995), *Reengineering Management: The Mandate for NewLeadership*. London: Harper Collins.

Crosbie, A. (1995), 'The Japanese Model, Transnational Production and the North East', in *Northern Economic Review*, No.24 (winter), pp.32–47.

Elbaum, B. (1991), 'The Persistence of Apprenticeship in Britain and Its Decline in the United States' in H.F. Gospel (ed.) *Industrial Training and Technological Innovation*. London: Routledge.

Fabian Society (1996), *Changing Work*. London.

Freire, P. (1972), *Pedagogy of the Oppressed*. London: Penguin.

Garrahan, P. and P. Stewart (1992), *The Nissan Enigma*. London: Mansell.

Gospel, H.F. (1994), 'The Survival of Apprenticeship Training: A British, American, Australian Comparison'. *British Journal of Industrial Relations* 32: 4: 505–22.

Guest, D. (1992), 'Right Enough to Be Dangerously Wrong: An Analysis of the "In Search of Excellence" Phenomenon' in G. Salaman (ed.) *Human Resource Strategies*. London: Sage.

Hudson, R. (1995), 'The Role of Foreign Inward Investment' in L. Evans, P. Johnson and B. Thomas (eds) *The Northern Region Economy*. London: Mansell.

Lynn-Meek, V. (1988), 'Organizational Culture: Origins and Weakness'. *Organizational*

Studies, Vol.9, No.4, pp.453–73.
Mead, M. (1978), *Culture and Commitment*. New York: Doubleday.
Morishima, M. (1984), *Why Has Japan Succeded?* Cambridge: Cambridge University Press.
Penn, R.D. (1986), 'Socialisation into Skilled Identities'. Unpublished paper to the Labour Process Conference.
Peters, T. and H. Waterman., (1982), *In Search of Excellence*. London: Harper & Row.
Roberts, I.P. (1997), 'The Culture of Ownership and the Ownership of Culture' in R.K. Brown (ed.) *The Changing Shape of Work*. London: Macmillan
Roberts, I.P. (1995), 'Rationality in Training: Change in the Engineering and Construction Industries', in M. Erikson. and S. Williams (eds) *Social Change in Tyne and Wear*. Sunderland: Black Cat Publications.
Roberts, I.P. (1993), *Craft, Class and Control: The Sociology of a Shipbuilding Community*. Edinburgh: Edinburgh University Press.
Stephenson, C. (1996), 'The Different Experiences of Trade Unionism in Two Japanese Transplants' in P. Ackers., C. Smith and P. Smith. (eds) *The New Workplace and Trade Unionism*. London: Routledge.
Strangleman, T.E. and I.P. Roberts (1997), 'Social Reproduction, Social Dislocation and the Labour Market', in C.J. Kristensen (ed) *The Meeting of the Waters: Individuality, Community and Solidarity*. Copenhagen: Scandinavian University Press.
Taylor, F.W. (1947), *The Principles of Scientific Management*. New York: Harper Row.
Thompson, E.P. (1968), *The Making of the English Working Class*. London: Penguin.
Wright, S. (ed.) (1994), *Anthropology of Organizations*. London: Routledge.

8

The Transformation of Employment Relations in the UK's Old Industrial Regions: A Regional Comparison of the Experience of Japanization

ANDREW CUMBERS

In the past two decades the employment landscape of the UK's old industrial regions has been transformed as a result of the destruction of the traditional industries and the shift towards service-based forms of employment and new manufacturing industries, often associated with foreign inward investment. A major component of this transformation has been the influx of Japanese owned firms, driven by globalization strategies and the desire to take advantage of opportunities in the emerging Single European Market. Older industrial regions have proved attractive locations for such investments because of the availability of large reserves of manual labour, released from traditional forms of work by processes of deindustrialization, and also because of the huge start-up subsidies available from national and European regional development agencies. Nissan, for example, received £112 million from the UK government for the first phase of development in setting up its car manufacturing plant outside Sunderland in the North of England in 1986 (Garrahan and Stewart, 1992a). Within the UK, the two regions that have attracted the lion's share of Japanese manufacturing investment – though not services (see Dicken et al., 1997) – in recent years are South Wales and the North East of England. The employment impact of Japanization has been substantial; in Wales 28 firms were established between 1972 and 1991 with the creation of over 13,000 jobs (Wilkinson et al., 1993). In the North East, Japanization has been a more recent and intense phenomenon than in Wales with over 11,000 jobs being created between 1985 and 1993 (Hudson, 1994). The dominant sectors for investment have been automobile

Andrew Cumbers, Department of Geography, University of Aberdeen manufacture (more dominant in the North East) and consumer electronics (more prominent in South Wales).

While there is no doubting the scale of the economic impact of Japanese firms,[1] it has also been claimed that these developments are fundamentally transforming the nature of employment relations in the two regions. There is some debate however about the nature of this transformation. According to one set of commentators, Japanization is resulting in the development of a new consensus on the shopfloor replacing more adversarial relationships between capital and labour, because of the particular requirements of the Japanese production system based around Just-in-Time management practices (Wickens, 1988; Wilkinson et al., 1993). Alternatively, another group of researchers have suggested that Japanization represents the attempt by management to reassert more direct forms of control, commensurate with the return of more coercive and Taylorist methods of work organization (Garrahan and Stewart, 1992a). Yet another school of thought suggests that the concept of Japanization as a new universal model of production organization and employment relations is itself open to question, given the enormous variation between firms, sectors and geographical context in which Japanese firms operate (Elger and Smith, 1994; Williams et al., 1992).

This contribution examines the experience of Japanization in South Wales and the North East, placing it within the context of on-going changes in employment relations in the two regions. It focuses explicitly upon the consequences of what Ackroyd et al. (1988) have termed 'direct' Japanization – the new forms of Japanese inward investment that have taken place since the mid 1970s – rather than the more pervasive and indirect influences of Japanese production practices on domestic firms. The argument is that, while there is no disputing the magnitude of current changes taking place, we need to be wary about conceptualizing Japanization as being unique or separate from other on-going changes in the employment environment. Rather than helping to bring about a new and more consensual employment environment Japanization must be seen as one strand of a shift towards a more coercive set of employment relations in an attempt by management to re-establish control over labour in the workplace. The remainder of the essay is divided into four main sections. The first section outlines in brief the nature of traditional forms of employment relations in the two regions. This is followed by an analysis of the broader changes taking place in the current period. This then forms the context in which to examine the experience of Japanization in the two regions in the third section. The essay then concludes with some remarks about the significance of Japanese firms in re-shaping the employment environment in the context of wider on-going changes.

THE EVOLUTION OF EMPLOYMENT RELATIONS IN SOUTH WALES AND THE NORTH EAST

The impact of Japanese firms in South Wales and the North East of England can only be understood in the context of the historical development of employment relations in the two regions. The regions share common industrial traditions and employment legacies as a result of their involvement in an early stage of industrial capitalism from about 1840 to 1920 geared to the production of capital goods – or Department 1 industries (Aglietta, 1979). During this period, the two regions developed their own particular systems of employment regulation and work organization centred upon the heavy industries of coal mining, chemicals, iron and steel and the related downstream industries of heavy engineering and shipbuilding. There was some variation in the culture of employment relations between places, reflecting the importance of different industries and employment experiences. In the coalfield areas a more inclusive working class consciousness developed. Typically, a single employer – the local colliery – would be the focus for entire communities, encouraging forms of social cohesion and collective resistance to capital that are rarely found in more diverse local labour markets. Consequently, South Wales in particular earned a reputation as a militant/radical region (Cooke, 1982). Alternatively, in the coastal districts of North East England, a very different labour market culture developed, centred upon craft-based production. Here, the basis for organized labour was the preservation of individual craft skills, rather than a collective class consciousness. Although union organization and worker representation were highly developed, they tended to be fragmented between the different trades, and internecine conflict was often a more important element in defining employment relations than the conflict between capital and labour. In addition, the labour markets in these areas were highly fluid and for the majority of workers the work experience was characterized by a succession of jobs with different firms rather than a more stable career with a single employer.[2]

In the twentieth century, the protracted decline of these industries and the failure to develop new consumer industries left its own legacy with respect to the organization of work in the two regions (see Table 1). For it meant that in the post-war period (1945–70) these areas never made the full transition to the Fordist forms of employment relations that have been viewed as characteristic of more modern industrial regions (Piore and Sabel, 1984). In shipbuilding and heavy engineering, for example, production continued to revolve around the manufacture of either single unit, non-standardized products, or small batch produced goods for markets where demand was often highly irregular. Under these circumstances the labour process continued to be craft based, corresponding to Friedman's (1977) concept of 'Responsible Autonomy'. In addition, there was only a very limited form of internal labour market development and firms continued to marginalize large elements of the workforce from permanent forms of employment.

Some forms of Fordist style production did develop from the 1930s onwards. In particular, mass consumption industries such as food, clothing and electronics became important sources of employment (Austrin and Beynon, 1979; Lovering, 1979; Massey, 1984; Hardill, 1990). These industries were predominantly involved in low-skilled branch plant operations, often under foreign ownership with US firms being especially important. Significantly though, up until the 1970s, these industries were aimed at drawing women into the labour market – often on a part time basis – rather than re-employing the existing (and predominantly male) workforce in standardized permanent forms of employment (Glucksman, 1990).[3]

Overall, it is clear that right up to the 1970s, employment relations in both South Wales and the North East continued to be organized on a 'non-Fordist basis of extensive rather than intensive accumulation' (Hudson, 1988: 158). Indeed, as late as 1978, and despite their long term decline, the traditional heavy industries of coal mining, steel production, chemicals, heavy engineering and shipbuilding still accounted for over half of all industrial employment in both regions (NOMIS database). A recognition of the enduring influence of these 'older' industries and the distinctive

TABLE 1
INDUSTRY AND EMPLOYMENT LEGACY IN SOUTH WALES AND THE
NORTH EAST 1840–1970

Product markets	Capital goods – Department 1
Type of industry	Large scale, heavy industry (e.g. coal, heavy engineering, shipbuilding, steel)
Labour process	Craft based, responsible autonomy
Employment structure	Limited internal labour market development, primarily occupational labour markets
Industrial relations	Voluntarist, bilateral agreements between trade unions and employers' associations

cultures of employment regulation with which they were associated is crucial to understanding the character and significance of changes in the contemporary era.

THE RESTRUCTURING OF EMPLOYMENT RELATIONS IN THE CONTEMPORARY ERA: PUTTING JAPANIZATION IN CONTEXT

In the period since the 1970s employment relations in the two regions have been transformed by the destruction of traditional industries and the growth of new forms of work in services and inward investment-led manufacturing. The growth in employment in services has only partially compensated for the decline in manufacturing work, so that the overall scale of job loss has been dramatic (Table 2). At the same time, there has been a major shift in the nature of employment with the most dramatic changes being a decline in the proportion of male and full-time forms of employment and an increase in female and part-time employment (Table 3).

Just what kind of change is taking place in the nature of employment relations alongside such developments is a matter for considerable debate. For some (Morris and Hill, 1991, Price et al., 1994), the most recent wave of manufacturing inward investment – especially that by Japanese companies – is helping to upgrade the employment environment and is of a much higher quality than the low-skilled screwdriver image of earlier waves of branch plant activity (Firn, 1975). For others however, the current period is characterized by attempts by management to reassert control over

TABLE 2
THE PROCESS OF DEINDUSTRIALIZATION, 1978–95
(EMPLOYMENT CHANGE IN MANUFACTURING AND SERVICES)

	Wales			Northern		
	1978	1995	% change	1978	1995	% change
Manufacturing	349,268	208,387	–40	472,191	232,765	–51
Services	557,245	667,117	20	643,283	735,484	14
All	1,015,316	945,707	–7	1,240,504	1,046,453	–16

[*Source*: NOMIS database]

TABLE 3
THE PERIPHERALIZATION AND FEMINIZATION OF WORK, 1978–95

	Wales				Northern			
	1978	(%)	1995	(%)	1978	(%)	1995	(%)
Male	613,211	60	475,949	50	748,329	60	522,361	50
Female	402,105	40	469,709	50	492,175	40	524,041	50
Part–time	177,768	18	262,193	28	230,124	19	300,118	29
Full–time	837,548	82	683,466	72	1,010,380	81	746,286	71
All	1,015,316	100	945,707	100	1,240,504	100	1,046,453	100

[*Source*: NOMIS database]

labour and, as Hudson puts it, to develop 'corporate strategies to preserve Fordist mass production of standardized commodities by carefully locating new capacity in OIRs and raising productivity via selective recruitment and intensification of the pace of work' (Hudson, 1988: 162). Here, the changes taking place are reviewed along three different dimensions (Table 4): first at the level of the labour process; second, with regard to employment structure; and, finally, by examining the industrial relations environment.

Overall, changes in the labour process have typically been depicted in terms of the erosion of archaic and traditional forms of work with the dismantling of existing systems of demarcation and the introduction of newer and more flexible working practices (Hudson, 1988; Morgan and Sayer, 1988). This is certainly true of the newer manufacturing industries. In their study of the electrical engineering industry in South Wales, for example, Morgan and Sayer have suggested that (1988: 177):

TABLE 4
CHANGES IN EMPLOYMENT RELATIONS IN SOUTH WALES AND THE NORTH
EAST SINCE 1970

Dimension	Nature of change taking place
Labour process	New forms of managerial control in incoming industries (e.g. automobile, consumer electronics)
	Increased flexibility = intensification of work in existing industries (e.g. coal, steel, financial services)
Employment organization	Widespread use of flexible employment strategies in incoming industries and growth sectors (e.g. automobile, consumer electronics, tourism, retail)
	Increased numerical flexibility in existing industries (e.g. steel, financial services, public sector)
	Partial take-up of flexible manpower strategies elsewhere (e.g. auto components, heavy engineering)
Industrial relations	Changing balance of power in labour market
	New agreements with incoming firms (e.g. single union deals, no-strike agreements)
	Derecognition of unions in some firms, especially following external acquisition
	Low levels of union recognition in service growth sectors (e.g. retailing, tourism

the most distinctive feature of the work practices of the newer firms is their emphasis on *flexibility*: reduced demarcation, allowing wider margins of discretion over job allocation was apparent not only in comparison to the traditional coal and steel industries but also to the longer established electrical engineering plants. Demarcation is now under attack from recession, new foreign firms and new management 'philosophies'. Such flexibility was most pronounced in the wholly-owned Japanese plants in the consumer electronics sector.

Similar points have been made about new manufacturing developments in the North East of England (Garrahan and Stewart, 1992a). Elsewhere however, the nature of change in working practices varies enormously between different sectors and industries. In some traditional industries – notably steel and heavy engineering industries (Blyton, 1993; Cumbers, 1994) – attempts have been made to introduce more flexible methods of working that mirror developments in the new industries, but in other areas changes have a completely different rationale. For example, in coal mining during the 1980s, there was considerable restructuring of production, which involved more automation and the reorganization of work. But this represented the increased Taylorization of production, rather than a move towards greater flexibility (Hudson, 1988). Similarly, the majority of jobs created in the service sector in both regions have been in routinized unskilled forms of work, especially retailing (Lovering, 1996; Brown, 1994).

In both regions there is also considerable evidence of a trend towards more flexible recruitment strategies and employment conditions. For example, Morris's (1988) study of 100 manufacturing firms in South Wales discovered an increase in both the subcontracting-out of work and in the use of contractual forms of employment, though notably only a small increase in the use of part-time workers. Although it is usually claimed that incoming firms have spearheaded the introduction of new patterns of labour force recruitment (Hudson and Sadler, 1992), some of the more profound changes have been in the traditional industries. For example, Fevre's (1986; 1987) work on the steel industry in South Wales has identified a considerable increase in subcontracting and other temporary forms of employment in place of more permanent forms of work. Similar trends have been apparent in the chemicals and steel industries in the North East (Beynon et al., 1994). But the greatest changes appear to be occurring in the service sector, in public sector services where there has been direct government pressure to contract out more work and in some of the growth areas of the private sector such as retailing and tourism, where as Brown puts it: 'much of the work ... is in low-paid, low-skilled, part-time positions, predominantly filled by women' (1994: 183). In the North East for example, Thomas (1994) suggests that two thirds of all new tourist-related jobs are part-time jobs for women.

Perhaps the most fundamental change in employment relations in the two regions in recent times has been in industrial relations. Once again, it is the case that where start-up plants are concerned new agreements have been commonplace, particularly on greenfield sites away from established areas of trade union strength. In addition, the continuing high levels of unemployment in many traditional industrial areas have created the conditions in which unions have been prepared to sacrifice long established agreements in return for any kind of job. However, while such developments clearly signal a pragmatic change in attitude by trade union officials, this does not automatically imply the final demise of organized labour in the two regions. For, as Martin *et al.* (1993, 1996) demonstrate, union densities in the North East and South Wales continue to be over 40 per cent of the total workforce – far higher than in other parts of the UK – during a period in which the government has actively encouraged employers to derecognize trade unions.

JAPANIZATION IN THE OLD INDUSTRIAL REGIONS: SOUTH WALES AND THE NORTH EAST COMPARED

The significance of Japanese firms in remaking the employment landscape in both South Wales and the North East has to be considered within the context of the changes outlined above. It also needs to be remembered that Japanese inward investment has taken place against the backdrop of a government in power committed to attacking the power of trade union organization and deregulating the labour market. Government policy under the Conservative regime from 1979 to 1997 was based around the desire to 're-establish the right of capital to manage' (Holloway 1987: 148). This has provided considerable momentum and opportunity for new firms setting up in the two regions to dramatically reshape the character of employment relations.

Japanization as a New Model of Employment Relations

In the minds of its supporters the Japanese employment model is a fundamental component of the system of Lean Production, which was instrumental in giving Japanese firms global competitive advantage in the 1970s and 1980s (Kenney and Florida 1988; Womack *et al.*, 1990). While there are various celebrated individual features of the Japanese production system (Just-in-Time, Quality Circles, Total Quality Control, flexible working practices) the underlying philosophy – and the feature that marks it out from Fordism – is a commitment to continuous learning, or *kaizen,* allied to more flexible production methods (Oliver and Wilkinson, 1992). The significance of this for the social relations of production is that they require much greater levels of interaction and communication between firms, suppliers and workers than was present under Fordism. The labour problem becomes one in which 'senior managers must find ways of living with high-dependency relations' (Oliver and Wilkinson, 1992: 3). The outcome of this is the development of forms of work based around high-trust and consensus between managers and workers, in which the latter are more fully incorporated into the decision-making process than was present in Fordism. These ideas have been subject to extensive criticism elsewhere (for example, Williams *et al.*, 1992; Wood, 1992; Garrahan and Stewart, 1992, Elger and Smith, 1994) and it is not the purpose here to add to the debate. Instead, I have drawn up a stylized version of the shift in employment relations entailed in moving from a Fordist employment regime to a Japanese one (Table 5). This is used as a heuristic device in examining the significance of Japanization in the North East and South Wales.

Taken in its entirety, an idealized Japanese employment system contains three components. In the first place, and perhaps the most significant departure from existing capitalist social relations, is a radical change in the nature of the labour process. Typically this is depicted as a shift away from the deskilled and intensive division of labour associated with Fordist assembly work towards the multi-skilling and multi-tasking of labour. Henry Ford's philosophy of single task, repetitive work becomes inverted so that the worker moves rapidly and efficiently between tasks as and when required. In addition the alienation of workers, both from one and other and from managers under the direct Taylorist control regime characteristic of Fordism (Braverman, 1974) has been replaced by an environment centred more upon team-working and responsible autonomy (Friedman, 1978). Secondly, Japanization is associated with a set of changes in the conditions of employment and in particular the need to construct high trust relations between managers and workers. This includes the replacement of 'hire and fire' attitudes with greater job security, the collapse of hierarchical internal labour markets into a smaller number of grades and the development of single status regimes; and a greater commitment to training and upgrading the skills of workers. More recent research has pointed out that in reality an extensive dual labour market exists in Japan itself with only about one quarter of the workforce – and usually those in the larger firms such as Nissan and Toyota – enjoying high levels of job security (Elger and Smith, 1994). The remainder constitute a peripheral workforce with employment becoming more precarious the further one moves from the centre of subcontractor networks. Finally, underpinning these developments is the shift away from adversarial class-based

TABLE 5
A STYLIZED DEPICTION OF THE SHIFT FROM FORDISM TO A JAPANESE
SYSTEM OF EMPLOYMENT REGULATION

	Fordism	Japanization
Labour process	direct control single task division of labour	responsibe autonomy multi-skilling and flexibility
Employment structure	hierarchical 'hire and fire' recruitment strategy	single status secure employment commitment to upgrading and skill enhancement
Industrial relations	class conflict adversarial	corporate ethos and identity consensual

industrial relations towards a more consensual harmonious set of relations on the shopfloor based upon identification with the company rather than a class position.

The Realities of Japanization in South Wales and the North East

The empirical evidence of Japanization in South Wales and the North East provides a picture of an employment environment a long way from the idealized model described above. Regarding the labour process, the evidence suggests that the changes taking place in both regions are more contingent upon particular market and sectoral conditions that on any universal Japanese model. Taking the North East for example, Peck and Stone's (1993) study found an enormous variation in the kind of working practices being pursued, ranging from strategies that were identifiable with a responsible autonomy management control philosophy in the more sophisticated engineering plants to strategies synonymous with direct Taylorist forms of control in consumer electronics factories. Other research suggests that in practice, claims of multi-skilling often equate with multi-tasking, where the purpose is to eliminate down-time rather than create a new category of flexible skilled craft-worker (Pike and Tomaney forthcoming).

In South Wales, where there is a greater concentration of assembly line activities, the idealized Japanese labour process is even more difficult to find. For example, Danford's survey of 15 Japanese firms across four industrial sectors suggests that if anything Japanization has led to the intensification of the labour process through stricter supervision and discipline procedures, reduced downtime and the increased pace of work (Danford, 1995). *Kaizen* in South Wales translates into a 'Japanese obsession with reducing idle time and squeezing out 60 minutes worth of useful work in every hour' (Danford, 1995: 20) rather than continuous improvement through eradicating material waste and upgrading quality. Symbolizing this system was a bell-to-bell working routine – found in all the companies he surveyed – which was strictly enforced by supervisors. Clearly, such a regime is far closer to Taylorism and Braverman's view of the labour process (1974) than the Lean Production model.

In both South Wales and the North East, the Japanese labour process is often structured along gender lines, reinforcing the type of employment regime that has developed in the new consumer industries in the post-war era (Delbridge, 1998; Pike and Tomaney, forthcoming). Women predominate in many of the low-skilled, low wage assembly line activities, while men are dominant in the higher skilled engineering and technician jobs.

The evidence of the idealized Japanese model is even more difficult to come by in regard to the conditions of employment and recruitment practices. While job security is relatively high among the more skilled workers in high profile firms such as Nissan, the experience elsewhere suggests a more transient and casualized employment environment. Danford's study (1995) in South Wales for example revealed high levels of labour turnover within Japanese firms, while Crosbie's research (1995) found signs of the Japanese dual labour market system being transferred to the North East, with Nissan's suppliers displaying highly flexible employment strategies centred upon a low-paid, low skilled and less secure peripheral workforce' (1995: 45). Evidence of single status workplaces was lacking in Danford's study, although Peck and Stone (1993) did come across some cases in the more sophisticated engineering sectors where the reality matched the rhetoric. These were however exceptions rather than the rule. It appears that in practice, most Japanese plants in Britain have extremely hierarchical internal labour markets, with a marked schism between workforce and management (see Taylor *et al.*, 1994 on this point). It is also worth noting that Japanese recruitment strategies are themselves highly discriminatory and divisive, carefully screening applicants to eliminate workers who are 'contaminated' with older and more traditional views about employment relations (Garrahan and Stewart, 1992a).

While Japanese firms do generally have a better record with regard to training than many other inward investors and indigenous firms, the training is often highly firm-specific in nature and does not provide workers with the diverse range of skills and experience that would make them marketable in the external labour market. As Garrahan and Stewart note with reference to Nissan:

> Nissan creates skills which are only of practical value inside the organisation. It is not the case that generalised multi-skilling occurs. From our interviews, it is clear that many ex-engineers and fitters, whose skills are still in demand outside Nissan, found that what passed for multi-skilling was really knowledge of a number of general and cognate tasks. These are almost entirely company specific (1992: 84).

The transformative role of Japanese firms appears greatest with regard to industrial relations. In particular, the shift from multi-union to single union and non-union workplaces and the introduction of no-strike agreements have been heralded as important new developments (Wilkinson et al., 1993). The evidence suggests that non-union deals have been greater in the North East, particularly in the new town areas and greenfield sites away from union strongholds in the coastal districts; in Peck and Stone's (1993) study over 50 per cent of firms were non-unionized. By comparison, in South Wales only two out of the 28 companies that have been established since 1972 are non-unionized (Wilkinson et al., 1993).

The 'new industrial relations' (Wilkinson et al., 1993) has been taken by some to represent the demise of worker resistance and organized labour. In this vein for example, Garrahan and Stewart (1992) note the irrelevance and impotence of the union at Nissan, where only 30 per cent of workers were members anyway, and the success with which the firm was developing its own corporate sense of identity among workers. In many cases, union convenors and officials have been co-opted onto company-based labour control schemes. This has led some to stress the role of Japanization in constructing a less adversarial and more consensus based work environment (for example, Wickens, 1987). The decline in the level of strikes and the pliant attitude of unions is also taken as indicating a more harmonious industrial relations environment (Wilkinson *et al.*, 1993). In the main, such findings are often based upon interviews with managers and trade union officials and could be interpreted as a best practice 'wish list' rather than as a set of concrete realities. Other more detailed research that has been conducted with workers and supervisors on the shopfloor, suggests a rather different picture in which a considerable degree of latent hostility and informal resistance to Japanese management strategies exists within the workforce (Delbridge, 1997; Graham, 1994; Danford, 1995; Palmer, 1996). While the level of overt industrial conflict in both South Wales and the North East might have been reduced so that the two regions can boast of 'excellent' industrial relations in trying to attract new sources of inward investment, this does not necessarily equate with a more deep-seated transformation of the industrial relations environment. It should also be remembered that other more covert forms of worker resistance exist, for as Thompson and Ackroyd (1995: 629) have pointed out: 'innovatory employee practices and informal organization will continue to subvert managerial regimes'. It might also be the case that Japanese firms in the two regions have been enjoying a 'honeymoon' period with regard to industrial relations (Elger and Smith, 1994: 54). Traditional forms of conflict might well re-surface in the longer term.

CONCLUSION

It is clear from the body of work reviewed in this essay that there is little evidence to suggest a shift towards the idealized Japanese style model of employment relations in either the North East or South Wales. At one level there is, as Hudson puts it (1994: 86): 'considerable heterogeneity in the labour requirements, recruitment strategies, forms of work organization and regimes of labour process control'. In other words the impact of Japanese firms varies enormously between different sectors and product markets. If anything, there is slightly more evidence of the upgrading of employment relations in the North East than in South Wales, although once again the pattern is highly variable (Peck and Stone, 1993). In South Wales, the changes reported by Danford suggest a shift towards a more Taylorist style of control regime with stricter supervision and management control. The most significant changes are in the area of industrial relations, where single-union deals and no-strike agreements in particular represent something of a departure from existing arrangements, although the extent to which they can be viewed as distinct from other on-going changes is another matter. Whether the low levels of worker resistance and industrial relations conflict reported are a permanent feature of the new landscape must however be open to question.

Overall, and with a few innovations in management culture aside, the impression is that the changes brought about by Japanese firms in South Wales and the North East have been working with the grain of the on-going changes in the employment landscape described earlier. In this sense, they represent part of an on-going shift in the past two decades away from an older and somewhat narrowly-based working culture dominated by heavy industry, craft-based forms of production and male-dominated work, towards a broader set of employment circumstances in new manufacturing and service activities, which involves women in the workforce in equal numbers, but often in non-standardized low wage and unskilled work. It is also worth recalling the enthusiasm with which the Conservatives pursued and sponsored Japanese inward investment during the 1980s. The then Prime Minister, Margaret Thatcher, encouraged Japanese firms to set up in the old industrial regions in the first place, precisely because she thought their management style fitted in with her own hegemonic mission to destroy the power of organized labour (Garrahan, 1986). In this sense, if there is a more general conclusion that can be reached about something called Japanization in the two regions, it is linked to attempts to establish what Garrahan and Stewart (1992b: 107) have termed a 'new regime of subordination and management control'. Japanization in South Wales and the North East does not represent a radical new departure in employment relations, but it has been one strand of a wider and extremely powerful project by both the state and management to delegitimize worker represen-tation, attack the principles of collective bargaining and encourage a cult of individualism.

NOTES

1. Although it should be noted that US firms are still the single most important source of inward investment in both regions.
2. For evidence of this see Mess's famous report on the Tyneside labour market (1928).
3. Indeed, during the 1950s the state, under pressure from the larger established employers, had actively discouraged diversification into new industries that would have drawn male workers away from traditional heavy industries due to worries about skill shortages (Beynon *et al.*, 1986).

REFERENCES

Ackroyd, S., G. Burrell, M. Hughes and A. Whitaker (1988) 'The Japanization of British Industry?' *Industrial Relations Journal*, Vol.19, No.1, pp.11–23.
Aglietta, M. (1979) *A Theory of Capitalist Regulation.* London: New Left Books.
Austrin, T. and H. Beynon (1979) *Global Outpost: the Working Class Experience of Big Business in the North East of England*, University of Durham mimeo.
Beynon, H., R. Hudson and D. Sadler (1986) 'Nationalised Industry Policies and the Destruction of Communities: Some Evidence from the North East of England', *Capital and Class*, Vol.29, pp.27–58.
Beynon, H., R. Hudson and D. Sadler (1994) *A Place called Teesside: A Locality in a Global Economy.* Edinburgh: Edinburgh University Press.
Blyton, P. (1993) 'Steel' in a. Pendleton and J. Winterton (eds), *Public Enterprise Industrial Relations.* London: Routledge.
Braverman, H. (1974) *Labour and Monopoly Capital.* New York: Monthly Review Press.
Brown, R. (1994) 'The Changing Nature of Work and Employment' in L. Evans, B. Johnson and B. Thomas (eds), *The Northern Region Economy: Progress and Prospects in the North of England.* London: Mansell.
Cooke, P. (1982) 'Class Interests, Regional Restructuring and State Formations in Wales', *International Journal of Urban and Regional Research*, Vol.6, No.3, pp.187–204.
Crosbie, A. (1995) 'The Japanese Model, Transnational Production and the North East', *Northern Economic Review*, Vol.24, pp.32–47.
Cumbers, A. (1994) 'New Forms of Work and Employment in an "Old Industrial Region"? The Offshore Construction Industry in the North East of England', *Work, Employment and Society*, Vol.8, No.4, pp.531–52.
Danford, A. (1995) 'Work Organisation and Labour Process inside Japanese firms in South Wales: A Break from Taylorism?' *13th Annual Labour Process Conference*, Blackpool, 5–7 April.
Delbridge, R. (1998) *Life on the Line in Contemporary Manufacturing.* Oxford: Oxford University Press.
Dicken, P., A. Tickell and H. Yeung (1997) 'Putting Japanese Investment in Europe in Its Place', *Area*, Vol.29, No.3, pp.200–212.
Elger, T. and C. Smith (1994) 'Global Japanization? Convergence and Competition in the Organization of the Labour Process' in T. Elger and C. Smith (eds), *Global Japanization? The Transformation of the Labour Process.* London: Routledge.
Fairbrother, P. and J. Waddington (1990) 'The Politics of Trade Unionism: Evidence, Policy and Theory', *Capital and Class*, Vol.41, pp.15–56.
Fevre, R. (1986) 'Contract Work in the Recession', in K. Purcell (ed.), *The Changing Experience of Employment.* London: Macmillan.
Fevre, R. (1987) 'Subcontracting in Steel', *Work, Employment and Society*, Vol.1, No.4 pp.509–27.
Firn, J. (1975) 'External Control and Regional Development: The Case of Scotland', *Environment and Planning A*, Vol.7, pp.393–414.
Friedman, A. (1977) *Industry and Labour: Class Structure at Work and Monopoly Capitalism.* London: Macmillan.
Garrahan, P. (1986) 'Nissan in the North East of England', *Capital and Class*, Vol.27,

pp.5–13.

Garrahan, P. and P. Stewart (1992a) *The Nissan Enigma: Flexibility at Work in a Local Economy*. London: Cassell.

Garrahan, P. and P. Stewart (1992b) 'Management Control and a New Regime of Subordination: Post-Fordism and the Local Economy' in N. Gilbert, R. Burrows and A. Pollert (eds), *Fordism and Flexibility*. London: Macmillan.

Glucksman, M. (1990) *Women Assemble: Women Workers and the New Industries in Interwar Britain*. London: Routledge.

Hardill, I. (1990) 'Restructuring in the Cleveland Clothing Industry' in P. Stewart, P. Garrahan and S. Crowther (eds), *Restructuring for Economic Flexibility*, Aldershot: Gower.

Holloway, J. (1987) 'The Red Rose of Nissan', *Capital and Class*, Vol.32, pp.142–64.

Hudson, R. (1988) 'Labour Market Changes and New Forms of Work in "Old" Industrial Regions', in D. Massey and J. Allen (eds), *Uneven Re-Development: Cities and Regions in Transition*. London: Hodder and Stoughton.

Hudson, R. (1994) 'The Role of Foreign Inward Investment' in L. Evans, P. Johnson and B.Thomas (eds), *The Northern Region Economy: Progress and Prospects in the North of England*. London: Mansell.

Hudson, R. and D. Sadler (1992) 'New Jobs for Old? Reindustrialisation Policies in Derwentside in the 1980s', *Local Economy* Vol.6, No.4, pp.316–25.

Kenney, M. and R. Florida (1988) 'Beyond Mass Production: Production and the Labour Process in Japan', *Politics and Society* Vol.16, No.1, pp.121–58.

Lovering, J. (1979) *The Theory of the 'Internal Colony' and the Political Economy of South Wales*. University of Wales mimeo.

Lovering, J. (1996) 'New Myths of the Welsh Economy', *Planet* Vol.116, pp.6–16.

MacInnes, J. (1987) *Thatcherism at Work*. Milton Keynes: Open University.

Martin, R., P. Sunley and J. Wills (1993) 'The Geography of Trade Union Decline: Spatial Dispersal or Regional Resilience?' *Transactions of the Institute of British Geographers* Vol.18, No.1, pp.36–62.

Martin, R., P. Sunley and J. Wills (1996) *Union Retreat and the Regions: The Shrinking Landscape of Organised Labour*. London: Jessica Kingsley.

Massey, D. (1984) *Spatial Divisions of Labour: Social Structures and the Geography of Production*. Basingstoke: Macmillan.

Mess, H. (1928) *Industrial Tyneside: a Social Survey*. London: Earnest Bevin.

Morgan, K. and A. Sayer (1988) 'A "Modern" Industry in a "Mature" Region: The Remaking of Management–Labour Relations', in D. Massey and J. Allen (eds), *Uneven Re-Development: Cities and Regions in Transition*. London: Hodder and Stoughton.

Morris, J. (1988) 'New Technologies, Flexible Work Practices and Regional Sociospatial Differentiation: Some Observations from the United Kingdom', *Environment and Planning D: Society and Space*, Vol.6, No.4, pp.301–19.

Morris, J. and S. Hill (1991) *Wales in the 1990s: A European Investment Region*. London: EIU Report.

Oliver, N. and B. Wilkinson (1992) *The Japanization of British Industry: New Developments in the 1990s*. Oxford: Blackwell.

Peck, F. and I. Stone (1993) 'Japanese Inward Investment in the North East of England: Reassessing Japanization', *Environment and Planning C*, Vol.11, No.1, pp.56–67.

Pike, A. and J. Tomaney (1999 forthcoming) 'Far Eastern FDI and the Political Economy of Local Development in North East England', *Asia Pacific Business Review*, Vol.5, No.2.

Piore, M. and C. Sabel (1984) *The Second Industrial Divide: Possibilities for Prosperity*. New York: Basic Books.

Price, A., K. Morgan and P. Cooke (1994) *The Welsh Renaissance: Inward Investment and Industrial Innovation*, Regional Industrial Research Report No.14, Cardiff, Centre for Advanced Studies, University of Wales.

Rubery, J. (1986) 'Trade Unions in the 1980s: The Case of the United Kingdom', in R. Edwards, P. Garonna and F. Todtling (eds), *Unions in Crisis and Beyond: Perspectives from Six Countries*. Dover, MA: Auburn House.

Taylor, B., T. Elger and P. Fairbrother (1994) 'Transplants and Emulators: The Fate of the

Japanese Model in British Electronics', in T. Elger and C. Smith (eds), *Global Japanization? The Transformation of the Labour Process*. London: Routledge.

Thomas, B. (1994) 'Tourism: Is It Undeveloped?' in L. Evans, B. Johnson and B. Thomas (eds), *The Northern Region Economy: Progress and Prospects in the North of England*. London: Mansell.

Womack, J., D. Jones and D. Roos (1990) *The Machine That Changed the World*. New York: Rawson Associates.

Wickens, P. (1987) *The Road to Nissan*. London: Macmillan.

Wilkinson, B, J. Morris and M. Munday (1993) 'Japan in Wales: A New IR', *Industrial Relations Journal*, Vol.17, No.4, pp.273–83.

Williams, K., C. Haslam, J. Williams, T. Cutler, A. Adcroft and S. Johal (1992) 'Against Lean Production', *Economy and Society*, Vol.21, No.3, pp.321–54.

Wood, S. (1992) 'Japanization and/or Toyotaism', *Work Employment and Society* Vol.5, No.4, pp.567–600.

9

Deciphering the East Asian Crisis

JEFFREY HENDERSON, NORIKO HAMA,
BERNARD ECCLESTON and
GRAHAME THOMPSON

For three decades and more, the world marvelled at the growth and prosperity of the 'miracle' economies of East Asia. From orthodox free-trade theorists and the World Bank to left-leaning political economists, everyone, it seemed, found in the development experiences of Japan and the newly industrialized countries (NICs) of the region, something that could vindicate their arguments about the most effective routes to dynamic economies. There were, of course, dissenting voices about how miraculous the various economies actually were. Many scholars pointed to the fact that the success of the NICs had been built on appalling labour – and sometimes political – repression and had resulted in untold environmental damage (for example, Deyo, 1989; Ho, 1990; Bello and Rosenfeld, 1992; and on China, Leung, 1988; Smith, 1997). Others emphasized that there were serious structural weaknesses in the NIC economies, and in their interface with the world economy, which ultimately would throw their growth trajectories into reverse (most famously, Krugman, 1994), or at best would circumscribe their possibilities of ever reaching the economic 'big league' (for example, Bernard and Ravenfield, 1995; Henderson, 1994, 1998). In spite of such words of caution, however, no one really foresaw that the symptoms of instability would appear so quickly, and the dynamics of crisis gather speed so rapidly.

As with some of the commentary that attended the economic rise of East Asia, the economic crisis that began in 1997 has been attended by a great deal of 'hot air' (particularly in the business press and other media), but little informed analysis of the origins and likely consequences of these events for the region and the international economy more generally (though on the one hand see

Jeffrey Henderson, Manchester Business School, University of Manchester; Noriko Hama, Mitsubishi Research Institute, Tokyo; Bernard Eccleston and Grahame Thompson, Faculty of Social Sciences, Open University

Krugman, 1998 and on the other, Wade and Veneroso, 1998; Wade, 1998; Chang, 1998, for radically differing interpretations). With this in mind, and having recently completed an edited volume on East Asia for the Open University's new Pacific Studies Programme (Thompson, 1998a), Grahame Thompson brought together Noriko Hama of the Mitsubishi Research Institute, Jeffrey Henderson of the Manchester Business School and Bernard Eccleston of the Open University to discuss the sources and implications of the current economic crisis in the region. The discussion was chaired by Grahame Thompson.

Grahame Thompson (GT): We are having this discussion at a time when a number of the economies in East Asia are experiencing what we can appropriately call 'crisis conditions'. This is certainly the case with respect to their financial systems, and this is possibly having some major implications for the real economies of the countries concerned. This is an appropriate time, then, to discuss the reasons for this crisis and the future prospects for the region and indeed the global economy generally.

The development of many of the East Asian economies in the post-Second World War period represented something of an unexpected disjuncture relative to experiences elsewhere on the globe. What was unexpected was that while starting from different moments in time, and different conditions, they have all experienced very rapid rates of economic growth, right up to the last few months. The question with which we need to start, I think, is whether or not the present period marks another disjuncture for these economies; whether they will now go on a completely different growth trajectory, perhaps losing the dynamism that we have seen in recent decades.

Perhaps I could begin by asking Jeffrey Henderson whether he thinks we are in a completely changed situation; whether, in other words, the East Asian economies have reached another disjuncture.

Jeffrey Henderson (JH): First let me make a methodological point. Nothing that is the product of human labour is for all time. Everything has 'sell-by' dates; and that is as true of social institutions, of business structures, of state–business relations, of relations between national economies and the world economy, as it is of anything else. One of the unfortunate things about the current situation is that there is a major international institution, the IMF, which does not believe that. It seems to believe that it is possible to fashion economies in more or less the same sort of way; that there is indeed – ultimately – only one route to a capitalist heaven. One of the things that the East Asian economies have so far demonstrated, is how patently untrue that belief is.

That is not to say, however, that these economies, both in their histories and in the particular types of political, economic and social processes that have delivered them in the condition they are in today, were essentially all the same. There were commonalties, but one of the interesting things about them was the significant differences in their routes (plural) to the modern world.

That, then, is a sort of methodological preamble. Let me now give you a short response to your question about whether the current period represents a disjuncture. My answer is that for some economies in East Asia, possibly yes; but for others, probably no. One of the interesting things about the current situation is that a number of the economies in East Asia – China clearly, but also Taiwan and Singapore – have so far been relatively unaffected by whatever is generating the current economic crises (again plural), and this needs to be explained.[1]

GT: Noriko Hama, do you think that this is a turning point for these economies?

Noriko Hama (NH): Yes I do, for a variety of reasons. First of all, there is always an element of pain in economic growth and the current situation is an indication that these economies have begun to experience those pains. Secondly, it has to be said that the East Asian economies have been involved in very much of a 'high wire act' in terms of their reliance on short term funds flowing into their economies, so that they could invest and grow. This was a 'high wire act' also in the sense that people were marvelling at the performance itself. While the funding kept coming in, the wire remained intact. Now, however, it has almost snapped, and the whole edifice has begun to crumble. And thirdly, from a wider perspective, I think this is (a) the result of problems in Japan, which is the largest creditor in the world, and not least to the East Asian part of the world economy; and (b) because of the weakness of the dollar regime. I think that in the East Asian crisis we are witnessing the end-game of the dollar currency system.

Additionally, Jeffrey Henderson raised a very interesting point about the IMF. I would agree that the IMF is becoming very anachronistic as shown by its attitude to this whole situation. I think that this is a product of the fact that the IMF is very much an edifice based on the dollar regime. If the dollar regime is in trouble, then so to is the IMF as a regulatory institution. It is in this sense that the East Asian crisis is at root a very global problem.

GT: Bernie, a 'high wire act', and the wire is about to collapse. Do you think that's true, and are these economies heading for a really genuine down-turn?

Bernard Eccleston (BE): One of the things we should not forget is that Japan has been bouncing along the bottom of its economic cycle since the early 1990s, and this is symptomatic of a number of things that the East Asian economies have in common; and one is the relationship between bank lending and property.

Many companies and some individuals borrow on the strength of property as collateral; and while the market is rising, that's fine. What we saw in Japan, however, from about 1990–91, was the collapse of a property boom, which left many companies and banks with huge debts. If you track round the Asia Pacific you can see similar things happening in Hong Kong, in Malaysia and in Singapore – though to a lesser extent there – and I think this reflects back a little bit on what Jeff was saying about diversity.

One of the things I have noticed is that international banks and other financial institutions seem to have considerable trust in some of the financial and monetary authorities of the region. The monetary authorities of Hong Kong, Taiwan and Singapore seem to get high marks from these institutions and in a way the latter seem to be protected by them. But a country's position on that 'confidence list' can change very quickly, as we have seen recently. For instance, it was only in the autumn of 1997 that the IMF was complimenting the South Korean monetary authorities. By December, South Korea's credit rating had been down-graded and this was one of the factors that triggered the recent crash.

GT: The growth rate in Japan has been one or two per cent over the last four or five years. That's similar to the growth rates of the advanced industrial economies of the West. In a way, then, it's been 'Welcome to the problems of advanced capitalism'. The other economies of East Asia have been growing at seven, eight, nine per cent; even if they go down to four or five, it will still be a rather spectacular growth rate. So, will the growth rates of these dip to, say, one or two per cent or are they going to bounce back fairly quickly to a very respectable performance?

NH: I think the growth rates could go down substantially below the four to five per cent that is being assumed at the moment. This crisis, in a sense, is a classic textbook credit crunch that is being confronted by what are still weak economies. These are young economies; exuberant, yes, but still very much unsophisticated economies in many ways. For such vulnerable economies to be hit by this kind of situation is something of a tragedy, especially as most have currencies pegged to the dollar, as I said earlier. This is an anachronism which will be a negative factor for them.

So the combination of situations and circumstances is a very harsh one for economies of this nature. Consequently I think the impact will be much more serious than people are assuming at this moment.

GT: But, Jeff, this is to some extent a crisis which has been precipitated in the financial system; but what about the real economies? Are the real economies more robust? It seems to me that one component of the problem is that there has been an 'Anglo-Americanization' of the financial systems of these economies, but this is resting on top of real economies that work quite differently to their Anglo-American equivalents. Consequently this has exacerbated the situation.

There seems to be another disjuncture, then, between the way in which the financial system is evolving and the way in which the underlying economies in East Asia are organized. What I am really trying to get at here is, how far will this financial turmoil affect the real economies?

JH: I think there's something in what you say, Grahame. But I'd first like to take issue with something which Noriko said earlier on.

I am not at all convinced that the current crises in East Asia are primarily traceable to the relationships of the various economies to the international financial system, or to the relative collapse of the dollar block. If that were the case, one surely would expect those economies that are most closely integrated into the international financial system – of which Singapore is the obvious example – to be also the most seriously affected by the current situation. Clearly that is not the case, and so the problem – and its explanation – is more complex than that.

To respond to your question, Grahame, I think that part of the problem that we see in East Asia is to do with the nature of the real economies; with how they've been structured, and the extent to which those structures have become increasingly inappropriate to current circumstances. The interesting thing, of course, is that there are enormous differences in the institutional structures of the various real economies, and the ways and extent to which these have become inappropriate has been a product of quite different processes in each case.

The inappropriateness of the structure of the South Korean economy, for instance, is a product of different historical processes, different relationships between state and business, different changes in the polity in South Korea, *vis-a-vis* some other economies such as, say, Taiwan. The South Korean economy has emerged out of synch with the requirements of effective operation in the international economy, but the reasons for this are quite different than in the cases, for instance, of Malaysia or Thailand.

GT: Bernie, it seems to me that talking about Malaysia and Thailand, for a minute, that these economies, and others like them, are neither 'fish nor fowl' at the moment. That is, they're neither sufficiently developed, in terms of technology and innovation etc., to take on the advanced economies, nor are they cheap enough to continue to be the depositories of assembly-type operations that have been offshoring from Japan and elsewhere. Do you think that is something typical and hence a problem for these economies?

BE: I think it is, and it's a great mistake to lump all of these economies together. One of the things you find in Malaysia is a really keen interest, not in what East Asian countries who've industrialized before them are doing, but in what the likes of Burma (Myanmar), Vietnam, even in some cases Cambodia etc.. are up to.

Malaysians see the differences between their labour costs and those of the others as very critical.

One of the key features of an economy like Malaysia, is that they rely heavily on foreign direct investment (FDI). One of the battles the Malaysian Government has had, particularly with Japanese companies, is that they will not re-locate high-tech operations. Consequently the labour force in Malaysia is kept towards the low skill end of foreign companies' global operations. This is clear, for instance, with the Proton motorcar, which is produced by a joint venture with Mitsubishi. Mitsubishi have refused to re-locate any of their advanced production engineering facilities to Malaysia, which they have kept firmly under headquarters' control.

What things like this mean is that the Malaysian human infrastructure has not been improving as rapidly as, say, that of Singapore, where the role of the foreign multi-nationals and FDI is somewhat different. So I think we've got to recognize the diversity within East Asia, as governments, politicians and economists from the region do themselves.

GT: Noriko, you've mentioned short-term portfolio investment, but obviously there's the longer term FDI type of investment. Do you think the rapid growth of FDI has contributed to current problems? A short-term capital inflow, as we know, can disappear as quickly as it arrives, but FDI is supposed to be a longer term involvement. Presumably, then, FDI is not such a problem for the East Asian economies, other than perhaps with regard to flows from Japan.

NH: Theoretically it should not be a problem, but I think everybody was putting their FDI eggs in the Asian basket in a very hurried manner. I think that happened because in the search for growth, people just flocked to this area without regard to what was going on with the fundamentals of the various economies – indeed to the diversity and the different underlying conditions. So I think that much of the FDI that flowed into the region went in there blindfold, as it were, and this is starting to have consequences.

To clarify, it was very much a case of you had to be there because everybody else was there; you had to be there because that was where the growth potential was. I think there was a lack of extensive and deep thought behind these investment activities and they are coming back to haunt the economies and investors in question.

GT: And much of this FDI got channelled, as we were saying, into the property market. So to some extent it supported the property boom, rather than being invested in directly productive assets.

JH: That was somewhat true, but it varied from country to country. It got channelled into property and real estate in Thailand and Malaysia, and to some extent in Hong Kong, and it is representative, in my view, of basic structural weaknesses in those three economies. But that was not especially true in Singapore, for instance, where the vast majority of FDI has gone into manufacturing and related services. Actually, it was initially less true of Malaysia, but things have changed there in recent years.

I think we have to bear in mind that foreign direct investment, with the major exception of Singapore (as of 1991, I think, something like 70 per cent of the Singaporean economy was foreign owned, and about 84 per cent of manufacturing at that point) and to a lesser extent Malaysia and Thailand, has not been an overwhelming feature of development in the region. So the story of the current crisis is not especially a story about FDI.

GT: What is it fundamentally a story of, then, if not that?

JH: It's a question of short term investment. It's a question of the need for investment, it seems to me, by some of those economies rather than others. It's a question of how it was acquired, the circumstances under which it was acquired, and the problems that the various economies have been lumbered with as a result of those circumstances.

It seems to me that the need for foreign investment and foreign-derived lines of credit has changed significantly in relatively short periods of time. The circumstances under which that investment has been acquired, in the case of South Korea, have changed dramatically in recent years in that the state is no longer an effective financial mediator between the major companies and the world economy. South Korea is in the trouble it is today, partly because of that fact.

GT: The World Bank in its *East Asian Miracle* report (World Bank, 1993) and others (for example, Krugman, 1994) have argued that the East Asian NIC economies have been successful because they have been recipients of large inputs of capital and labour, but have not been able to use these to increase significantly their total factor productivity (through innovation and moving into higher value-added products etc.). So their economic growth, it has been suggested, is purely a result of the quantities of capital and labour that have been employed, and is not particularly a consequence of using these more effectively. The prediction has been, therefore, that there's going to be a big problem of transition when these factor inputs dry up.

Does anybody think that this is one of the problems behind the financial crisis in East Asia? Is there a problem of productivity in these economies?

BE: I don't like the frame of analysis that uses total factor productivity. For one thing, it is almost impossible to separate these kind of inputs from their productivity. When you look at replacement capital investment, you see an enormous amount of embedded technological progress. I mean, no one deliberately chooses to reinvest by using an old-fashioned machine. This is one reason why I have great problems with 'total factor productivity' analysis; these elements cannot easily be split into neat boxes.

GT: But the Korean chaebol, for instance, are thought to be very unproductive. This is the reason why they are thought not to be generating sufficient profits to service loans. So there may be a problem, here. Jeff, what do you think?

JH: It's unclear, Grahame. My reading of the situation, and my response to this issue, is to take the criticisms of this type of analysis presented by Singh (1998) and others. But again, as I have said already, there are significant differences here, depending on which economy you look at. I think that 'total factor productivity' analysis makes more sense when you look at, for instance, Thailand and Malaysia. I doubt that there have been significant improvements in productivity, innovation etc. there. In the case of Singapore, and certainly in the case of Taiwan, it's more difficult to argue that technological progress is not taking place.

Korea is an interesting case, however. Hyundai Motor, for instance, have moved from a situation 20 years ago of producing essentially geriatric GM models – taking something like 2,000 person hours to screw them together (Williams *et al.*, 1995) – to a respectable situation today of well under 300 hours. Now clearly that's just one indication, but it sure looks to me as though improvements in productivity allied to higher order technology etc. has been happening. Additionally Hyundai have begun to design their own cars, and they now have a greater Korean-made content.

One problem with Korea is that its development is uneven. Hyundai Motor would be one of the better examples of progress in that context. One could clearly point to others, however, that would better approximate your argument about the relative absence of increases in total factor productivity in Korea.

GT: Let's leave that for a moment, and come back to something that Noriko was saying about the end of the dollar-peg. I was interested in what you said on this, because it's true that most of these economies did align their currencies to the dollar, and you think this crisis is going to shatter that, do you?

NH: Yes, very much so. The next chapter in this continuing saga will be how long Hong Kong can retain the dollar-peg. My feeling is that the sooner they abandon it, the better. But they will try to resist as France did back in the 1930s when they held-on for dear life to the gold standard. As a result they suffered tremendous pain, but in the end had to abandon it anyway.

I think the currency element is very important in this whole situation. For all the diversity amongst the Asian economies, of which I take full account, I think this preoccupation with the dollar-peg has prevented that diversity from working in their favour. A more flexible currency regime could have allowed a quicker and more dynamic response to this whole situation.

The East Asian NICs are now locked into a very strange situation. They are being forced into a re-evaluation of their competitiveness, and they don't like that at all. This is a war of attrition which they would have preferred not to be involved in. Currency stability has been the focal point of their success story in the past. This is similar to the way Japan had earlier managed to be the miracle economy of the world under a fixed exchange regime.

But the more the dollar regime becomes outdated, the more the fraying at the edges will begin to show.

So I think this is the issue at the heart of the current situation. It is why these divergent economies now find themselves in the same problematic basket.

BE: When economic historians write about this crisis in 20 years time, I think the currency issue will be one of the things on which they'll focus, because it's not just one or two countries depreciating, it's a whole group. And the extent of depreciation is phenomenal. In the past year the Indonesian rupiah, for instance, has declined by over 100 per cent, as has the South Korean won. The Thai baht has declined by about 75 per cent, and the Malaysian ringgit by around 50 per cent. These are quite remarkable rates of depreciation.

These economies, however, are going to become fiercely competitive in export markets, including against each other. This could lead to much more conflict within ASEAN (Association of South East Asian Nations) which has been proud of its collegiality over the past 20 years or so.

GT: In my mind this would raise a question about the ability of the rest of the international economy to absorb these exports if these economies are going to become suddenly so competitive. Clearly they benefited from linking their currencies to the dollar when it was depreciating, particularly against the yen. At that point, then, they gained the competitive advantages of a depreciating currency. Since 1995–96, however, the reverse has been true, and it is since then that the problems with the NIC economies have come home to roost. But are you both (Bernie and Noriko) saying that it's a floating rate regime that is going to take over, rather than these currencies being re-stabilized by, say, linking to the yen? Noriko, are you arguing for a floating rate regime in these countries rather than a re-pegging to some other currency?

NH: Well, it looks as though it is going to be a stronger linkage to the yen. Neither side may like that very much, but I think the way the situation is going it will make increasing sense to the Asian nations to look towards the yen as the dominant regional currency.

This will certainly cause problems for the Japanese domestic economy, and it may not be the best solution, but I think that the way things look at the moment, it is an option that will be pursued as the last resort. Whether over and beyond that a fully flexible floating regime emerges remains to be seen. But the current situation could be the starting point of an Asian currency area with the yen as its focal point.

JH: I'd like to come in, not on Noriko's last point, but on the general issue of the extent to which it is possible to understand current developments in Asia as a reflex of the dollar link. It seems to me that that clearly is part of the problem, but I would again insist, only part of the problem. The reason, first of all, is that the sociologist in me resists monocausal explanations for anything that is the product of human behaviour. And secondly, the political economist in me seeks to weight the various determinants within a framework of multi-causality. If we were to go down that route and attempt to weight the various causes of the current situation in East Asia, I would tend to weight some of the issues specific to the political economies of the countries in question at least as much as the issues that Noriko has been talking about.

GT: What about the role of the IMF? We've talked a little about this, but are the IMF's policy proposals sensible? Noriko, do you think it's sensible for them to encourage the competitive devaluations you mentioned?

NH: Well, given its current position, I think that the proposals it has come up with so far are pretty much the only type of thing that the IMF is capable of. That is to say that they are still living within the Bretton Woods framework, and there is an inconsistency there which tends very much to date the way they address these issues. If the IMF does not change, and start to live in the post-Bretton Woods world that we've entered, I don't think that the current situation in Asia is going to change very much.

It's almost like the current European concerns with a single currency, which is being forced on a very diverse area and a very diverse collection of economies. If you have that kind of a situation in Asia, with a 'one-size fits all' solution thrust on everybody, then the burden of adjustment that will be brought to bear on individual countries, in order to regain stability, will be a very harsh one. But that's essentially what the IMF is saying to these countries, because it is living within an outdated currency and regulatory framework.

BE: I think that one of the interesting things is the huge scale of IMF involvement in a number of these economies. In Asia the IMF's policy prescriptions are seen as deflating economies which were already beginning to deflate for the reasons you have written about, Grahame, such as declining export performance (Thompson, 1998b). So there is a question about whether the IMF strategy, which may have worked in Mexico, may not work in Asia. Most recently, stories filtering out of Washington point to major disputes within the IMF, and between the IMF and the World Bank about how to handle the East Asian situation. This further raises a question about transparency within the IMF. Just who, precisely, is driving this policy agenda; what is their rationale, and can we see the basis of their policy prescriptions? Indirectly, then, the East Asian crisis is raising all sorts of interesting questions about the way the IMF police the international financial system.

NH: And the rules whereby they police the situation are becoming very much out of date.

JH: Yes, I absolutely agree with that. But let me take a particular twist on this issue of the IMF if I may Grahame, because one of the things I'm interested in is whether indeed the policy package which the IMF is trying to impose on South Korea, in particular, is likely to work. In other words, is this package likely to be absorbed and consequently is the IMF indeed going to be able to remake South Korea in the image of the United States?

One of the interesting things for me is that the IMF has not seemed to suffer from declining self-confidence in its general policy package in the same way that the World Bank appears to have done; in its case, initially as a result of an increasingly high profile by the Japanese government in World Bank operations. That process – namely the pressure to shift the other major Bretton Woods institution, the IMF, away from its standard policy package, to try and get it to recognize that there are different routes to prosperous high value-adding, high wage economies, than the ones fashioned by Britain and the United States – doesn't seem to have got too far.

But to answer my own question about the IMF and South Korea, I doubt very much indeed whether the IMF will be able to impose its package of reconstruction on the South Korean economy in the way that it clearly hopes, and I'll indicate three reasons why I suspect this will be the case. Firstly, with South Korea we have probably the most nationalistic political economy in the capitalist world. For historical reasons there is going to be massive resistance to an outside foreign agency re-working the institutional basis of the Korean state and economy. Secondly, Korea in the last 20 years or so has had arguably the most militant working class in Asia. They are the ones that will suffer from this IMF package. The chances are there'll be significant working class mobilization which will put enormous pressure upon the South Korean government from the opposite end, from the need to stabilize the domestic polity, from the need to deal with the disruption of social order. And thirdly, there are the chaebol themselves. In them you have an extraordinary business organization with extraordinary power in the South Korean economy. Bear in mind that South Korea, in terms of the ownership of assets, has probably the highest level of concentration of any capitalist economy in the world. For the IMF to assume that it's simply going to be able to remake the business structure of the Korean economy, in the light of the United States, is incredibly naive on their part.

NH: Can I ask Jeffrey a question? I fully take your point that the IMF is going to have immense difficulties trying to restructure the Korean economy. On the other hand, I think that by implication you are saying that the current system, the current ways of doing things in Korea, are not working and that they are starting to out-live their usefulness. If so, where is Korea going? Surely it can't stay the way it is now, but you say that the IMF reforms will not work for it either. So where will it end up, do you think?

JH: The answer to that question is: I don't know, and I don't think anybody else does. But my guess is that it will mutate into some other form of capitalism, some different sets of relations between state and business which cannot be foreseen at the present time. I would stick my neck out and say, once again, that the chances of the South Korean economy being re-made, more or less along the lines of the dream world of orthodox neo-classical economic theory, is not a possibility.

GT: We've talked a lot about Korea, but I'd like to raise the question of one or two other countries that have not figured in the discussion as much as they might. One is China, one is Japan, and thirdly, perhaps, the USA. What are the implications of the Asian crisis for the other side of the Pacific and for the world more generally?

Let's begin with China. It seems to be out of this little dance at the moment; it doesn't seem to be affected, significantly, by these dramatic changes in the other East Asian economies. Is this because it isn't integrated sufficiently into the network of economic relationships here. Is its economy driven by a completely different set of issues? Does anyone want to make a few remarks about China?

BE: I think the extent of China's global connections is quite different from that of the other East Asian economies, because of the continuing degree of state control over the economy. The extent of state control in China over the banking system, the foreign exchange system, the conditions of foreign investment is quite different from the others.

There will come a crunch over the next few months, though, and this will hinge on whether the government allows the Chinese Yuan to fall in order for the economy to remain competitive against some of the other countries. Clearly if Indonesia, Thailand or South Korea are experiencing 100 per cent currency depreciation, then that's going to erode substantially the labour cost differential which China currently benefits from.

GT: What about Japan, Noriko? What is the future for Japan given the evolving situation in Asia? It is also suffering from problems with its banking system, isn't it? Is the banking system going to collapse and cause major problems domestically?

NH: Well absolutely. Japan is very much the crux of the whole question in that it is the creditor nation of the world. When structural problems of this kind occur in such a country, everybody suffers. I think that Japan is facing a situation in which fundamental demolitions of the established ways of doing things are necessary. The things that went so well for Japan in the past are now turning into liabilities. What stood for stability, now stands for stagnation.

What used to stand for security, now stands for a lack of creativity and a very rigid system indeed. So I think that Japan does need to overhaul completely what has been known as the 'Japan Inc.' system, in order for it to have a viable existence in the twenty-first century. It needs to become an internally diverse place, as opposed to the homogeneous myth that was 'Japan Inc.' in the post-war years.

GT: You mentioned that Japan is the creditor nation of the globe, so presumably the problems that Japan may suffer would have wider impact, particularly on the US. That relationship between Japan and the US is important, isn't it?

NH: Very important indeed. And I think that the exuberance, irrational or otherwise, of the American economy, has very much been dependent on funds flowing in from Japan. Japan has been a very artificially low interest-rate country for some time and that has pushed funds into the United States' economy and into its stock markets. Take away that flow of funds and the American economy, as it stands today, will be totally non-existent. We have, if you like, an alliance of fear, a terrorist–hostage relationship between the Americans and the Japanese at the moment – the Americans being the terrorist and the Japanese the hostage, in terms of the flow of funds. Neither likes each other very much but they have to hang on to each other to stay afloat. This is a very precarious situation which I think is reaching the end of its sustainability.

GT: Jeff, a global crisis as a consequence of this? Is this something we should all be worried about in the last years of the twentieth century?

JH: Well interestingly enough, Grahame, I noticed in the *New Yorker* recently a piece on 'Dusting off Marx'.

GT: Karl Marx?

JH: Karl Marx, yes, in terms of his significance for the analysis of capitalism in a phase of globalization. But my response to your question is that I don't think so. I think that this is going to damage some economies in Asia more than others, and I've already indicated the ones that I think are going to be the most badly damaged: Malaysia, Thailand, Indonesia certainly, maybe some others. But it will be a phase of reconstruction, certainly in South Korea, certainly I would have thought in Japan, but perhaps less so – because it's less necessary – in Taiwan and Singapore.

China, as Bernie has indicated, is somewhat outside of the net, precisely because as a whole, it is still relatively disengaged from the world economy in the way that many of the others are not. Additionally, the state effectively still controls the commanding heights of the economy which in any case remains only partially capitalist.

So my first point is that the fall-out from the current crisis will be specific to particular economies and it will have an asymmetrical impact across the region. Secondly, the interesting question with regard to the global picture is the one that Noriko was just talking about; the connection between Japan and the United States and the issues raised by the fact that Japanese corporations own most of the US debt.

GT: Yes, but why on earth should they liquidate that debt? It is, after all, the source of much of their earnings. It's the most profitable part of their investments. It seems to me pretty unlikely that they'd liquidate that. They'll liquidate their non-performing assets within the region initially, but you'd have to have a really serious structural crisis in Japan for the banking system or the companies there to liquidate their assets – their high performing assets – in the United States. So it seems to me that this is unlikely to happen.

NH: Well, one hopes so, but it could be that the credit crunch in Japan itself could become so serious that Japanese investors will have no alternative but to start repatriating funds from the United States and elsewhere. I think that is the real focal point of the concerns we have about what's happening, about the circumstances that are unfolding in Japan.

GT: It seems to me also that the European economy is expanding now. We're told that it's about to come out of recession, and the US economy is buoyant also. So isn't the structural crisis really in only one part of the triad?[2] Surely to have a global crisis you would have to have major structural problems in all three parts, I would have thought, and some rather stupid policy making as well on the part of the leaders in these areas. This leads me to think that a genuine global crisis is unlikely since the conditions for it are far from being in place.

But I'm going to have to bring the discussion to a halt. We have emphasized the diversity and particularities of the economies in question, the causes of the crisis, and likely reactions to it. We have also had some disagreement, particularly on the significance of international financial issues and on the global impact of the crisis. The economic turmoil in East Asia is undoubtedly one of the important issues of the moment, and its consequences will linger for a long time to come.

ACKNOWLEDGEMENTS

This discussion was recorded at the BBC's Open University Production Centre in December 1997. The transcript of this discussion, which forms the basis for the article, has been prepared for publication by Jeffrey Henderson and incorporates new material from all the contributors. We are grateful to Jeremy Cooper, on behalf of the BBC, for allowing us to use the transcript of the discussion in this way.

NOTES

1. For an attempt at expanation see Henderson (1999).
2. The economic domains of the United States, European Union and Japan respectively.

REFERENCES

Bello, W. and S. Rosenfeld (1992), *Dragons in Distress: Asia's Miracle Economies in Crisis*. Harmondsworth: Penguin.

Bernard, M. and J. Ravenfield (1995), 'Beyond Product Cycles and Flying Geese: Regionalization, Hierarchy and the Industrialization of East Asia', *World Politics*, Vol.47, No.2, pp.171–209.

Chang, H.J. (1998), 'Korea: The Misunderstood Crisis', *World Development*, Vol.26, No.8, pp.1555–61.

Deyo, F.C. (1989), *Beneath the Miracle: Labor Subordination in the New Asian Industrialism*. Berkeley and Los Angeles: University of California Press.

Henderson, J. (1994), 'Electronics Industries and the Developing World: Uneven Contributions and Uncertain Prospects' in L. Sklair (ed.), *Capitalism and Development*. London: Routledge, pp.258–88.

Henderson, J. (1998), 'Danger and Opportunity in the Asia-Pacific' in G. Thompson (ed.), *Economic Dynamism in the Asia-Pacific*. London: Routledge: pp.357–84.

Henderson, J. (1999), 'Uneven Crises: Institutional Foundations of East Asian Economic Turmoil', *Economy and Society*, Vol.28, No.3 (in press).

Ho, S.Y (1990), *Taiwan – After a Long Silence: The Emerging New Unions of Taiwan*. Hong Kong: Asia Monitor Resource Center.

Krugman, P. (1994), 'The Myth of Asia's Miracle', *Foreign Affairs*, Vol.73, No.6, pp.63–75.

Krugman, P. (1998), 'What Happened to Asia?' Unpublished paper, Department of Economics, Massachusetts Institute of Technology.

Leung, W.Y. (1988), *Smashing the Iron Rice Pot: Workers and Unions in China's Market Socialism*. Hong Kong: Asia Monitor Resource Center.

Singh, A. (1998), 'Growth: Its Sources and Consequences' in G. Thompson (ed.), *Economic Dynamism in the Asia-Pacific*. London: Routledge: 55–82.

Smith, R. (1997), 'Creative Destruction: Capitalist Development and China's Environment', *New Left Review*, No.222, pp.3–41.

Thompson, G. (ed.) (1998a), *Economic Dynamism in the Asia-Pacific : The Growth of Integration and Competitiveness*. London: Routledge.

Thompson, G. (1998b), 'Financial Systems and Monetary Integration' in G. Thompson (ed.), *Economic Dynamism in the Asia-Pacific*. London, Routledge, pp.83–111.

Wade, R. (1998), 'The Asian Debt-and-Development Crisis of 1997-?: Causes and Consequences', *World Development*, Vol.26, No.8, pp.1535–53.

Wade, R. and F. Veneroso (1998), 'The Asian Financial Crisis: The High Debt Model versus the Wall Street–Treasury–IMF Complex', *New Left Review*, No.228, pp.3–23.

Williams, K., C. Haslam, J. Williams, S. Johal, A. Adcroft and R. Willis (1995), 'The Crisis of Cost Recovery and the Waste of the Industrialised Nations', *Competition and Change: The Journal of Global Business and Political Economy*, Vol.1, No.1, pp.67–93.

World Bank (1993), *The East Asian Miracle*. New York: Oxford University Press and The World Bank.

Abstracts

Fast but Fragile: British Restructuring for FDI in a Global Era
by Louise Amoore

In the 'globalization' debates of the early 1990s, the Anglo-American practices of rapid restructuring to achieve 'attractiveness' to foreign direct investment tended to be presented as the universal panacea for dealing with the pressures of global change. However, the East Asian economic crises of the late 1990s have precipitated a widespread questioning, both of the export-oriented 'Asian model' of development, and of the possible contagion spreading to the western financial market and 'FDI attracting' western states. This article considers the 'fast but fragile' nature of Anglo-Saxon style restructuring in the light of the political-economic and social crises experienced by East Asian state-societies. The discussion focuses specifically on the British approach to restructuring for FDI, arguing that this reflects and embodies both a distinctive set of state-societal relations, and a distinctive understanding of what the process of globalization implies for these relations.

The Road from Nissan to Samsung: A Historical Overview of East Asian Investment in a UK Region *by Marie Conte-Helm*

Japan's relationship with the North East of England is often charted from the 1984 investment by the car manufacturer, Nissan, in its Sunderland plant. The aftermath of that investment decision saw not only a wave of Japanese manufacturing investment descending upon the North East but also other investments from Korea, Taiwan and Hong Kong following in its wake. This article attempts to situate the experience of Japanese investment in the North East in the wider context of the region's more long-term associations with Japan. It looks to the legacy of the past in the building of Japanese battleships on Tyneside and other episodes of technology transfer in the late nineteenth century. It juxtaposes the subsequent changes in the region's industrial base with the post-war history of Japanese investment in the UK. With the arrival of NSK, the Japanese ball-bearings manufacturer, in County Durham in 1974, a new relationship can be seen to have emerged along with a regional infrastructure which supported further East Asian investment at the height of the bubble economy. The spreading out of that investment, its social and cultural impact and the consequences of the bubble bursting are explored at a time when claims for the dawning of 'the Pacific century' have been seriously called into question.

East Asian FDI and the UK Periphery *by Ian Stone*

This article has two main components. The first section charts the emergence of Japanese and (subsequently) other East Asian countries as major sources of FDI on a global scale. It outlines the timing, characteristics and spatial pattern of these FDI flows, especially as they relate to Europe and the UK, which is a primary host economy for such investment. The second element analyses the development and character of the East Asian investment flows into the North of England. It assesses the contribution of these flows to overall job generation in the region, alongside that in other peripheral UK regions, which compete with the North to attract inward investment. The article ends by considering implications for the region's foreign-owned sector arising out of the current crisis affecting Asia.

Working Miracles? Regional Renewal and East Asian Interlinkages *by John Ritchie*

This contribution considers the arguments surrounding claims that a 'New' North East is arising as a particular result of an upsurgent regional economic miracle whose frontal East Asian interlinkages promise continuing business and organizational transformations ahead. Largely off-circuit for other economic miracle claims before, this 'New' North East benefits from both any supposed British economic miracle at large and that recently associated with East Asia generally. But while current British state–public narratives constantly reiterate miraculous transformational possibilities, others constitute their chances very differently. Using a concept-led social constructionist perspective this contribution explores alternative interpretations of the North East economic trajectory which constitute any East Asian interlinkages several other ways. It finally acknowledges differing debates over what roles these interlinkages actually play while posing further questions about where else the North East regional economic trajectory might be headed instead.

East Asian Investment and Reinvestment in the 1990s: Implications for Regional Development *by Carol Burdis and Frank Peck*

There has been considerable debate in recent literature concerning the regional implications of corporate organization based on complex forms of networking. In particular, it has been suggested that recent international investments are more sophisticated and more beneficial to host economies. This article explores the relevance of these ideas using case studies of reinvestments within East Asian plants located in the North East of England. Examples show how reinvestment decisions can create incremental improvements in the status of production locations. The implications of this for the design and delivery of aftercare services through regional development organizations are explored.

East Asian FDI and the Political Economy of Local Development *by Andrew Pike and John Tomaney*

This article situates the experience of the North East region within the context of the debates concerning East Asian FDI and the political economy of local development. The analysis looks in detail at the Sedgefield Borough economy to offer a more critical reading of the role of East Asian FDI in local economic development. The study concludes that East Asian FDI is a small but significant segment of the local economy which reveals evidence of some 'leading edge' developments in particular areas in tandem with a recurrence of the structural characteristics reminiscent of previous 'branch plant' investments. The conclusions for the business support network concern the need to change the focus and apparent control over the local economic development strategy and to forge strong links to the agenda of more active regional institutions and policy being promoted by the current Labour government.

Managing Culture and the Manipulation of Difference: A Case Study of Second Generation Transplant *by Ian Roberts and Tim Strangleman*

This contribution studies the processes and tensions involved in the introduction of management techniques, largely inspired by the Japanese example, into a non-Japanese manufacturing firm in the North East of England. In treating culture as something an organization *has* rather than something an organization *is,* management were able to introduce a new approach by actively using divisions existing among workers, particularly those along the axes of age and gender and skill. While successful in the short term the changes appear as brittle in the longer term context of skill deficits and the fluctuating demand for labour within the firm.

The Transformation of Employment Relations in the UK's Old Industrial Regions? The Experience of 'Japanization' *by Andrew Cumbers*

This contribution presents a comparative analysis of the impact of Japanese inward investment on employment relations in the North East of England and South Wales. In particular, it examines the experience of 'Japanization' in both regions within the context of on-going processes of employment restructuring. While there is some variation in impact between regions, overall the evidence suggests that Japanization is helping to transform the work environment. However, it is not resulting in the idealized model of harmonious employment relations depicted by some commentators, but is part of a wider shift towards a more coercive set of employment practices.

Deciphering the East Asian Crisis *by Jeffrey Henderson, Noriko Hama, Bernard Eccleston and Grahame Thompson*

Based on a roundtable discussion, the article surveys the causes and consequences of the East Asian economic crisis as it began to take root from the middle of 1997. While retaining the form of a debate, and thus exhibiting some disagreement between the participants, it deals with the macroeconomic and international dimensions of the problem, as well as the domestic and institutional sources of the crisis in each of the relevant societies. It concludes with a commentary on some of the likely long-term effects of the crisis for East Asia and for the global economy more generally.

Index

Printed in the United States
by Baker & Taylor Publisher Services